Innovation and Technological Catch-Up

T0329879

To the memory of Jo Lorentzen,
for his passion in development
and his ironic and often unusual vision of life

Innovation and Technological Catch-Up

The Changing Geography of Wine Production

Edited by

Elisa Giuliani

University of Pisa, Italy and SPRU, University of Sussex, UK

Andrea Morrison

Utrecht University, The Netherlands and KITeS-Bocconi University, Italy

Roberta Rabellotti

Università del Piemonte Orientale, Italy

Edward Elgar
Cheltenham, UK • Northampton, MA, USA

Published by
Edward Elgar Publishing Limited
The Lypiatts
15 Lansdown Road
Cheltenham
Glos GL50 2JA
UK

Edward Elgar Publishing, Inc.
William Pratt House
9 Dewey Court
Northampton
Massachusetts 01060
USA

A catalogue record for this book
is available from the British Library

Library of Congress Control Number: 2011925708

MIX
Paper from
responsible sources
FSC
www.fsc.org   FSC® C018575

ISBN 978 1 84844 994 7 (cased)

Typeset by Servis Filmsetting Ltd, Stockport, Cheshire
Printed and bound by MPG Books Group, UK

Contents

Contributors

Kym Anderson is George Gollin Professor of Economics and Executive Director of the Wine Economics Research Centre at the University of Adelaide, Australia. He has published a global wine statistical compendium and edited a 2004 book, *The World's Wine Markets: Globalization at Work*. He has served on the board of directors of Australia's Grape and Wine Research and Development Corporation (2000–05), and is a co-founder of the American Association of Wine Economists and co-editor of the *Journal of Wine Economics*.

Lorenzo Cassi is Associate Professor of Economics (Maître de Conférences) at University Paris 1 Panthéon-Sorbonne (France), Research Fellow at the Centre Économie de la Sorbonne (Paris 1) and Affiliated Fellow at the Observatoire des Sciences et des Techniques of Paris and at KITeS Bocconi University, Milan, Italy. His research interests include economics of innovation and technical change, technology policy and cooperative R&D, knowledge transfer and social network analysis.

Rafael A. Corredoira is Assistant Professor at the Robert H. Smith School of Business, University of Maryland, College Park, USA. He received his PhD from the Wharton School at the University of Pennsylvania, USA. His current research focuses on the role of social networks in inter-organizational knowledge flows, economic development, and entrepreneurship.

Lucia Cusmano is Assistant Professor of Political Economy at Insubria University, Varese, Italy, and Research Fellow at KITeS (Knowledge, Innovation and Technology Studies), Bocconi University, Milan, Italy. In 2010 she joined the OECD Centre for Entrepreneurship, Small and Medium-sized Enterprises and Local Development as a senior economist. She holds a PhD in economics from Pavia University, Italy, and a master of science in economics from Warwick University, UK. She has published extensively in international journals on innovation and economic development in advanced and developing regions.

Elisa Giuliani is Assistant Professor at the University of Pisa in Italy and Visiting Fellow at SPRU, University of Sussex in the UK. Her research interest has been directed essentially to understanding how the private sector contributes to economic development – mainly via innovation. She has a PhD from SPRU and she has been ESRC and Jean Monnet Post-Doctoral Fellow at SPRU and at the Robert Schuman Center for Advanced Studies at the European University Institute. Her works have been published by numerous international journals and she has done consultancy work for the United Nations Economic Commission for Latin America and the Caribbean (ECLAC) and the Inter-American Development Bank.

Martin Kunc has worked in Chile for three years where he was involved with research related to the linkage between universities and industry in clusters. His work has been published in *European Planning Studies* and the *International Journal of Learning and Intellectual Capital*. He is currently working at Warwick Business School, UK. His research interests are in the area of regional innovation systems and the use of modeling and simulation to explore the dynamics of regional innovation systems.

The late **Jo Lorentzen** ran a research unit on innovation and development at the Human Sciences Research Council in Cape Town (South Africa). He worked with city and regional governments in South Africa on innovation and industrial policy and with national entities on assessments of the national innovation system. He was part of the Globelics network and co-directed a large global consortium on the emerging geography of knowledge-intensive activities in the global economy (www.ingineus.eu). He was also involved in research on innovation in the agricultural and health systems of low-income countries.

Gerald A. McDermott is Associate Professor of International Business in the Darla Moore School of Business at the University of South Carolina, Columbia, USA. He received his PhD in political science at the Massachusetts Institute of Technology. His work focuses on the interaction between institutional change and inter-firm networks by analyzing industrial restructuring and innovation in emerging market countries, especially in East Central Europe and Latin America.

Andrea Morrison is Assistant Professor at the Department of Economic Geography, Utrecht University, the Netherlands, and research affiliate at KITeS-Bocconi University, Milan, Italy. His research interests lie in the area of evolutionary economic geography, with particular attention to the evolution of industrial clusters. Most recently his research has focused on the geography of innovation and science. His work has been published in leading international journals, such as *Regional Studies, European Planning Studies, the Journal of Evolutionary Economics, Research Policy* and *World Development*.

Roberta Rabellotti is Professor of Economics at the Department of Economics, Università del Piemonte Orientale, Italy. She holds a PhD from the Institute of Development Studies, University of Sussex, UK, and an MSc in development studies from the University of Oxford, UK. She has been a consultant for the Inter-American Development Bank, the European Union, UNIDO, UNCTAD, ILO and ECLAC-UN. Her publications include books with Harvard University Press and Macmillan as well as numerous articles published in major academic journals. Her main research interests are in the field of local development and innovation.

Scott Tiffin is a Canadian who has lived in Santiago, Chile, Montevideo, Uruguay and Boston, MA, USA for the past decade. His work in this period has been to carry out research and university management projects across the region related to business school development and the linkage of universities to industrial stakeholders through innovation and entrepreneurship in clusters. He has performed a number of projects on this area for IDRC, UNESCO and the World Bank. He is author of *Entrepreneurship in Latin America* (Praeger Press, 2004).

Acknowledgments

This book draws on the empirical findings of the *Innovation and Globalization in the Wine Sector: An International Comparison between Argentina, Chile, Italy and South Africa* project, carried out with the financial support of Progetto Alfieri (Fondazione CRT) and Interlink (Ministero dell'Istruzione, dell'Università e della Ricerca), directed by Roberta Rabellotti. The editors would like to thank Massimo Pernicone and Gabriela Cares for their collaboration in the collection of data. For their support in the field research, in Argentina we thank Ana Maria Ruiz and Adriana Bocco; in Chile, Mario Castillo, Jimena Gonzalez Alvarado, Pablo Ugarte and Cruz Coke from CORFO, Jose Miguel Benavente, Jorge Katz and Graciela Moguillansky; in Italy, Daniele Della Valle from Vignaioli Piemontesi and Giuseppe Martelli of Assocnologi and Vittorino Novello of Università di Torino; in South Africa, Nick Vink, Melanie Vivier and Eric Wood. Moreover, we have greatly benefited from the participation and discussion of our works in many seminars around the world, where preliminary drafts were presented. We thank all the colleagues who on these occasions discussed our work and helped refine it by putting it under a true global scrutiny. Special thanks go to the entrepreneurs, wine experts and researchers in Argentina, Chile, Italy and South Africa, who shared with us their knowledge and generously gave us their time. Finally, we are very grateful to Susanna Burchielli for reviewing and editing the volume.

Elisa Giuliani, Andrea Morrison and *Roberta Rabellotti*
Pisa and Milan
August 2010

1. Innovation and technological catch-up in the wine industry: an introduction

Elisa Giuliani, Andrea Morrison and Roberta Rabellotti

1 THE AIM OF THE BOOK

Why choose the wine industry to investigate catching up in emerging countries? And why focus on science and innovation as the main drivers of catching up in a traditional agro-food industry such as wine? These two questions may well be asked by many potential readers of this book. Numerous recent studies about catching up are focused on countries such as China and India and on high-tech sectors such as electronics, software, pharmaceuticals and telecommunications. These cases are indeed globally known for having sparked economic growth in some selected locations, such as Bangalore in India or Shenzhen in China. Nevertheless, in spite of being in the spotlight, very little is known about the impact of these success stories on the rest of the country. Furthermore, there is little doubt that a large number of less developed countries are still highly dependent on agriculture and agro-food industries. The agro-food industry, though often depicted as low value added and with little innovation content, can instead represent a sector with significant opportunities of technological and rent upgrading. Hence, the real challenge is to understand how such sectors can contribute to the process of growth in these countries.

What has happened in the global wine industry is extremely interesting from a development point of view because the latecomers in the international market have radically changed how wine is produced, sold and consumed. Until the end of the 1980s, the international market for wine was dominated by European countries, and particularly by France and Italy. But since the beginning of the 1990s this supremacy has started to come under attack due to the spectacular performance, in terms of both exported volumes and values, of new international players. Among these new global leaders are affluent nations relatively new to the wine sector, such as the USA and Australia, and emerging economies, such as Argentina, Chile and South Africa.

The main argument supported in this book is that innovation in product and process, spurred by consistent investments and research efforts, has played a prominent role in the emergence of New World producers in the international market. Scientists have performed a key innovative role in the wine industry since the 1860s' *phylloxera* outbreak, but traditionally the production of good wines has been a privilege of a few *terroir*[1] and a few producers, with the secrets transmitted from generation to generation. The empirical evidence collected in this book shows that New World producers have radically improved the quality of their wines, investing in research in universities and laboratories, strengthening the link between university and industry and importing external knowledge through experts. An investigation into the wine industry in countries such as Argentina, Chile and South Africa represents an extraordinary opportunity to show how a traditional agro-food industry can become highly competitive and catch up in the global market, when following a different trajectory from the long-standing leading countries, a new pathway in which innovation, science and research play a prominent role.

Therefore, the research questions in this book are as follows. What are the main conditions for successful catching up in the wine industry? Are scientific and technological knowledge, and institutions devoted to its production and diffusion, key ingredients for catching up? And if so, to what extent have New World countries developed indigenous technological and scientific capabilities? Were they able to enter the international scientific community successfully? Are there diverse catching-up trajectories emerging with the recent upsurge of New World countries? What can be learned from the successful case of the wine industry that can be extended to agro-food industries in general?

To answer these questions, a research project – Innovation and Globalization in the Wine Sector: An International Comparison between Argentina, Chile, Italy and South Africa – was carried out by the editors of this book, collecting new empirical evidence on wine firms, researchers in wine-related disciplines and industry-supporting institutions. To complement and enrich the findings of this project, some prominent scholars in the field were invited to contribute to the book. Some of these contributions were discussed in a workshop organized in 2009 at Università del Piemonte Orientale in Novara, Italy. The selected contributions are collected in this book, which is divided into two parts. In Part I, Chapters 2–4 adopt a macro-level perspective to analyze the process of catch-up in a variety of contexts (that is, both emerging and developed economies), with a focus on the role played by scientific research and innovation. Part II comprises a set of case studies on the main drivers of catch-up: universities and researchers, public institutions and firms, in Argentina, Chile and South Africa.

The book contributes to the existing knowledge in several ways. While contemporary accounts of catching up have mainly followed the high-tech fad (Malerba and Mani, 2009), here we shift the focus to the agro-food industry. We do so by providing fresh empirical evidence on places and countries that have seldom been at the centre of the analysis, but from which original and important lessons can be drawn. One such lesson is that beneath the surface of traditional industries there can be significant investments in knowledge-intensive activities, which create unique opportunities for catching up with leading countries. Moreover, the book challenges the conventional rhetoric about the backwardness of innovation systems in less developed countries, which are often thought to be plagued by few university–industry linkages and poor technological advancements on the side of domestic firms. In contrast, this research shows that in Argentina, Chile and South Africa, although at different levels of advancement, innovation systems, in which firms and other organizations have configured new inter-organizational relational models, have contributed significantly to the generation of higher-value products and new business opportunities. In the light of this, the empirical evidence collected in this book may be of relevance not only for scholars of innovation and development, but also for policy makers interested in understanding how to engage in catching up in the agro-food sectors.

This introductory chapter is organized as follows. Section 2 contains a discussion about the concept of catching up, which in our view goes beyond the idea of a unique path of convergence towards the leader, showing that latecomers can succeed by following different learning trajectories. In Section 3 we introduce the idea of an innovation system, which is discussed considering both a national perspective, in particular looking at the institutional difference between developed and emerging economies, and a sectoral one, which looks at the industry-specific commonalities across countries. Section 4 focuses on the role of science, universities and researchers within the wine system of innovation. We contend that building indigenous technological and scientific capabilities is a necessary requirement for latecomers that want to compete in international markets. Section 5 concludes with a presentation of the structure of the book.

2 CATCHING UP: THEORY AND EXPERIENCES

The concept of catching up has been commonly used in the economic literature to indicate the ability of a country to reduce income and productivity gaps with the leaders. In the earlier debate, catching up was straightforward: the larger the productivity gap between backward economies and the leaders, the higher the potential for the former to make a large leap. Therefore, backward countries were expected to grow more quickly than leaders, so that in the long run they would inevitably converge towards a similar per capita income. The above argument rests on the idea that latecomers can easily import technology and, through it, access and reap the benefits of international technological spillovers. In this view, catching up is considered to be a question of relative speed in a race along a fixed track, and technological learning is understood as a cumulative and linear process, which consists in copying the blueprint made by the leaders, rather than running in a new direction (Perez, 1986).

Since the end of the 1980s the spectacular performance of the newly industrializing countries (NICs) in Asia has encouraged novel conceptualizations of economic growth and structural change, given that the Asian experience could not be explained as the result of the import and adoption of technologies and organizational models developed in advanced countries, as implied by the theory of economic growth that prevailed in the 1950s and 1960s (Solow, 1956). There is a broad consensus in the literature that the progress of Asian NICs has involved significant deviations from earlier industrialization experiences, entailing distinctive strategic innovations, learning paths, accumulation of absorptive capacities and institutional building (Lall, 1992; Bell and Pavitt, 1993; Hobday, 1995; Kim, 1997; Altenburg et al., 2008).

According to the pioneering contribution by Abramovitz (1986), catch-up is a process going far beyond the mere adoption of new technologies, and depends on the ability of countries to build some 'technological congruence' with leaders as well as their own 'social capabilities'. The first concept indicates the conditions that latecomers need to share, at least to a certain degree, with leaders, in order to adopt their models. These might refer to economic factors such as market size, availability of inputs, consumer tastes, and so forth. The latter concept concerns issues such as technical competence as well as educational infrastructure, and more broadly those institutions supporting technological capabilities. In a similar vein, Nelson and colleagues have argued that catching-up countries need to master not only 'physical' technologies; they rather have to build 'social' technologies (Nelson and Sampat, 2001), which include 'organisational forms, bodies of law, public policies, codes of good business and administrative practice, customs norms' (Mazzoleni and Nelson, 2007: 1513).

All in all, the above-mentioned approaches clearly indicate that catching up is more than simply copying new technologies; it requires creative adaptation and innovation along and beyond the model followed by forerunners. Therefore, in their catching-up effort, latecomers do not simply follow the technological path of the advanced countries; they may skip some stages or even create their own individual path (Lee and Lim, 2001). Late entrants build on existing knowledge, but they would eventually depart from it by following their own trajectory of development. As suggested by Perez and Soete (1988), this occurs when windows of opportunity in the prevailing techno-economic paradigm (that is, the set of interrelated technical and organizational innovations that characterize the existing mode of production) open up. At such turning points, taking over is possible since incumbents are locked in existing technologies, management practices and labor skills. The burden of previous investments makes it difficult for them to fully recognize changes taking place in the external environment and endorse them. This eventually hampers the adoption of new technologies among leaders, which instead will diffuse more quickly elsewhere, in countries not bound to the old technology and the related institutional context. An excellent illustrative case comes from the history of economic development: the latecomer Germany developed its own way to industrialization based on the system of investment banks, and in so doing outpaced the UK in the early twentieth century. Similarly in the 1970s and 1980s, first Japan, then Korea and Taiwan, took over western economies in several high-tech sectors thanks to engineering excellence and government support (Mazzoleni and Nelson, 2007).

While much of the discussion on catching up has been carried out at the country level, there is also an interesting stream of literature extending this idea (or conceptualization) to sectors within and between national boundaries (Mytelka, 2004; Niosi and Reid, 2008; Malerba and Mani, 2009). In the chapters of this book, we investigate catching up and forging ahead in the wine industry, making the point that in this specific sector, the rise of latecomers in the global wine market, including some emerging countries (that is, Argentina, Chile and South Africa) has occurred thanks to significant discontinuities in both technologies and market demand. The discontinuities reflect the fact that in the 1980s to 1990s, new pathways for the production and marketing of wines have been explored by latecomer countries, which departed from the established business models of Old World countries, such as Italy and France. In other words, New World producers have prompted the process of technological modernization, product standardization and marketing innovation, which have proved to be in line with the requirements in the international market. More than that, these countries set the foundation for a new paradigm in the wine industry, based on a market-driven scientific approach to wine production. Such modernization has challenged Old World producers, and has had a remarkable impact not only on the industry knowledge base, but also on the relevant industry actors (for example, universities, regulatory bodies, companies) in both New and Old World producers.

3.   INNOVATION SYSTEMS AND CATCHING UP

In the catching-up debate, the adoption of an innovation system perspective (Freeman, 1987; Lundvall, 1992; Edquist, 1997) has contributed to shifting the emphasis from resource endowments and comparative advantages to institutional variables, capabilities and the dynamic creation of competitive advantages. Focusing attention on innovation systems in development economics has followed from the realization of the need for conscious and purposive innovation effort and capacity building in less developed countries (Lundvall et al., 2009; Malerba and Mani, 2009). The burgeoning literature on innovation systems in less developed areas exemplifies the increased attention placed on the broad institutional set-up affecting learning as well as searching and exploring (Lundvall et al., 2009). As Nelson and Nelson (2002) emphasize, the innovation system idea is an institutional conception *par excellence*, articulated at the national, regional and local levels and characterized by the interaction of different actors – firms, universities, technology transfer organizations, service providers – as well as by frameworks and norms, set within relatively well-defined boundaries.

In less developed countries, where new frontier innovation is still scarcely generated and the bulk of knowledge and technology is imported, scholars have stressed the importance of extra-national influences on the innovation process, given that linkages with foreign firms and organizations play a central role in helping to operate innovation systems. The sectoral system approach (Malerba, 2004) complements the national and regional perspectives by underlying the transnational dimension of sectoral systems, that is, the role of international actors, linkages and transmission mechanisms, and the limits of national policies in the framework of increased global integration. In addition to the structuring of national and local innovation systems, inflows of knowledge and technology from external sources, as well as the dynamics of demand along the internationally fragmented chains of production, are essential components for upgrading and learning in emergent economies (Pietrobelli and Rabellotti, 2009).

State-of-the-art literature has therefore suggested that innovation systems in less developed countries are mainly *learning* systems and that connections outside national boundaries are crucial to acquire and absorb external knowledge (Viotti, 2002). These views have often been complemented by a widespread acknowledgment of the weaknesses of developing countries' innovation systems (for example, Intarakumnerd et al., 2002; Aubert, 2004). Nevertheless, this idea has recently been debated (Lundvall et al., 2009), and in this book we aim to contribute to the current debate by providing new empirical evidence about how firms and other organizations in the wine industry have in fact created successful innovation systems that have permitted the production of innovative and high-value products. We show that connections with global pipelines of technological knowledge have been significant in wine catch-up countries. Most of them run through international experts, such as consultant wine-makers, and star scientists who play a role in spreading global knowledge on methods of production and ideas for product innovations in the domestic industry. Connections to consultants are common in advanced as well as in emerging countries' wine producers, showing that globalization in some instances has been an opportunity to access knowledge and technology rather than a threat for the latter countries. With regard to researchers, we show a rapidly increasing participation of catching-up countries in international research networks.

At the domestic level, the book illustrates how, in the new international context, old institutions, such as extension agencies, were forced to enter into a restructuring process, which transformed them into knowledge facilitators that enhance the formation of local social capital. At the country level, the growing engagement of public and private actors, often in partnership, has led to the development of supportive industrywide institutions. Remarkable examples can be found in some New World countries, such as South Africa and Australia, where two bodies funded by producer levies (respectively, Winetech and the Grape and Wine Research and Development Corporation) have contributed to creating public goods in the form of research and development (R&D) promotion, and in so doing they have enhanced local wineries' innovation activity.

4   INNOVATION SYSTEMS AND THE ROLE OF SCIENCE, UNIVERSITIES AND RESEARCHERS

Within innovation systems, firms are the key actors in the innovation and learning processes, but an essential role is also played by other institutions and organizations and by the interactions taking place among them. The literature on innovation systems in less developed countries has mainly focused on the importance of organizations dealing with technology diffusion and extension, which have been considered as key in these contexts, given the nonexistence and/or the weakness of science and technology organizations (Lundvall et al., 2009). Nevertheless, in many developing countries increasing attention is being paid to the role that might be played by actors such as universities and public research organizations (PROs) – an awareness that stems from the strengthening of ties among science, technology and innovation in many industries – and also beyond those sectors traditionally defined as knowledge intensive.The contribution to economic development of science and research conducted at universities and PROs has been recognized by Mazzoleni and Nelson (2007) as one of the key elements of past and recent experiences of catching up.

Literature comparing the scientific and research productivity of advanced economies (for example, the USA versus Europe) as well as their institutional underpinnings has flourished in recent years, showing how different institutional contexts and policy models enable countries to reduce the gap with the frontier (Etzkowitz and Leydesdorff, 2000; Dosi et al., 2006). Instead, as pointed out by Mazzoleni (2008), a good understanding of the contribution and the functioning of research organizations in less developed countries is still far away. In fact, in backward countries it is widely disputed whether they should invest in tertiary education and whether universities and PROs should be encouraged to undertake advanced research. Nonetheless, it is less controversial that research organizations are necessary to support the development of indigenous capabilities and to build a national absorptive capacity (Albuquerque, 2004; Brundenius et al., 2009).

This is particularly true in the agricultural field where there is a need to undertake research and develop knowledge and technologies suited to the specific conditions of each country and region (Vessuri, 1990; Albuquerque, 2004). In agriculture, imported technologies need to be adapted to the local climate, soil conditions and other biophysical characteristics. Moreover, research issues addressed in temperate zones, where developed countries are generally located, are not necessarily the most relevant in tropical climates. A case in point is viticulture, where for example irrigation issues matter considerably more for wine growers in the South than for those in the North; similarly, plagues and viruses as well as soil conditions differ from country to country. This implies that accessing foreign sources of knowledge is important; nevertheless, in order to fully exploit the potential development of local crops and technology, it must be accompanied by investment in indigenous research, which can spur local technological capabilities and enhance both adoption and adaptation of international discoveries (Pardey and Beintema, 2001; Bernardes and Albuquerque, 2003; Giuliani, 2007). Furthermore, investing in indigenous capabilities is even more urgent today than it was in the past, as tighter international property rights regulations are restricting the opportunities for less developed countries to tap into international public knowledge (Mazzoleni and Nelson, 2007).

The wine sector represents a very interesting case in which to investigate whether the economic catch-up (if not forging ahead) is associated with a similar catch-up process in scientific capabilities. The evidence presented in this book clearly shows that New World countries are closing the gap with the established producers in terms of scientific research. First and foremost, national universities in catching-up countries are important generators of applied science, which is critical for the industry. Second, university researchers are not isolated but are part of a global knowledge network formed by academic scholars worldwide, who carry out research on wine-related topics, ranging from biotechnology to agronomics, chemistry and mechanical engineering. We show that scientists involved in wine-related research in the wine-producing latecomers have considerably expanded their participation in the international scientific community over the past 10 years: not only have they increased co-publications with peers in the Old World, but increasingly they have established research linkages with colleagues at universities in other New World countries. This evidence clearly points on the one hand to the growing importance of such countries as a source of scientific knowledge, and, more importantly, on the other it suggests that they are capable of setting their own research priorities and in doing so of influencing the international scientific agenda. Finally, we show that by tapping into international scientific knowledge, a few talented university researchers act as bridging agents and contribute to channelling international knowledge towards the domestic wine industry.

5 THE STRUCTURE OF THE BOOK

The book is structured in two parts. Part I investigates catching up undertaken by some New World producers, stressing the role played by scientific research and innovation in this process. Part II focuses on some of the main drivers of catch-up: universities and researchers, firms and supporting institutions.

In Chapter 2, Cusmano, Morrison and Rabellotti illustrate the significant discontinuities in both technologies and market demand that favored the emergence to the global stage of the New World producers. The interplay between national features and sector-specific dynamics, which emerges at the global level, is interpreted through the conceptual framework of the sectoral system of innovation (SSI) approach. The transformations that occurred in the wine industry are explained as a tale of co-evolution on the demand and supply sides, which has led to the emergence of a novel, knowledge-based, market-driven model, challenging the producer-driven approach of incumbents. The chapter shows that emerging countries with diverse institutional models and innovation strategies actively participate in the process of technological modernization and product standardization. These newcomers in the wine sector have responded particularly effectively to changes in demand, aligning emerging scientific approaches with institutional-building efforts and successful marketing strategies.

In Chapter 3, Cassi, Morrison and Rabellotti investigate the scientific performance, measured in terms of number of publications, of the successful latecomers in the global wine market. In addition, based on the analysis of co-authorships, the chapter explores to what extent the scientific wine community has become global, and in particular whether Argentina, Chile and South Africa undertake international linkages within the scientific and research system. Finally, analyzing the network of co-authorships, attention focuses on the structure of the national research systems in these three countries for highlighting the distinct roles played by PROs, universities and the industry in the existing domestic and international links.

In Chapter 4, Anderson focuses on Australia's wine industry, which has been through major structural changes over the past six decades and has grown especially rapidly since the early 1990s. Investments in generic promotion and in grape and wine R&D have been significant features of the industry throughout that period, and have grown in importance following the formation in the early 1990s of the Australian Wine Export Council and the Grape and Wine R&D Corporation, which coordinates the investing of grape grower and winemaker national levies and matching federal government funding. This chapter assesses the role that the innovation system has played in the industry's recent growth and concludes by speculating on the scope for more diversification and attention to regional diversities in the promotion and R&D strategies in the future of the Australian wine industry.

Part II investigates the main drivers of the catching-up process, and in Chapter 5 the focus is on universities in emerging regional innovation systems. According to Kunc and Tiffin, universities have the ability to understand existing technologies, maintain connections with external networks and are usually the main, if not the only, regional knowledge source. In order to fulfil their role, universities have to provide for a qualified workforce, locally adapted research, appropriate services and technologies for their regional stakeholders. The chapter proposes a set of measures for analyzing the involvement of universities in the development of their regional systems of innovation, applying it to investigate two universities located in two important wine regions in Argentina and Chile.

The results suggest that the investigated wine regions follow two different development paths: in the case of Chile, exogenous sources of knowledge, such as foreign consultants, prevail with respect to those related to the local university, while in Argentina there are strong linkages between the university and the local companies, facilitating the circulation of knowledge from endogenous sources.

Chapter 6 focuses on the wine industry in Argentina, and McDermott and Corredoira examine a case regarding the institutional evolution of the country's wine industry. They show how the impressive catching-up process of the Mendoza wine industry is due to a large extent to a local institutional renovation, which has led to the emergence of a new generation of public–private institutions (PPIs). Because of their governance properties, the PPIs helped reshape both policy and inter-firm networks as well as improve firm access to a variety of knowledge resources. In turn, their unique survey data and statistical analysis suggest that firms improved their product upgrading because of the ways in which PPIs acted as social and knowledge bridges among previously isolated producer communities.

In Chapter 7, Giuliani and Rabellotti investigate the role that universities play in channeling international scientific knowledge into the Chilean and South African wine industries. Universities are critical actors for catching up and, within universities, the links of individual researchers with international research networks appear to be critical channels for directing external scientific knowledge into the local economy. The authors investigate the characteristics of such 'bridging researchers' and find that they are significantly more 'talented' than the average, both because they publish more in international journals and/or because they have received awards for their academic work. The authors suggest that this result may have significant policy implications, as policies aimed at strengthening the skills of these researchers should be welcomed in catching-up industries.

In Chapter 8, Lorentzen studies innovation in the wine industry of the Western Cape Province in South Africa. The focus of this chapter is on the nature and role of linkages between relevant actors in the wine sector as well as on the knowledge flows such interactions facilitate, in order to understand the relationship between the knowledge infrastructure and those linkages on the one hand and innovation on the other. It also raises the issue of spatial proximity, namely whether being close to one another is a necessary condition for such knowledge exchange. Finally, the question addressed is what, if anything, policy has to do with this being a success story.

In Chapter 9, Giuliani, Morrison and Rabellotti summarize the main findings of the book, drawing some lessons from the rich and varied empirical evidence collected. Skills, access to external knowledge, domestic research and innovation capability and networking between public and private actors are identified as the key drivers of the catching-up process successfully undertaken by some emerging countries in the wine sector. Finally, policy implications are discussed and an open agenda for future research is proposed.

NOTE

1. *Terroir* is a French term used to denote the special characteristics of an agricultural site, in terms of soil, weather conditions and farming techniques, each contributing to the unique qualities of the wine.

REFERENCES

Abramovitz, M. (1986), 'Catching up, forging ahead, and falling behind', *Journal of Economic History*, **46** (2), 385–406.

Albuquerque, E. (2004), 'Science and technology systems in less developed countries', in H. Moed, W. Glänzel and U. Schmoch (eds), *Handbook of Quantitative Science and Technology Research*, Dordrecht, the Netherlands: Kluwer Academic, pp. 759–78.

Altenburg, T., H. Schmitz and A. Stamm (2008), 'Breakthrough? China's and India's transition from production to innovation', *World Development*, **36** (2), 325–44.

Aubert, J.E. (2004), 'Promoting innovation in developing countries: a conceptual framework', World Bank, accessed September 2010 at http://info.worldbank.org/etools/docs/library/137729/0-3097AubertPaper%5B1%5D.pdf.

Bell, M. and K. Pavitt (1993), 'Technological accumulation and industrial growth: contrasts between developed and developing countries', *Industrial and Corporate Change*, **2** (2), 157–210.

Bernardes, A. and E.M. Albuquerque (2003), 'Cross-over, thresholds, and interactions between science and technology: lessons for less-developed countries', *Research Policy*, **32** (5), 867–87.

Brundenius C., B.-A. Lundvall and J. Sutz (2009), 'The role of universities in innovation systems in developing countries: developmental university systems – empirical, analytical and normative perspectives', in B-A. Lundvall, K.J. Joseph, C. Chaminade and J. Vang (eds), *Handbook of Innovation Systems and Developing Countries – Building Domestic Capabilities in a Global Setting*, Cheltenham, UK and Northampton, MA, USA: Edward Elgar Publishing, pp. 311–33.

Dosi, G., P. Llerena and M. Sylos Labini (2006), 'The relationships between science, technologies and their industrial exploitation: an illustration through the myths and realities of the so-called "European Paradox"', *Research Policy*, **35** (10), 1450–64.

Edquist, C. (ed.) (1997), *Systems of Innovation: Technologies, Institutions and Organisations*, London: Pinter.

Etzkowitz, H. and L. Leydesdorff (2000), 'The dynamics of innovation: from national systems and "mode 2" to a triple helix of university–industry–government relations', *Research Policy*, **29** (2), 109–23.

Freeman, C. (1987), *Technology Policy and Economic Performance: Lessons from Japan*, London: Pinter.

Giuliani, E. (2007), 'The wine industry: persistence of tacit knowledge or increased codification? Some implications for catching-up countries', *International Journal of Technology and Globalisation*, **3** (2/3), 138–54.

Hobday, M. (1995), *Innovation in East Asia: The Challenge to Japan*, Aldershot and Brookfield, VT, USA: Edward Elgar.

Intarakumnerd, P., P. Chairatana and T. Tangchitpiboon (2002), 'National innovation system in less successful developing countries: the case of Thailand', *Research Policy*, **31** (8–9), 1445–57.

Kim, L. (1997), *Imitation to Innovation: The Dynamics of Korea's Technological Learning*, Boston, MA: Harvard Business School Press.

Lall, S. (1992), 'Technological capabilities and industrialization', *World Development*, **20** (2), 165–86.

Lee, K. and C. Lim (2001), 'Technological regimes, catching-up and leapfrogging: findings from the Korean industries', *Research Policy*, **30** (3), 459–83.

Lundvall, B.-A. (1992), *National Systems of Innovation: Towards a Theory of Innovation and Interactive Learning*, London: Pinter.

Lundvall, B.-A., K.J. Joseph, C. Chaminade and J. Vang (eds) (2009), *Handbook of Innovation Systems and Developing Countries: Building Domestic Capabilities in a Global Setting*, Cheltenham, UK and Northampton, MA, USA: Edward Elgar.

Malerba, F. (ed.) (2004), *Sectoral Systems of Innovation: Concepts, Issues and Analyses of Six Major Sectors in Europe*, Cambridge: Cambridge University Press.

Malerba, F. and S. Mani (eds) (2009), *Sectoral Systems of Innovation and Production in Developing Countries: Actors, Structure and Evolution,* Cheltenham, UK and Northampton, MA, USA: Edward Elgar.

Mazzoleni, R. (2008), 'Catching up and academic institutions: a comparative study of past national experiences', *Journal of Development Studies*, **44** (5), 678–700.

Mazzoleni, R. and R. Nelson (2007), 'Public research institutions and economic catch-up', *Research Policy*, **36** (10), 1512–28.

Mytelka, L. (2004), 'Catching up in new wave technologies', *Oxford Development Studies*, **3** (3), 389–405.

Nelson, R.R. and K. Nelson (2002), 'Technology, institutions, and innovation systems, *Research Policy*, **31** (2), 265–72.

Nelson, R.R. and B.N. Sampat (2001), 'Making sense of institutions as a factor shaping economic performance', *Journal of Economic Behavior and Organization*, **44** (1), 31–54.

Niosi, J. and S. Reid (2008), 'Biotechnology and nanotechnology: science-based enabling technologies as windows of opportunity for LDCs?', *World Development*, **35** (3), 426–38.

Pardey, P.G and N.M. Beintema (2001), *Slow Magic: Agricultural R&D a Century After Mendel*, Washington, DC: International Food Policy Research Institute.

Perez, C. (1986), 'New technologies and development', in C. Freeman and B.-A. Lundvall (eds), *Small Countries Facing the Technological Revolution*, London: Pinter, pp. 85–97.

Perez, C. and L. Soete (1988), 'Catching up in technology: entry barriers and windows of opportunity', in G. Dosi, C. Freeman, R.R. Nelson, G. Silverberg and L. Soete (eds), *Technical Change and Economic Theory*, London: Pinter, pp. 458–79.

Pietrobelli, C. and R. Rabellotti (2009), 'The global dimension of innovation systems – Linking innovation systems and global value chain', in B-A. Lundvall, K.J. Joseph, C. Chaminade and J. Vang (eds), (2009), *Handbook of Innovation Systems and Developing Countries – Building Domestic Capabilities in a Global Setting*, Cheltenham, UK and Northampton, MA, USA: Edward Elgar Publishing, pp. 214–40.

Solow, R.M. (1956), 'A contribution to the theory of economic growth', *Quarterly Journal of Economics*, **70**, 65–4.

Vessuri, H.M.C. (1990), 'O inventamos o erramos: the power of science in Latin America', *World Development*, **18** (11), 1543–53.

Viotti, E.B. (2002), 'National learning systems: a new approach on technological change in late industrialising economies and evidence from the cases of Brazil and South Korea', *Technological Forecasting & Social Change*, **69** (7), 653–80.

PART I

Catching up in the wine industry

2. Catching-up trajectories in the wine sector

Lucia Cusmano, Andrea Morrison and Roberta Rabellotti

1 INTRODUCTION

Up to the end of the 1980s, 'Old World' countries, and particularly France and Italy, dominated the international wine market. Since the beginning of the 1990s, their supremacy has been challenged by new international players, who are recording spectacular performances in terms of both exported volumes and values. These 'New World' countries include affluent frontrunners that are relatively new to the wine sector, such as the USA and Australia, and less developed but rapidly growing latecomers such as Chile, Argentina and South Africa.

A number of different factors has contributed to the emergence in the international market of New World players, and, among them, the late rapid expansion of developing economies. On the supply side, a process of technological modernization and pervasive organizational change has been spurred by consistent investment and research effort by newcomers and supported by the establishment of specialized research institutions. The research-driven industry transformation was first promoted by the affluent New World players, but has rapidly diffused to emerging economies, which have been dynamic adapters and adopters of the new business model. The demand side has also been important in this evolution. In fact, New World players have been particularly responsive to changes in wine consumption habits across the world, aligning emerging scientific approaches and institutional building efforts with their branding and marketing strategies.

This chapter illustrates the significant discontinuities in both technologies and market demand that favored the emergence to the global stage of affluent newcomers in the first instance and fast-growing developing regions in more recent times. The interplay between national features and sector-specific dynamics, which emerges at the global level, is interpreted through the conceptual framework of the sectoral system of innovation (SSI) approach. This focuses on co-evolutionary mechanisms on the demand and supply sides and is adopted in the present chapter to single out relevant trends, key factors and feedback mechanisms underpinning the catching-up process.

The chapter is organized as follows. Section 2 presents the dynamics of the global wine industry. Section 3 introduces the conceptual framework. Section 4 analyzes the four pillars of the wine sectoral system. Section 5 concludes.

2 THE DYNAMICS OF THE GLOBAL WINE INDUSTRY

Although the so-called Old World countries, that is, Italy, France, Spain, Portugal and Germany, are still among the main producers, exporters and markets, they no longer dominate the wine industry as they once did. New World producers, such as the USA, Australia, Argentina, South Africa and Chile, have rapidly been gaining market shares, including the medium–high-quality segments that once were the exclusive domain of traditional, long-established producers.

Before the late 1970s, New World production, which was typically started by colonial settlers and based on imported root stock, was concentrated in bulk wine of variable quality, posing no real threat, either in terms of volume or in terms of quality, to the European hegemony in the international market. The initial entry of new competitors in the second half of the 1970s took place at a time of sharp decline in volumes of wine production and consumption, which recovered gradually only in the 1990s, following integration of global markets and diffusion of wine consumption in emerging areas (Tables 2.1 and 2.2).

In terms of world production shares in volumes, in the late 1980s Europe still accounted for 78 percent of world wine production, and by 2007 its share had dropped by 10 points, generally to the advantage of producers from the American continent, followed, in order, by Asia, Africa and Oceania.

The shift in production shares coincided with the emergence of new consumption areas, particularly in Asia, which increased its share of world consumption from 2 percent in the late 1980s to 7 percent in 2007. In terms of consumption, the erosion of the European market has been more gradual, dropping from 74 to 67 percent of world consumption, whereas the American market remained rather stable around 20 percent (OIV, 2009).

The challenge posed by New World producers to established ones

Table 2.1 *World wine production (volume, tonnes '00), 1975–2008*

Yearly average	1975–79	1980–84	1985–89	1990–94	1995–99	2000–04	2005–08*
France	67,484	68,062	66,378	56,215	57,588	53,505	50,292
Italy	71,482	76,787	67,329	61,058	56,150	49,641	47,202
Spain	31,256	35,675	32,140	30,441	29,509	38,883	33,764
Portugal	9,276	9,327	7,930	7,916	6,727	7,350	6,594
USA	15,388	17,043	18,782	17,575	20,994	24,098	24,345
Argentina	24,047	22,799	20,255	15,106	14,237	13,986	15,255
Australia	3,550	3,855	4,298	4,693	6,773	11,061	12,676
South Africa	5,812	7,443	7,477	7,382	7,953	7,748	9,462
Chile	5,423	5,331	3,951	3,488	4,364	6,186	8,082
China	90	1,196	2,692	4,248	8,881	11,500	14,250
World	317,160	342,096	299,971	269,516	268,456	279,280	274,613

Source: FAOSTAT (2009).

Note: Estimates.

Table 2.2 *World wine consumption (volume, tonnes '00), 1975–2007*

Yearly average	1975–79	1980–84	1985–89	1990–94	1995–99	2000–03	2004–07
France	52,522	48,517	41,891	37,025	33,990	30,739	32,658
Italy	54,084	47,773	38,052	33,784	32,435	29,778	26,835
Spain	22,136	20,188	17,800	16,316	14,528	14,253	15,503
Germany	16,376	17,781	17,795	19,562	19,593	20,401	20,217
Portugal	7,399	7,659	6,192	5,699	5,377	5,014	5,291
USA	15,572	19,850	21,332	18,324	21,006	21,617	21,455
Argentina	22,339	20,692	18,117	16,485	13,218	12,229	11,021
Australia	1,972	2,871	3,349	3,181	3,489	4,031	4,613
South Africa	5,740	7,347	3,749	3,799	4,413	4,232	3,532
Chile	5,245	4,958	3,715	2,662	2,382	2,481	2,450
China	114	1,234	2,734	4,274	9,305	11,599	14,927
World	279,694	285,166	240,687	222,141	222,544	225,130	236,298

Source: FAOSTAT (2009).

becomes most evident when we consider the dynamics of world wine exports: in volume terms, the share of world trade by European exporters has declined from almost 95 percent in the late 1980s to 71 percent in 2007 (Table 2.3).

Table 2.3 World wine exports (volume, tonnes '00 and country share), 1975–2007

Yearly average	1975–79	%	1980–84	%	1985–89	%	1990–94	%	1995–99	%	2000–04	%	2005–07	%
France	7,196	17.2	9,662	20.2	12,730	28.2	11,553	24.7	14,328	23.9	15,005	22.0	14,408	16.8
Italy	13,238	31.6	16,419	34.3	12,790	28.3	12,920	27.7	15,062	25.1	14,479	21.2	17,240	20.0
Spain	5,048	12.1	5,492	11.5	5,056	11.2	6,987	15.0	8,053	13.4	10,224	15.0	13,785	16.0
Germany	1,246	3.0	2,382	5.0	2,738	6.1	2,733	6.0	2,307	3.8	2,515	3.7	3,150	3.7
Portugal	1,682	4.0	1,448	3.0	1,524	3.4	1,950	4.2	2,020	3.4	2,345	3.4	2,932	3.4
USA	97	0.2	310	0.6	467	1.0	1,104	2.4	2,026	3.4	3,089	3.4	3,793	4.5
Argentina	341	0.8	172	0.4	196	0.4	384	0.8	1,386	2.3	1,320	1.9	2,967	3.4
Australia	55	0.1	78	0.2	242	0.5	852	1.8	1,612	2.7	4,682	6.9	7,464	8.7
South Africa	92	0.2	112	0.2	88	0.2	276	0.6	1,081	1.8	2,080	3.0	3,739	4.3
Chile	124	0.3	138	0.3	170	0.4	774	1.7	2,709	4.5	4,185	6.1	6,802	7.6
China	0	0.0	0	0.0	14	0.0	41	0.1	33	0.1	28	0.0	53	0.1
World	41,848	100	47,854	100	45,159	100	46,690	100	60,010	100	68,221	100	86,234	100

Source: FAOSTAT (2009)

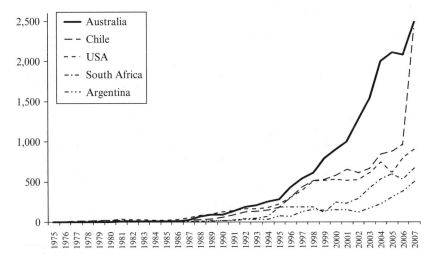

Source: FAOSTAT (2009).

*Figure 2.1 Wine exports, New World countries (value US$m),
1975–2007*

The catching-up dynamics by New World producers accelerated over
the 1990s when the 'first tier' of advanced newcomers (the USA and
Australia) was joined in the race by a 'second tier' of developing countries
(Figure 2.1). Among these, the fast-growing Chilean wine industry stands
out in terms of export values, having rapidly overcome the USA and
caught up with the leader, Australia.

A few emerging areas account for the recent remarkable trade performance of the New World. At present Australia leads the group of followers,
but, as highlighted in Figure 2.1, other countries have lately experienced
faster growth. Over the 10 years from 1996 to 2006, the export volumes
have increased at the rate of 350 percent in South Africa, around 280
percent in Australia and Chile and 190 percent in the USA (European
Commission, 2007). Most recently the fastest-growing wine exporter is
Argentina, recording between 2002 and 2007 export volume increases at
an annual compound growth rate of 22 percent. In some markets the New
World producers have even been able to overcome those in the Old World.
For example, Australia overtook France as the second-largest exporter,
after Italy, to the USA, and it became the biggest exporter to the UK; similarly, Chile became the fifth-largest exporter to the USA and the world's
first table grape producer.

The remarkable performance of the New World countries is even more

Table 2.4   Unit value of wine exports ('000 US$/tonnes), 1975–2007

Yearly average	1975–79	1980–84	1985–89	1990–94	1995–99	2000–04	2005–07
France	1.49	1.66	2.32	3.50	3.70	3.83	5.56
Italy	0.42	0.48	0.73	1.13	1.44	1.88	2.41
Spain	0.52	0.57	0.93	1.11	1.46	1.35	1.51
Germany	1.49	1.51	1.49	1.65	1.91	1.76	2.58
Portugal	0.94	1.38	1.87	2.32	2.58	2.33	2.44
USA	1.08	1.09	1.32	1.42	1.93	1.90	2.03
Argentina	0.35	0.54	0.49	0.76	0.91	1.29	1.33
Australia	1.22	1.70	1.86	2.07	3.30	2.87	2.98
South Africa	0.68	0.83	1.11	1.50	1.61	1.65	1.66
Chile	0.79	0.95	1.19	1.36	1.43	1.59	2.08
World	0.70	0.85	1.30	1.78	2.07	2.25	2.75

Source: FAOSTAT (2009).

evident when we consider the *value* of exports, whose growth testifies to the upgrading along the quality ladder and the entry into the premium market segments that used to be contended by French and Italian wines.[1] For instance, since the early 1990s premium exports have contributed to 97 percent of the growth in the value of Australia's wine exports. Accordingly the unit price for Australian wines went up from US$1.22 per liter to US$3.14, placing the country just after France and ahead of a historically quality producer such as Italy[2] (Table 2.4). Similarly, in Argentina since the mid-1990s, the majority of export revenues come from fine wines, as opposed to cheap table wine, and the unit value of export has increased by 30 percent between 2002 and 2008 (McDermott and Corredoira, ch. 6 in this book). Chile and South Africa still specialized in lower-quality segments, but the unit value of their exports has gradually been converging towards the world average, and more than doubling, in absolute terms, since the early 1990s.

As a consequence of quality upgrading and volume expansion, the value of exports increased in Chile from US$72 million in the first half of the 1990s to almost US$900 million in 2004, and in South Africa from less than US$200 million in the second half of the 1990s to more than US$500 million in 2004. The resilience of the catching-up trajectory by the New World is proved by the capacity that these areas recently exhibited to recover rapidly from downturns caused by extreme weather seasons.

Overall these figures suggest that the catching-up trend is sustained and increasingly taking the form of 'quality upgrading', although, as Ponte and Ewert (2009) underline for the case of South Africa, going up the value-added ladder is only one of the possible trajectories of upgrading. Others may reside in general exposure to different managerial models in end-markets, or may also consist of more sophisticated commercial strategies and learning in basic-quality segments.

3 THE INTERPRETIVE FRAMEWORK

The New World catching-up trajectory in the wine industry cannot merely be explained by the conventional development theories that, in the 1950s and 1960s, represented latecomers as users of technology, and assigned a primary role to diffusion or imitation of established techniques and organizational models. Along these lines, catching up is basically a question of relative speed, in a race along a fixed track, in which latecomers take advantage of mature technologies, forerunners' experience and reduced market uncertainty (Mytelka, 2004). In the wine industry, the progress across the New World has involved significant deviations from earlier experiences of traditional regions. Newcomers drove the process of technological modernization and brought about new organizational models, shifting the competitive game with incumbents to new playgrounds. The challenge to the Old World has been favored by interrelated changes on the demand and supply sides and by consistent institutional innovations across the New World. These latter made it possible for newcomers to take advantage of windows of opportunity opening up in the international market. According to Perez and Soete (1988), these windows are opened to followers particularly at a time of pervasive transformations in the techno-economic paradigm (that is, the set of interrelated technical and organizational innovations that gradually come together to form the best-practice model), because the burden of structural adjustment for forerunners is heavier. Catching up, however, is not guaranteed and depends on the extent to which countries are equipped with the relevant capabilities and supporting institutions, or can manage to build appropriate new institutions rapidly and effectively (Abramovitz, 1986; Perez and Soete, 1988; Justman and Teubal, 1991; Nelson, 2008; Niosi and Reid, 2008).

Following the pioneering contribution by Abramowitz (1986), numerous studies have been conducted on the institutional and political conditions needed for successful catch-up (Hobday, 2003; Fagerberg and Godinho, 2005). Great emphasis has been placed on investments in 'social technologies', the mechanisms of distribution and coordination of tasks and activities that are consistent with evolving physical technologies, and on efforts to mold supporting institutions, especially higher education and research infrastructure (Nelson, 2008).

The burgeoning literature on national and regional innovation systems in developing areas exemplifies the increased attention placed on the broad institutional set-up affecting learning, as well as searching and exploring (Lundvall et al., 2009). The concept of sectoral systems of innovation complements the national and regional approaches by expanding the analysis to international linkages and transmission mechanisms, which play a central role in developing countries. Inflows of knowledge and technology from external sources, as well as dynamics of demand along the internationally fragmented chains of production, are essential components for upgrading and learning in emergent economies (Pietrobelli and Rabellotti, 2009). Concerning these aspects, there appears to be important room for research that might unveil the large variety of catching-up experiences across countries and sectors.

The SSI perspective provides useful insights into the dynamic interplay between, on the one hand, sectoral dynamics, in terms of co-evolution of markets, technologies, production modes and organizational forms, whose determinants and influence cut across national boundaries, and, on the other, idiosyncratic elements, which might explain the capacity of specific latecomers to take advantage of technological and/or market windows of opportunities.

The Sectoral System Approach

Following the path set by the national and regional innovation system literature, the SSI approach departs from the traditional concept of sector adopted in industrial economics, as it considers a wider range of actors compared to firms, pays more attention to institutions, focuses on market as well as non-market interactions and places emphasis on knowledge and learning processes, both on the supply and the demand sides. These dimensions certainly reflect idiosyncratic national and local characteristics but the SSI perspective also places emphasis on the emergent globalization of production networks and knowledge flows, which are indeed a relevant source of differentiation across industries in terms of innovation dynamics and opportunities for latecomers to catch-up and leapfrog (Malerba and Mani, 2009). A systemic perspective on the sectoral dynamics of innovation is relevant to analyze the determinants of the catch-up process because it identifies the key elements that are different and specific to each industry, and emphasizes the international, national and local conditions that can amplify or hinder the sector-specific evolutionary mechanisms.

Knowledge domains, learning processes and technologies, demand, actors and networks, and institutions are the interrelated dimensions of analysis of a sectoral system, investigated with regard to the role of global, country and sector-specific determinants of innovation performance and catching up.

Sectors differ in terms of *knowledge domains*, that is, in terms of the scientific and technological fields at the basis of their innovative activities, and in terms of the applications and types of users involved (Nelson and Rosenberg, 1993). In a sectoral system, features and sources of knowledge affect the organization of production and innovation, the paths of exploration and learning dynamics, the sequences of variety generation and selection, and the roles and interactivity of the main actors.

Identification of *key actors* and an understanding of the *relationships* among them are other critical steps in the characterization of SSI. Firms (producers, suppliers, users) are the main object of investigation in the innovation literature, but they are not the only organizations relevant to the dynamics of technological change at the sectoral level. Business associations, technical, training and financial organizations, trade unions, government agencies and universities play an important role, as they set conditions for business activity and innovative investments, provide capabilities and inputs to the business community, and engage directly in technological advancement and commercial application. In particular, public research organizations (PROs) are acknowledged to be key players in building indigenous technological capabilities, especially in applied fields such as agriculture, and are likely to become even more important as international property rights regimes become tighter (Mazzoleni and Nelson, 2007).

Demand is also vital for the evolution of an SSI. It may spur the emergence of an SSI and it represents, in general, an important stimulus to change; in other cases, however, it can become a major constraint to evolution. Demand influences both the scale of activities and the cognitive boundaries – the nature of the problems firms have to solve and the incentives for their innovation behavior. Changes in demand imply substantial modification to the context in which firms operate, and may favor the entry of new firms and/or the outpositioning of established ones that find it difficult to recognize or adapt to new markets when they open up (Christensen and Rosenbloom, 1995). In globalized markets, changes in international demand and organization of commercial functions directly affect export-oriented players, but can also percolate at the local level through vertical chains.

The *institutional framework* is a dimension of the SSI that cuts across all the others. It encompasses the laws, standards, norms, routines and established practices that shape agents' cognition and behavior and influence their interactions (Coriat and Weinstein, 2002; Malerba, 2004). At the institutional level, there is a strong interplay between sectoral specificities and national or regional factors. On the one hand, national institutions, such as the system of property rights, the regulation of standards and procedures, the education system, the norms ruling university research and its interaction with industry, the antitrust or labor market rules, largely explain the different development paths and innovative dynamics within the same sectors across countries (Lundvall et al., 2002). In particular, they explain the capacity of national systems to respond effectively to changes in techno-economic paradigms and catch-up (Perez and Soete, 1988). On the other hand, national or local institutions can exhibit, across sectors, different degrees of 'congruence' in relation to the other defining elements of the SSI. Thus they can support or hinder sector-specific catching-up trajectories to a different degree.

The long-run dynamic interaction between national factors and sectoral systems is an open research question requiring robust comparative analysis. The recent empirical literature on sectoral systems and catching up has focused mostly on high-tech and large-scale manufacturing (Malerba and Mani, 2009). There is a need to extend the analysis to other sectors and, considering their relevance in the developing world, traditional sectors and the agro-food industries represent a key research target (Arocena and Sutz, 2000). This chapter tackles this open agenda by focusing on the significant transformations experienced in the wine industry, a highly dynamic agro-food sector. This provides an interesting case of catching-up opportunities, exploited to different degrees, by newcomers in developing areas.

4   CATCHING UP AND THE EVOLUTION OF THE WINE SECTORAL SYSTEM OF INNOVATION

Demand

The demand side plays a central role in the wine industry's evolutionary trajectory. New World producers have not only upgraded the quality of their wines, but also addressed and taken advantage of changing consumer tastes, thus ending what Aylward (2003) describes as the historical monopoly of Europe over the wine culture. The changing consumption habits are part of a wider transformation in consumer attitudes, which, since the 1980s, have characterized the market in European countries with a tradition of wine drinking (for example, Italy, France, Spain) and other affluent countries with an incipient wine culture (for example, the UK, Scandinavia, the USA). In the 1980s a 'gourmet culture' began in the rich countries, increasing the popularity of wine as a 'beverage', and consolidating a preference for Cabernet Sauvignon, Merlot and Chardonnay varietal wines, typically produced in the New World (Cohen and Labys, 2006). Among the more affluent and educated consumers, wine drinking gradually became a 'cultural experience', a sensory approach to other cultures where history, origin and variety complement taste. This cultural change was quickly embraced and promoted by European wine producers, who encouraged the diffusion of knowledge about *terroir*[3] and quality varieties, and a link between wine drinking and lifestyle. However, it also raised interest in experiencing products from other areas.

These changes in taste were accompanied by a sharp decline in wine consumption in almost all wine-producing countries (see Section 2 in this chapter), a decline that was partly compensated for by growing demand from the Northern European countries, Russia and China (European Commission, 2007). However, the volume reduction was matched with an increase in unit value, as in affluent markets a shift occurred in the type of consumption, from bulk to premium wines.

What is interesting is that this pervasive demand-side change has substantially modified the role of the consumer in the industry. Definition of wine 'quality' is no longer the exclusive domain of wine producers; beyond any intrinsic characteristics the ultimate criterion of quality is the value perceived by the market (Aylward and Zanko, 2006). Furthermore, the diffusion of wine-drinking habits to a large share of relatively inexperienced consumers, whose wine purchases are mainly made in supermarkets, has increased the relevance of marketing and consistent 'product building'.

In this sense the consolidation of distribution, at both the wholesale and retail levels, has had a major effect on competition in the wine market (Gwynne, 2008). In the USA the 20 largest wholesalers control 70 percent of the market, and supermarkets and hypermarkets account for more than 40 percent of retail wine sales, with a similar trend emerging in all affluent countries (Castaldi et al., 2006). This consolidation among distributors has made it increasingly difficult for smaller producers to get their wines on the shelves. Wholesalers and supermarkets prefer to stock only the top selling brands, at the expense of small or new labels. This sales strategy is damaging wine industries that are characterized by small, often micro, wineries. In the Old World, Italy is a case in point, as its traditional producing regions present an incredibly rich variety of vines, and enter markets with wines sold under a myriad of different labels.

These quantitative and qualitative changes in the market were embraced first by California, whose wines played a crucial role in attracting interest and improving the reputation of wine areas that were not part of the traditional establishment. In this respect, US wine experts played a major role in changing established patterns of perception, thus altering the reputation and media recognition of wine regions traditionally associated with low-quality segments and low status in international markets. Australia was also quick to take note of this market evolution, and responded with increased branding and marketing efforts. In particular, and in order to send a clear and strong message to consumers, Australia chose to promote 'Brand Australia', putting aside differences among wines and regions in a bid to target the 'popular-premium' segment of the world market (Aylward, 2006).

Following the way opened by California and Australia, other New World producers have been changing their position in the international market, adopting aggressive branding and marketing strategies. In the case of Chile, for instance, the earlier strategies of supplying wines with good value for money and competing in a low price range, have evolved into brand-building investment by the largest producers, in order to market wines in higher-quality segments (Felzensztein, 2002).

This market-oriented New World expansion has forced adaptations in the organization of production and in the marketing strategies of Old World producers. Incumbents first responded to the aggressive marketing strategies of New World countries by emphasizing the concept of *terroir*, thus maintaining a producer-driven approach. Accordingly, emphasis was placed on strengthening the regulation on production and appellations of origin (Pompelli and Pick, 1999; Aylward and Zanko, 2006).[4] This response left much room for the penetration of New World producers in a changing world market, as previously illustrated in Section 2.

Lately, traditional wine regions have revised their strategies by attempting to embrace and support an evolution in consumers' attitudes that is more favorable to them. Producers from the Old World are increasingly targeting market niches dominated by highly sophisticated consumers, who are attracted by small independent producers and local wine varieties.[5]

Knowledge Base and Technologies

The responsiveness of New World players to the changing patterns of demand in wine markets is largely related to technological modernization and alignment of scientific efforts with marketing strategies. Because scientific knowledge in the field is generally rapidly diffused to wine producers worldwide (Aylward and Turpin, 2003), competitive advantage is not merely built on appropriability of research output. The relative competitive advantage of New World areas has been founded on the ability to 'build up' products, thus, on the alignment of research and development (R&D) priorities with both production and marketing requirements. The interplay between the industry and the research system has been key to this alignment.

Until the 1980s, scientific research on wine-related issues was largely producer driven and mainly aimed at responding to the specific needs of the traditional *terroir*, implying context-specific learning processes and knowledge cumulativeness. Inputs from science were mainly used to inform the areas of microbiology and wine fermentation, in traditional production methods, typically based on the idiosyncratic knowledge, experience and manual dexterity of farmers.

In the New World the local industry, which was mainly confined to local markets and the production of bulk wine, was sustained traditionally by simple oenological culture and research. However, since the mid-1980s it was precisely in the New World that an intense process of modernization took off, consisting in large investments in human resources and scientific research, and innovative approaches to markets, branding and business systems.

Among New World producing areas, California has been the pioneer in introducing the novelty of a full-fledged 'scientific approach'. Its wine-related research has been significantly oriented towards responding to (and further strengthening) changes in demand. Research programs have largely been focused on the introduction of new grape varieties and the reduction of the variability of output, in order to produce wines of regular taste and quality, despite the variability in climate conditions, soil characteristics and other local specificities. In general, the recent changes in technologies and production methods have been based on consistent modernizing research-based approaches rather than scientific breakthroughs.

This scientific drive of newcomers has emerged in a global context of increased knowledge codification and formal investigation effort across a wide range of disciplines related to the wine industry (Glänzel and Veugelers, 2006). From the early 1990s to 2006, scientific publications on wine-related issues, mostly within food science and technology, but increasingly spanning biology and biotechnology, recorded a growth rate five times larger than the average across the spectrum of scientific disciplines (Figures 2.2 and 2.3).

The New World's dynamism in terms of scientific research output has been sustained over the last decade, with the number of publications doubling annually. Also, the number of co-authored publications by academic researchers is evidence of the increasing international nature of research in wine: the number of countries connected through co-authorship has

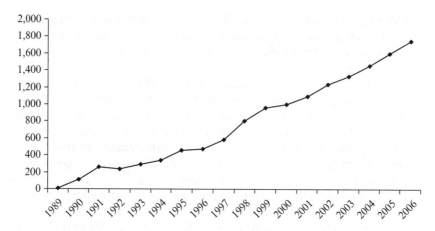

Source: Our elaboration based on Web of Science–ISI data.

Figure 2.2 Number of wine publications, 1989–2006

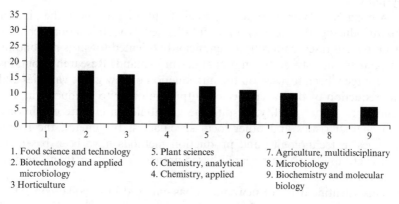

1. Food science and technology   5. Plant sciences   7. Agriculture, multidisciplinary
2. Biotechnology and applied   6. Chemistry, analytical   8. Microbiology
   microbiology   4. Chemistry, applied   9. Biochemistry and molecular
3 Horticulture   biology

Source: Our elaboration based on ISI data.

Figure 2.3 Subject coverage of wine research by most important ISI subject categories

increased from seven (France, Italy, Germany, Spain, Canada, the USA and Israel) in the period from 1992 to 1997, to 36 in the period from 2002 to 2006. Differences also emerge for the geographical span of collaborations; although Italy, France, Spain and Germany are still perceived by New World producers as important centers for the generation of scientific knowledge, the USA and Australia have emerged recently as key players (Cassi et al., ch. 3 in this book).

Innovation and firms

The increased importance of scientific research is demanding changes in producers' competences. Production techniques that used to be driven by farmers' experience and practical, problem-solving approaches, have become highly codified and need to be managed by highly skilled professionals, making formalized training and access to external knowledge extremely important. The so-called 'flying winemakers' symbolize the New World's leading role in modernization (Lagendijk, 2004; Aylward and Zanko, 2006). These are consultants contracted worldwide by the most dynamic wine producers and sometimes by wine regions, who have emerged as key actors in the global wine system, significantly contributing to the rapid transfer of scientific advances and technologies across emerging areas. Whereas the knowledge base of Old World producers is strongly related to the local wine culture and the locally accumulated competencies (Aylward, 2003), innovative firms in New World countries largely rely on foreign agronomists and oenologists, who support advanced experimental activities. In fact, experimentation consists not only in copying external technologies, but also in the creative adoption of and selection among, accompanied by mastery of, best practices, which can be adapted to local and firm-specific needs.

The alignment of innovative efforts with export-oriented strategies takes mainly the form of investment in new grape varieties and clones, aimed at changing and broadening the type of product supplied to the market, in accordance with international tastes. Traditional producers, on the other hand, address established national (or even regional) markets and international outlets, with traditional varieties. Hence, they prefer to focus on process innovation and largely rely on in-house competencies and skills at the local level (Cusmano et al., 2010).

Actors and U–I Networks

The interplay and co-evolution of the elements of the SSI presented above (that is, demand factors, knowledge base and technologies) also shape the nature and opportunities of the actors in the system. Indeed, the new competitive context, based on technological modernization, global marketing and predominance of international, large-scale retail chains, has affected the structure of the industry in a significant way (see Anderson, ch. 4 in this book, for a detailed analysis of the Australian case). A remarkable process of consolidation has taken place worldwide. Since the late 1990s national and transnational mergers, acquisitions and strategic alliances have intensified. The branding and volume capabilities of the leading global wine firms – as well as their ability to produce wines of an even quality – satisfy the requirements of supermarket channels, which prefer a few large suppliers in order to reduce procurement costs (Kaplan and Wood, 2004). However, international acquisitions have also been driven by quality concerns, brand diversification strategies and innovation-related motives. The opportunity to source grapes at competitive prices from multiple areas, the need to capture key brands and the acquired confidence with the most innovative oenological techniques are the driving forces behind the late wave of consolidations and alliances in the wine industry worldwide (Anderson et al., 2003). The process of concentration and rationalization concerns most of the New World, although to different extents, with the largest wine companies coming from the USA. In 2008 the world's largest wine producers are Foster's of Australia and Constellation Brands of the USA, followed by Distell of South Africa and by the Chilean company Concha y Toro (Mediobanca, 2009).

Among the 'second tier' of newcomers, increase in firm size and consolidation of the sector have corresponded to an inflow of foreign investments. This is the case in Chile, where although the wine industry is still dominated by a few family-based companies, with the four largest groups accounting for more than 45 percent of export value (Visser, 2004), there is increasing participation of foreign capital in the sector (Moguillansky et al., 2006). A partial exception to this trend is South Africa. Indeed, the South African Distell grew into one of the largest wine corporations in the world, but, compared to other New World regions, the country has failed to attract significant foreign investment. According to Ponte and Ewert (2007), this is explained, among other factors, by perceived political and currency risk, and lack of strong brands in the premium segment of the market – the segment that is growing fastest and providing the largest margins. Moreover, the lack of suitable land has affected the trend towards consolidation in the South African industry, limiting expansion of vineyards.

When compared to the average firm structure observed in New World regions, the long-established wine-making regions in Europe in general are characterized by fragmented industry structures and a predominance of small and very small firms. However, there are also significant differences among Old World wine countries. The comparison between the world leaders, France and Italy, points in this sense at differentiated evolutionary patterns. While French companies have grown in size and expanded overseas,[6] Italian companies are still small and mainly family based. The two largest Italian companies are cooperatives – GIV and Caviro – with turnovers in 2008 of about €280 million. The total sales of the top five Italian wine producers amount to about €1 billion, much less than the sales of world leaders such as Constellation Brands and Foster's, both with a turnover of about €2.5 billion in 2008. Also, Chilean and South African companies stay well ahead of the Italians; for example Concha y Toro from Chile and Distell from South Africa both double the turnover of the biggest Italian company (Mediobanca, 2009).

In addition to increasing the role of large firms, the technological changes of recent decades have brought research institutions, technology transfer organizations and innovation-oriented alliances to center stage in the industry. The creation and continued strengthening of institutions specialized in research and training have been a major driver of growth in New World areas such as California and Australia. And institutions engaged on industrywide applicable research are being targeted by policy in emergent producing areas such as New Zealand, South Africa and Chile. Bodies dedicated to the funding and promotion of wine-related research projects, often in partnership with national research organizations and universities, are being established.

The evidence about university–industry (U–I) linkages (McDermott et al., 2009; Giuliani et al., 2010) suggests that joint research agreements have played a relevant role in the most dynamic New World regions, allowing for the emergence of 'bridging researchers' (Giuliani and Rabellotti, ch. 7 in this book), well connected with international knowledge networks, thus favoring the access of local firms to global knowledge flows and the diffusion of technology at the local level. At the same time, case-based evidence shows that in traditional Old World regions, researchers have fewer links with the industry, through joint research programs or consultancy, and wineries perceive less of a pivotal role of public or university institutions in diffusing relevant information (Cusmano et al., 2010).

As further described in the next subsection, the different degrees of contact and involvement of researchers in industry projects also depend on the different institutional frameworks and on the policy initiatives implemented at the country and local levels.

The Institutional Framework

Institutional changes have played an important role in the trajectories of evolution and catch-up of New World producers. The successful experience of Australia has become best practice for adoption by latecomers, although implementation has proved more difficult in those emerging countries, such as South Africa, characterized by political instability or incipient institutional capital.

The Australian experience in institutional building is a case of successful centralization and coordination at the national level of industry organizations and research institutions, converging on a long-term vision for the industry and export-related objectives. The Australian model is indeed rather centralized, with two main actors, the Australian Wine and Brandy Corporation, which is the national sectoral organization, and the Australian Wine Research Institute, which is the national research body, playing a pivotal role, but strongly linked to government action, in particular with the Grape and Wine Research and Development Corporation, a governmental body devoted to financing R&D projects. This model has proved successful for rationalizing, coordinating, setting export-oriented priorities and targets, and promoting and socializing a vision for the industry at large (Anderson, ch. 4 in this book).

Spurred by the successful experience of Australia, other New World countries have engendered top-down institutional building or rationalization aimed at boosting international competitiveness. Accordingly, the main targets of the institutional reforms have been marketing, training and R&D. South Africa was one of the first latecomers to adopt a similar institutional strategy. A national system of market-oriented R&D institutions has been developing progressively since the late 1990s. Stimulated by government, the South African Wine and Brandy Corporation (SAWB) was established to enhance competitiveness. R&D and marketing promotion are among its main areas of intervention along with training of human resources and social promotion. SAWB has also set up a business unit (Wine Industry Network of Expertise and Technology – Winetech) specifically to finance and promote applied research in the wine sector. Thus the export orientation of the industry, the major concern of the early industry bodies, has become integrated within a more comprehensive governance structure. The South African industry has found a champion in the South Africa Wine Trust (SAWIT), which has acted as a catalyst in the launch of a visionary industrywide exercise (Strategy 2020) and also contributed to the South African Wine Industry Strategy Plan (WIP) (SAWB, 2003). This was meant as a step towards consensus among industry stakeholders, in particular to overcome the legacies of the apartheid regime and give proper representation to the interests of black workers and investors. The process led to the foundation, at the end of 2006, of the South African Wine Industry Council, the new single representative body of the industry. However, the transformation of the wine industry is far from being completed. Power relations between old and new economic and political groups are still unstable, and the process of 'black empowerment', which would enhance the participation of black investors and workers in the wine business, is still incipient and subject to controversy (Williams, 2005; Du Toit et al., 2008).

The process of institutional renewal has been slower in Chile. Following years of internal division, in 2007 the wine industry announced the creation of a single representative body. The two major winery associations in Chile, Viñas de Chile and Chilevid, have merged to form Vinos de Chile to provide a single voice, in a bid to achieve a more coherent strategy to guide the entire industry. There has also been some collaboration in the research field, with the establishment in 2006 of two consortia, supported by the Chilean Economic Development Agency (CORFO) through Innova Chile and involving the two industry associations in partnership with the main research institutions and universities. Both consortia aim at promoting investments in innovation and research in wine-related areas in order to enhance wine quality, and to strengthen the linkages between the universities and industry. The creation or strengthening of linkages between researchers and firms is also the target of specific policy instruments.[7]

The Old World countries have been slow in reacting to this evolution. The institutional picture is one of greater and persistent fragmentation, which results from the historical differentiation of traditional wine regions and from the competitive relevance of local specificities. In addition to institutional fragmentation related to regional specificities and inertial mechanisms, the strict regulatory framework has imposed additional constraints and reinforced differences across regions. European producers have to satisfy numerous restrictions on which grape varieties can be used in an appellation, on maximum yield and alcohol content, on vine density and on irrigation systems. Local wine industries are generally embedded in a dual layer of regulation: national level, especially in the appellation wines categories, and European level within the framework of the Common Agricultural Policy (CAP) (Corsi et al., 2004).

To address this situation, EU countries are currently engaged in a restructuring of their wine regulatory frameworks, reforming the agriculture Common Market Organization (CMO). These changes are aimed at increasing competitiveness among EU wine producers through marketing and promotion, simplification of winemaking practices and labeling policies, as well as reducing the amount of direct subsidies to producers (European Commission, 2007). These measures, however, are beset with controversy as they seem to address the interest of large industrial groups to the detriment of small wineries, which represent the backbone of competitive wine industries, such as that in Italy (Castriota and Delmastro, 2009).

Under pressure to adapt to ongoing EU agricultural policy reforms, institutional renewal is occurring at the national level. France is undertaking a profound restructuring of wine-related institutions, aimed at rationalization and simplification through the establishment of a national bureau to manage research and EU funds, and to coordinate

10 regional offices representing the main geographical wine production areas.

On the other hand, the Italian institutional framework is still highly fragmented. All the main regional production areas have their own supporting institutions and research centers. Policy decisions are taken at many different levels, leading to high coordination costs and often misleading and contradictory objectives; research activities involve a large variety of institutions, whose specialist fields often overlap. Both PROs and universities conduct research on wine, with the latter playing a leading role, along with some well-established oenological colleges. Although the direct link between the industry and the research centers may appear rather weak, in the case of traditional wine regions this is reinforced by the presence of important quasi-public intermediate extension organizations, which act as hubs for the dissemination of knowledge to companies (Morrison and Rabellotti, 2007).[8]

The highly differentiated extension services and R&D systems in traditional wine regions are at odds with the global trend of centralization and top-down rationalization described above. Indeed, this institutional fragmentation couples with the productive fragmentation and the strict regulatory environment to raise questions about the competitiveness of Old World producers in changing international markets, increasingly characterized, as described, by large-scale retailing, brand recognition and taste standardization. However, if this producer-driven and highly regulated approach has left much room for the penetration of New World producers in international markets in the last couple of decades, this same institutional framework presents advantages in the light of late evolution in markets. In fact, traditional producers are increasingly targeting market niches dominated by highly educated consumers, who are reacting to the standardization of tastes and the dominance of supermarkets and international retail chains in the global wine market by drawing attention to small independent producers and local wine varieties. Regional R&D infrastructures and extension services specifically address local needs and appear to be well suited to dealing with the development of market niches for differentiated and unique products. Indeed, in traditional regions, it is felt more and more that highly centralized R&D policies, such as those implemented by New World countries, would be inadequate to tackle the new emerging patterns of diversified demand favored by these traditional producers (Aylward, 2006). Evidence of this shift of perspective can be also found in South Africa, where, for example, the industry marketing organization Wine of South Africa (WOSA) has undertaken marketing initiatives to promote the diversity and uniqueness of local *terroir* along with an image of fair and environmental friendly industry.[9]

5 CONCLUSIONS

The last several years of technological evolution and global competition in the wine industry show clear examples of catching up, which may add to the knowledge of catching-up opportunities and strategies in the agro-food industry. Indeed, the wine industry represents an extremely interesting case of technological renovation driven by emerging countries, which, following different trajectories, have moved the competitive game into new playgrounds. The present contribution interprets the wine industry transformation as a tale of co-evolution on the demand and supply sides, which has led to the emergence of a novel, knowledge-based, market-driven model that challenged the producer-driven approach of incumbents.

Since the late 1970s, changes in consumers' attitudes and tastes – mainly the increasing popularity of wine as a beverage and the diffusion of wine drinking to relatively inexperienced consumer groups – along with the growth in mass distribution channels, have opened the way for standardized and easily identifiable wine varieties. New World producers, first from California and Australia, and more recently from developing countries such as Chile, Argentina and South Africa, have been quick to take advantage of this discontinuity.

Contrary to what has occurred in other industries, the spectacular performance of latecomers is not only the result of adaptive strategies or market segmentation and focus on specific niches. Rather, emerging countries, following the path opened by other New World producers (that is, California, Australia) have contributed significantly to the process of technological modernization, product standardization and marketing innovation, which have proved consistent with and even favored changes in demand. The strategy of 'building up' wine products to fit with international tastes is based on an innovative scientific approach to production, in which economies of scale, and the timing and alignment of R&D strategies with market objectives, are key competitive drivers. Access to foreign knowledge and linkages between local research communities and global networks have been feeding this process of modernization, contributing to the diffusion of this approach across both the New and Old Worlds.

This market-driven scientific turn has had enormous effects not only on the industry knowledge base, but also and importantly on the relevant industry actors. Universities and scientists have emerged as key players, and the ties between industry and research institutions have become ever more important, and are being strengthened across the New World by institutional changes. Following the early successful Australian experience, a top-down planning approach has diffused, with industry associations and research bodies strongly linked to government action and research efforts, explicitly tuned to export-oriented strategies. These institutional innovations have taken place within a framework of increasing concentration at industry level, mirroring global marketing strategies and large-scale retailing.

The initial response of traditional producers has been to strengthen the long-established producer-driven approach, based on context-specific and cumulative learning processes, traditional varieties and winemaking techniques, all highly embedded in specific local cultures. The strict regulatory framework has imposed additional constraints on the ability – or possibility – of reacting as flexibly as New World producers to the rapidly changing international markets. In traditional wine regions, with the partial exception of France, the industry has been largely unaffected by the international wave of consolidation, remaining highly fragmented and constrained in the access to large-scale retailing. Fragmentation has also characterized the policy level and that of supporting institutions, such as business associations and the research infrastructure.

However, more recently the Old World has begun to respond to the increasing competition from the New World through strategies related to diversification and experimentation for upgrading. These strategies address the demand-side evolutions, mainly the diffusion of a gourmet culture, in which wine drinking is perceived as contributing to a richer cultural experience, and variety and specificity are positive attributes. In this perspective, highly centralized R&D policies, such as those implemented by New World countries, are perceived to be increasingly inappropriate to tackle the emerging pattern of diversified demand. Indeed, in this perspective, the traditional regions' endowments of wine culture, labor market, localized linkages and dense institutional infrastructure represent a valuable asset. If what has happened in the global wine industry illustrates that opportunities for sectoral-driven catching up arise at times of significant industry transformation, the most recent changes on the demand and supply sides have opened the way for the co-existence of highly diverse institutional models and innovation strategies.

NOTES

1. Wines are commonly ranked on a six-point scale, from the best quality to the lowest (that is, icon, ultra premium, super premium, premium, popular premium and basic). Wines included in the premium segment are characterized by brand recognition and appellation of origin; their price ranges between 5 and 7 euros (Heijbroek, 2003).
2. It is worth highlighting that Italy has also been a traditional producer and exporter of bulk wine. Nevertheless in the last few decades we observe for this country, as for New World producers, a significant shift towards quality wine.

3. For a definition of terroir, see note 1 in Chapter 1.
4. The attribution of appellations depends on strict regulations that establish production area, grape varieties that can be used in a particular regional blend, vine yield, wine/grape yield, alcoholic content, production and aging methods and the type of information that is put on the wine label. As discussed in Section 4, in the EU this regulation is in the process of change, as part of the EU agricultural policy reform.
5. An Italian non-profit organization promoting this philosophy, and gaining increasing international popularity, is the Slow Food movement, founded in Piedmont, a traditional wine region, in 1989 (www.slowfood.com).
6. Some French wineries have become part of large multidivisional groups, such as the wine branch of the luxury group LVMH, mainly specialized in champagne, and Castel Frères, the largest European wine company, which is among the top 10 wine producers in the world. With regard to foreign operations, the Paris-based beverage group Pernod Ricard has become the third-largest winemaker in Australia and the foremost wine producer in Spain, New Zealand and Argentina.
7. Among these instruments there are a number of initiatives promoted by CORFO, such as the Proyectos de Fomento (Profos) and the Consorcios (Moguillansky et al., 2006).
8. A prominent example is the Piedmont association Vignaioli Piemontesi, the largest association of wine and grape producers in Italy, with more than 8,000 members. Vignaioli Piemontesi participates directly in many of the research projects ongoing in the region, acting mainly as a technical partner and providing access to technical information and knowledge for small firms and farmers (Morrison and Rabellotti, 2007).
9. For a critical analysis of this and related initiatives see Du Toit (2002) and Du Toit et al. (2008). See also http://www.varietyisinournature.com.

REFERENCES

Abramovitz, M. (1986), 'Catching up, forging ahead, and falling behind', *Journal of Economic History*, **46** (2), 385–406.
Anderson, K., D. Norman and G. Wittwer (2003), 'Globalisation of the world's wine markets', *The World Economy*, **26** (5), 659–87.
Arocena, R. and J. Sutz (2000), 'Looking at national systems of innovation from the south', *Industry and Innovation*, **7** (1), 55–75.
Aylward, D.K. (2003), 'A documentary of innovation support among New World wine industries', *Journal of Wine Research*, **14** (1), 31–43.
Aylward, D.K. (2006), 'Innovation lock-in: unlocking research and development path dependency in the Australian wine industry', *Strategic Change*, **15** (7–8), 361–72.
Aylward, D.K. and T. Turpin (2003), 'New wine in old bottles: a case study of innovation territories in "New World" wine production', *International Journal of Innovation Management*, **7** (4), 501–25.
Aylward, D.K. and M. Zanko (2006), 'Emerging interorganizational structures in the Australian wine industry: implications for SMEs', Proceedings of the 5th Global Conference on Business and Economics, Cambridge, July, Faculty of Commerce Papers, University of Wollongong, NSW.
Castaldi, R., S. Cholette and M. Hussain (2006), 'A country-level analysis of competitive advantage in the wine industry', Dipartimento di Economia e Ingegneria Agraria working paper 2, Università di Bologna.

Castriota, S. and M. Delmastro (2009), 'L'Europa non apprezza il buon vino' ['Europe does not value good wine'], *LaVoce.info*, accessed 31 January 2010 at www.lavoce.info/articoli/pagina1001228.html.

Christensen, C.M. and R.S. Rosenbloom (1995), 'Explaining the attacker's advantage: technological paradigms, organizational dynamics and the value network', *Research Policy*, **24** (2), 233–57.

Cohen, B. and W.C. Labys (2006), 'Trends vs. cycles in wine export shares', *Australian Journal of Agricultural and Resource Economics*, **50** (4), 527–37.

Coriat, B. and O. Weinstein (2002), 'Organizations, firms and institutions in the generation of innovation', *Research Policy*, **31** (2), 273–90.

Corsi, A., E. Pomarici and R. Sardone (2004), 'Italy', in K. Anderson (ed.), *The World's Wine Markets: Globalization at Work*, Cheltenham, UK and Northampton, MA, USA: Edward Elgar, pp. 73–97.

Cusmano, L., A. Morrison and R. Rabellotti (2010), 'Catching up trajectories in the wine sector: a comparative study of Chile, Italy and South Africa', *World Development*, **38** (11), 1588–602.

Du Toit, A. (2002), 'Globalising ethics: social technologies of private regulation and the South African wine industry', *Journal of Agrarian Change*, **2** (3), 356–80.

Du Toit, A., S. Kruger and S. Ponte (2008), 'Deracializing exploitation? 'Black economic empowerment" in the South African wine industry', *Journal of Agrarian Change*, **8** (1), 6–32.

European Commission (2007), *Towards a Sustainable European Wine Sector*, Brussels: European Commission.

Fagerberg, J. and M. Godinho (2005), 'Innovation and catching up', in J. Fagerberg, D.C. Mowery and R.R. Nelson (eds), *The Oxford Handbook of Innovation*, Oxford: Oxford University Press, pp. 514–43.

FAOSTAT (2009), Trade statistics, accessed 31 January 2010 at http://faostat.fao.org.

Felzensztein, C. (2002), 'Approaches to global branding: the Chilean wine industry and the UK market', *International Journal of Wine Marketing*, **14**, 25–32.

Giuliani, E., A. Morrison, C. Pietrobelli and R. Rabellotti (2010), 'Why do researchers collaborate with industry? An analysis of the wine sector in Chile, Italy and South Africa', *Research Policy*, **39** (6), 748–61.

Glänzel, W. and R. Veugelers (2006), 'Science for wine: a bibliometric assessment of wine and grape research for wine producing and consuming countries', *American Journal of Enology and Viticulture*, **57** (1), 23–32.

Gwynne, R.N. (2008), 'UK retail concentration, Chilean wine producers and value chains', *The Geographical Journal*, **174** (2), 97–108.

Heijbroek, A. (2003), *Wine is business. Shifting Demand and Distribution: Major Drivers Shaping the Wine Industry*, Utrecht the Netherlands: Rabobank International.

Hobday, M. (2003), 'Innovation in Asian industrialization: a Gerschenkronian perspective', *Oxford Development Studies*, **31** (3), 293–314.

Justman, M. and M. Teubal (1991), 'A structuralist perspective on the role of technology in economic growth and development', *World Development*, **19** (9), 1167–83.

Kaplan, D. and E. Wood (2004), 'Marketing, innovation and performance in the South African wine industry', paper presented at the 2004 GLOBELICS Conference, 12–20 October, Beijing.

Lagendijk, A. (2004), 'Global "lifeworlds" versus local "systemworlds": how flying winemakers produce global wines in interconnected locales', *Tijdschrift voor Economische en Sociale Geografie*, **95** (5), 511–26.

Lundvall, B.-A., B. Johnson, E.S. Andersen and B. Dalum (2002), 'National systems of production, innovation and competence building', *Research Policy*, **31** (2), 213–31.

Lundvall, B.-A., K.J. Joseph, C. Chaminade and J. Vang (eds) (2009), *Handbook of Innovation Systems and Developing Countries: Building Domestic Capabilities in a Global Context*, Cheltenham, UK and Northampton, MA, USA: Edward Elgar.

Malerba, F. (ed.) (2004), *Sectoral Systems of Innovation: Concepts, Issues and Analyses of Six Major Sectors in Europe*, Cambridge: Cambridge University Press.

Malerba, F. and S. Mani (eds) (2009), *Sectoral Systems of Innovation and Production in Developing Countries: Actors, Structure and Evolution*, Cheltenham, UK and Northampton, MA, USA: Edward Elgar.

Mazzoleni, R. and R.R. Nelson (2007), 'Public research institutions and economic catch-up', *Research Policy*, **36** (10), 1512–28.

McDermott, G.A., R.A. Corredoira and G. Kruse (2009), 'Public–private institutions as catalysts of upgrading in emerging market societies', *Academy of Management Journal*, **52** (6), 1270–96.

Mediobanca (2009), *Indagine sul Settore Vinicolo* [*Wine Industry Survey*], Milan, Italy: Ufficio Studi Mediobanca.

Moguillansky, G., J.C. Salas and G. Cares (2006), *Innovacion en la industria del vino* [*Innovation in the Wine Industry*], Santiago: CORFO.

Morrison, A. and R. Rabellotti (2007), 'The role of research in wine: the emergence of a regional research area in an Italian wine production system', *International Journal of Technology and Globalisation*, **3** (2–3), 155–78.

Mytelka, L. (2004), 'Catching up in new wave technologies', *Oxford Development Studies*, **3** (3), 389–405.

Nelson, R.R. (2008), 'What enables rapid economic progress: what are the needed institutions?', *Research Policy*, **37** (1), 1–11.

Nelson, R.R. and N. Rosenberg (1993), 'Technical innovation and national systems', in R.R. Nelson (ed.), *National Innovation Systems: A Comparative Analysis*, Oxford: Oxford University Press, pp. 3–21.

Niosi, J. and S.E. Reid (2008), 'Biotechnology and nanotechnology: science-based enabling technologies as windows of opportunity for LDCs?', *World Development*, **35** (3), 426–38.

OIV (International Organization of Vine and Wine) (2009), *State of Viticulture World Report*, accessed 31 January 2010 at www.oiv.int.

Perez, C. and L. Soete (1988), 'Catching up in technology: entry barriers and windows of opportunity', in G. Dosi, C. Freeman, R.R. Nelson, G. Silverberg and L. Soete (eds), *Technical Change and Economic Theory*, London: Pinter, pp. 458–79.

Pietrobelli, C. and R. Rabellotti (2009), 'Innovation systems and global value chains', in Lundvall, K.J. Joseph, C. Chaminade and J. Vang (eds), *Handbook of Innovation Systems and Developing Countries. Building Domestic Capabilities in a Global Context*, Cheltenham, UK and Northampton, MA, USA: Edward Elgar Publishing, pp. 214–38.

Pompelli, G. and D. Pick (1999), 'International investment motivations of U.S. wineries', *International Food and Agribusiness Management Review*, **2** (1), 47–62.

Ponte, S. and J. Ewert (2007), 'South African wine: an industry in ferment', Tralac working paper 8, October, accessed 31 January 2009 at www.tralac.org.

Ponte, S. and J. Ewert (2009), 'Which way is "up" in upgrading? Trajectories of change in the value chain for South African wine', *World Development*, **37** (10), 1637–50.

SAWB (2003), *The South African Wine Industry Strategy Plan*, Stellenbosch, South Africa: South African Wine and Brandy Company, accessed 31 January 2008 at http://www.sawb.co.za/strategyplan.htm.

Visser, E. (2004), 'A Chilean wine cluster? Governance and upgrading in the phase of internationalization', Desarollo Productivo working paper 154, CEPAL, Santiago.

Williams, G. (2005), 'Black economic empowerment in the South African wine industry', *Journal of Agrarian Change*, **5** (4), 476–504.

3. The changing geography of science in wine: evidence from emerging countries

Lorenzo Cassi, Andrea Morrison and Roberta Rabellotti

1 INTRODUCTION

Universities and public research organizations (PROs) are key actors in national innovation systems, their primary mission being to enhance indigenous scientific and technological knowledge (Amsden, 1989; Lall, 1992; Nelson, 1993; Fagerberg and Godinho, 2005; Brundenius et al., 2009). Increasingly, beyond their traditional activities in education, training and research they also undertake a 'third mission', interacting with industry and contributing to the development and upgrading of the domestic technological and production capabilities (Mowery and Sampat, 2005; Yusuf and Nabeshima, 2007).

In the advanced economies, a literature on scientific and research productivity of the different institutional contexts (for example, USA versus Europe) has flourished in recent years (Dosi et al., 2006; Etzkowitz and Leydesdorff, 2000). Instead, as pointed out by Mazzoleni (2008) in less developed countries, a good understanding of the contribution and the functioning of research organizations is still a long way off. Nonetheless, in scientific areas such as agriculture there is clearly a need to undertake research locally and develop knowledge and technologies suited to the specific conditions of each country and region (Vessuri, 1990; Albuquerque, 2004).

A study on the wine sector represents a very interesting case in which to investigate whether the economic catch-up (if not forging ahead) between latecomers and forerunners is associated with a similar catch-up process in their scientific capabilities. As discussed in Chapter 2 by Cusmano et al., since the beginning of the 1990s the supremacy of Old World long-standing wine leaders such as Italy and France has been challenged by new international players, recording spectacular performance in terms of both exported volumes and values. These 'New World' countries include affluent frontrunners that are relatively new to the wine sector, such as the USA and Australia, and less developed but rapidly growing latecomers such as Chile, Argentina and South Africa.

In this chapter we shall investigate the scientific performance, measured in terms of number of publications,[1] of these successful latecomers in the global wine market. In addition, based on the analysis of co-authorships, we shall investigate to what extent the scientific wine community has become global, and in particular whether Argentina, Chile and South Africa undertake international linkages within the scientific and research system. Finally, analyzing the network of co-authorships, we shall focus on the structure of the national research systems in these three countries for highlighting the distinct roles played by PROs, universities and the industry in the existing domestic and international links. A more thorough investigation on the relation between research and industry, which accounts for other type of linkages besides scientific publications, is presented in Giuliani and Rabellotti (see Chapter 7).

The chapter is structured as follows. In the next section we outline the main theoretical arguments on the mission and the contribution to economic development of universities and PROs. Section 3 focuses on the database. Section 4 outlines the global trends in wine research, showing the extent to which New World countries, and therein emerging economies, are challenging incumbents not only by taking shares of exports, but also by catching up in terms of scientific production. In Section 5, relational data about international co-publications are used to investigate how global the wine scientific community is, and particularly, to what extent emerging countries (that is, Argentina, Chile and South Africa) participate in this global network. Section 6 is an account of how the national research systems are organized in the three countries under investigation. Concluding remarks are presented in the last sections.

2   SCIENCE AND RESEARCH FOR DEVELOPMENT: AN OVERVIEW

Universities and PROs have traditionally contributed to the development of countries by means of their well-known key missions: education, training and research (Mowery and Sampat, 2005; Brundenius et al., 2009). Past accounts of successful catch-up (for example, Germany in the nineteenth century) clearly indicate that the availability of skilled workers and teachers, along with the migration of technicians from leader countries and the return of qualified students, have played a key role in building relevant capabilities across countries and industries. Similarly, recent experiences of catching up (for example, Japan, South Korea, Taiwan) have further confirmed the relevance of the above factors, and in particular the importance of cross-border linkages (for example, students trained abroad), as enabling conditions for building up indigenous technological capabilities (Lall, 1992; Kim and Nelson, 2000; Mowery and Sampat, 2005).[2]

In addition to education, universities and PROs contribute to development by undertaking basic and applied research. The argument that science and basic research are essential for growth and innovation was put forward in the late 1940s (Bush, 1945) and a decade later further supported by the market failure argument (Nelson, 1959; Arrow, 1962), inspiring a lively and long-lasting debate about the validity of the 'linear model' (Rosenberg, 1982; Dosi et al., 2006; Balconi et al., 2010). It goes beyond the scope of this chapter to review the terms of this controversy; what matters here is that despite criticisms, basic and applied research represent, along with other ingredients, key determinants for building domestic scientific capabilities, which might be regarded as an enabling 'input' for innovation and growth (Bernardes and Albuquerque, 2003).

The above considerations apply stringently in the context of agricultural development. Indeed, although agricultural modernization has raised several concerns among scholars and in civil society (IASSTD, 2009; Vanloqueren and Baret, 2009), there is a direct link between higher agricultural productivity, increasing yields and research conducted at universities and PROs (Pardey and Beintema, 2001). The network of PROs, along with their interactions with farmers and input suppliers, has contributed significantly to the development of new crops and cultivars as well as to the adoption and adaptation of foreign technologies (Vessuri, 1990; Pardey and Beintema, 2001). As discussed in Chapter 1, this latter point is of key importance, since knowledge and technologies in viticulture are context specific. Hence, imported technologies need to be adapted to local climate, soil conditions and other biophysical conditions. In order to do that, investment in indigenous research, which can spur local technological capabilities and enhance both adoption and adaptation of international discoveries, is strictly necessary (Pardey and Beintema, 2001; Bernardes and Albuquerque, 2003).

Today the role of universities in the context of catching-up countries is becoming more complex due to two main sets of reasons: on the one hand, the changing nature of technology and science, and on the other, the impact of globalization on the diffusion of knowledge and on the relative importance of scientific actors (Mazzoleni and Nelson, 2007).

As far as the former issue is concerned, knowledge as well as products and technologies now have a much shorter life cycle. In several scientific domains, the distinction between what is a scientific input and technology has become more blurred, which implies that scientific discoveries are often intertwined with technological development, in a way that the lag between discoveries and product development is now very short if not non-existent (OECD, 2002). Moreover, most of the new technological paradigms, both in industrial and in agricultural sectors, have much stronger scientific underpinnings and, as a consequence, in several scientific domains, the communities of academic and industry researchers are increasingly interconnected, as confirmed by growing empirical evidence (Fontana et al., 2006; D'Este and Patel, 2007).

The above suggests that catching-up countries, along with firms and universities therein, need to be adequately equipped to adapt rapidly to the changing conditions in the external environment. In order to do so, they have to set up a scientific infrastructure, which would enable them to renew their repertoires of competences and knowledge, or at least to identify the relevant sources of knowledge (Nelson, 2008). All these efforts call for the development and nurturing of indigenous scientific capabilities, in terms of both skill formation and research activity. On the basis of similar arguments, several approaches such as the national systems of innovation, the triple helix model, and the Mode 2 knowledge production claim, even if in varying degrees and with different emphasis, that a third mission of universities is to directly contribute to industrial research (Etzkowitz and Leydesdorff, 2000; Nowotny et al., 2003). These approaches rest on the idea that universities, in addition to research and training, also provide a more direct contribution to society by engaging in research activity directly related to industrial development.

With regard to the impact of globalization, the new regulatory framework in which catching-up countries currently operate is a rather different context compared to that faced by early catch-up countries (for example, Japan and South Korea). The access to knowledge is today more restricted than in the past, due to tighter intellectual property rights, which further constrain the ability of backward countries to catch up with the technological and scientific frontier, making the adoption of external technology harder and more costly (Mazzoleni and Nelson, 2007). Futhermore, in sectors such as agro-food, there are increasingly stricter regulatory frameworks, based on health and quality standards, to comply with for competing in the international market (Nadvi, 2008). In this context, the development of domestic science, educational and training infrastructures becomes an indispensable condition for promoting indigenous technological capabilities.

Nevertheless, globalization also offers new opportunities to developing countries because the worldwide scientific community is today more strongly interconnected than ever. Scientists in less developed economies have more opportunities to engage with their peers in advanced countries and this might allow them easier access to relevant and updated scientific knowledge. These interactions might occur because of migration, which despite the initial negative effect of brain drain, may ultimately spur the advancement of human capital and knowledge creation in the sending country (see among others: Koser and Salt, 1997; Meyer, 2001; Agarwal et al., 2008). Indeed, a small but increasing number of successful migrants are returning home, bringing with them knowledge, capital and networks (Saxenian, 2006). Moreover, information exchange has been enhanced by the diffusion of information and communication technology (ICT), by the reduced costs of communication at long distance and by the decreased costs of traveling, which render international collaboration and knowledge transfer easier, cheaper and more feasible.

The above arguments suggest that research activity carried out at scientific organizations such as universities and PROs matters for catching up. Emerging countries increasingly need to set up a domestic scientific infrastructure capable of undertaking research and able to establish channels for tapping into international scientific knowledge.

In this chapter, with a focus on three emerging wine producers – Argentina, Chile and South Africa – which, as seen in Cusmano et al (Chapter 2), are characterized by a successful participation in the international market – we investigate their scientific performance in relevant fields for this industry and their participation in international scientific collaborations, as an indicator of their ability to tap into the global scientific knowledge pool. With regard to scientific networks, we provide a detailed analysis of their structures, looking at the type of linkages established locally and internationally and at the nature of the organizations involved.

3 DATA SOURCES

The analysis is based on bibliographical data covering a period of 15 years (from 1992 to 2006),[3] extracted from the Web of Science edition of the Science *Citation Index Expanded*™ (SCIE) of the Institute for Scientific Information (ISI, Philadelphia, PA, USA). As in many similar studies, by restricting our analysis to the Science Citation Index, we acknowledge a well-known language bias because there are few non-English journals included in the SCIE database and this, of course, underrates the scientific output of Old World wine-producing countries such as France and Italy, as well as of Chile and Argentina, on which we focus our attention in this chapter (Van Leeuwen et al., 2001). Nevertheless, this database has the advantage of allowing comparison in different fields and countries. In this study, only 'citable' publications, that is, papers recorded as article, letter, note or review were selected. To define the wine research area, we have followed Glänzel and Veugelers's (2006) strategy, which considers two search criteria:[4]

1. *Specific search strings* applied to keywords, title and abstract of the publications, using the following search terms: GRAPEVIN* OR WINES OR WINE GRAP* OR WINE PRO* OR RED WINE* OR WHITE WINE* OR WINEMAKING OR ENOLOG* OR VITICULT* OR OENOLOG* OR WINE CELL* OR WINE YEAST* OR WINERY OR WINERIES OR VITIS.

   This set of search terms is the result of a series of strategies tested for the retrieval. In the first step, the most obvious term 'wine' was used but this keyword resulted in a lot of noise. Then, we verified that relevant publications using the term 'wine' in the title, abstract or as a keyword could also be found on the basis of the other search terms, listed above, since several words frequently co-occurred. Therefore we removed the term 'wine'.

2. *Specialized journals* included in the SCIE database, all papers of which have been included in the study. The journals considered are: the *American Journal of Enology and Viticulture*, the *Australian Journal of Grape and Wine Research* and *Vitis*.

The combination of the two components of the above search strategy resulted in a broad coverage of the field under study with the extraction of 15,692 publications. This figure might underestimate the amount of research conducted in wine-related fields, given that some keywords might have been overlooked in the first criteria. Nevertheless, including all the articles published in core wine journals reduces this bias. Then, the raw data were processed in order to clean and standardize the affiliations of the authors, assigning an identifying code to each research organization. In order to do that, a two-step procedure was implemented. First, the identity of the organizations was automatically recognized and the same code assigned when the standardized name and address strings corresponded. In particular, for each organization two codes were assigned: one (that is, *groupcode*) based on the group identity (for example, CNRS) and the other (that is, *orgcode*) based on both name and localization (for example, CNRS in Rhône-Alpes). Following this automatic procedure, a manual check was performed for a selected number of countries.

In the second step each identified organization was classified according to the following taxonomy: public research organization (PRO), higher education organization (HE), government organization (GOV) and private firm (IND). Similarly to the first phase of the procedure, this task was performed automatically for all the records and then manually checked for a selected number of countries. The final resulting dataset includes 12,373 publications and about 4,700 organizations with at least one publication.

Based on the assigned codes, it has been possible to identify co-publications between two or more organizations when two or more different codes (that is, *orgcode*) are associated with the same article as well as international co-publications when two or more organizations are located in two or more different countries.[5]

4   GLOBAL TRENDS IN WINE RESEARCH

In Chapter 2, Cusmano et al. show the growing importance of New World countries in the international market and at the same time the extent to which the Old World has lost ground in the last two decades, stressing the key role played by scientific research in the global restructuring of the wine industry. In this section, we investigate which countries contribute to the advances in scientific research on wine-related issues as well as their participation in national and international collaborations, as measured by scientific co-publications, as a way to examine whether the changing geography of the global wine industry has been accompanied by a similar shift in the international scientific community. The countries considered are the leading producers in the worldwide industry, which include the emerging economies that are the subject of our study, namely Argentina, Chile and South Africa.

As a way of introducing scientific research on wine-related issues, the first general consideration concerns the recent increase in the number of scientific publications on issues related to wine over the 1992–2006 period (see Figure 2.2 in Chapter 2). This increase appears even more impressive if compared to the pattern of publications without any field restriction; in 2003 the overall number of publications compared to the beginning of the 1990s grew by almost 30 percent, while the number of 'wine publications' increased more than five times. As Glänzel and Veugelers (2006: 29) noted: 'the growth of cumulated number of publications is thus stronger than linear. . . . These patterns are typical of an emerging but not exponentially growing science field'.

Table 3.1 reports the number of publications in wine-related fields over three periods (1992–1996, 1997–2001, 2002–2006). We observe for all countries a significant increase in the absolute number of scientific articles and,

Table 3.1   Publications in wine and index of specialization (IS – Balassa Index)*

Country	1992–96			1997–2001			2002–2006		
	No (%)	IS	Ranking	No (%)	IS	Ranking	No	IS	Ranking
United States	369 (25.93)	0.73	1	866 (21.54)	0.68	1	1,211 (18.05)	0.59	1
France	222 (15.53)	0.78	2	562 (13.98)	0.87	3	786 (11.71)	0.71	3
Spain	202 (14.20)	7.56	3	611 (15.20)	6.60	2	1,117 (16.64)	6.82	2
Italy	150 (10.54)	3.51	4	436 (10.85)	3.27	4	777 (11.58)	3.30	4
Australia	79 (5.55)	2.48	5	196 (4.88)	2.08	7	453 (6.75)	2.96	5
Germany	72 (5.06)	3.15	6	240 (5.70)	2.80	5	307 (4.57)	2.54	6
Portugal	39 (2.74)	17.24	10	150 (3.73)	13.93	9	293 (4.37)	12.19	7
Argentina	15 (1.05)	3.30	16	31 (0.77)	1.80	25	71 (1.06)	2.27	22
Chile	5 (0.35)	2.29	30	29 (0.72)	4.24	26	87 (1.30)	6.29	19
South Africa	18 (1.26)	3.01	15	48 (1.19)	3.27	19	111 (1.65)	4.63	15
All countries	1,423	–	–	4,020	–	–	6,711	–	–

Note: * The index of specialization is measured as the ratio of the world share of a given country in wine-related publications to the overall world share of publications of the same country in all scientific fields.

Source: Own elaboration of ISI data.

at a cursory look, we also see that leading countries have not changed their position in the ranking during the period investigated, though their share of total publications has changed. For example, France and the USA have lost ground, while Spain and Italy have slightly increased their share. Taking into account the three emerging countries under investigation, they all show a very small number of publications in the first period (1992–96), which increases abruptly 10 years later (2002–06). In particular, Chile stands out for its performance: with only five articles published in ISI journals in the first period, it has significantly increased its share, from 0.35 percent in the 1992–96 period to 1.3 percent in the 2002–06 period. Moreover, Chile also displays an increasing specialization trend: its share of publications in wine-related fields grew more significantly than in other fields. South Africa also raised its share from 1.26 percent in the first period to 1.65 percent, and its specialization index has increased steadily since the second half of the 1990s. On the contrary, Argentina has increased the absolute number of publications, but its share has remained unchanged.

5   THE GLOBAL SCIENTIFIC WINE COMMUNITY

To investigate the openness of the wine research system, we consider international collaboration as a share of total publications, observing an increase throughout the period under investigation (Figure 3.1). For a selected number of countries, Table 3.2 shows that the number of inter-national collaborations has increased, both in absolute terms and, more interestingly, relative to the number of co-publications. In particular, the

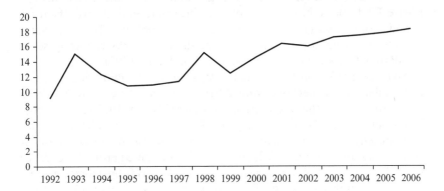

Source: Own elaboration on ISI data.

Figure 3.1   International co-publications as share of total publications

*Table 3.2   International co-publications in wine: number and share in
terms of co-publications*

Country	1992–96		1997–2001		2002–2006	
	No	%	No	%	No	%
United States	73	56.15	216	56.40	355	57.17
France	44	46.32	130	47.27	256	52.67
Spain	23	40.35	86	37.07	172	40.38
Italy	41	44.57	92	37.70	199	43.93
Australia	8	25.81	48	41.38	130	43.33
Germany	22	68.75	63	63.64	135	68.88
Portugal	12	52.17	43	55.84	100	53.48
Argentina	1	8.33	13	59.09	29	67.44
Chile	1	50.00	11	64.71	34	77.27
South Africa	6	75.00	15	60.00	48	65.75
All countries	360	51.72	1,243	53.58	2,514	55.28

Source: Own elaboration of ISI data.

three catching-up countries under investigation have increased their shares
of international co-publications, which are greater than the worldwide
average since 1997.[6]

The analysis of the network of international collaborations clearly illustrates the increasing globalization of the wine research community. This is
the focus of the rest of this section, in which on the basis of co-authorships
at country level we compare the relative position of Argentina, Chile and
South Africa with respect to the other global players in the wine industry.[7]
Figure 3.2 displays the networks of scientific collaborations over the three
periods considered (1992–96, 1997–2001, 2002–06) and Table 3.3 summarizes the structural features of these three networks reporting some
standard network measures (Wasserman and Faust, 1994).

A visual analysis provides a first glimpse of the evolution of the worldwide collaboration network, with different groups of newcomers joining
the network along the three periods considered. From 1992 to 1996, only
European (France, Germany, Italy and Spain) and North American countries are engaged in international collaborations (with the exception of
Israel). As shown in Figure 3.2a, the network is centered around the USA,[8]
with whom all the other countries are connected apart from a direct connection between Italy and France. This outcome emerges even more clearly from
the index of network centralization, which indicates the presence of a star
network configuration.[9] In this period, the New World countries are absent
from the international scientific arena, as measured by co-publications.

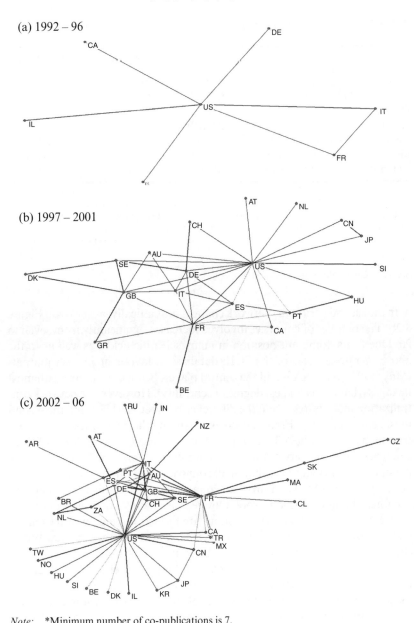

(a) 1992 – 96

(b) 1997 – 2001

(c) 2002 – 06

Note: *Minimum number of co-publications is 7.

Source: Own elaboration of ISI data.

Figure 3.2 Network of research collaborations* between countries

Innovation and technological catch-up

Table 3.3   Main structural features of research collaboration networks

	1996–2000	1997–2001	2002–2006
Number of countries	7	20	36
Number of links	7	78	144
Density	0.33	0.20	0.11
Average degree (std dev.)	2 (1.69)	3.90 (3.54)	4 (5.05)
Network centralization*	93.33 %	70.76%	63.53%
Most central country (degree)	US (6)	US (16)	US (25)
2nd most central country (degree)	Italy (2)	France (9)	France (17)

Note: *The network centralization index measures how much a network structure corresponds to the most central network structure theoretically possible. In undirected networks, such as those under analysis, the theoretically most centralized network is the star (i.e., all countries are directly connected to only one of them). This index ranges from 0 to 1.

Source: Own elaboration of ISI data.

In the second period the network changes dramatically, as shown in Figure 3.2b. The number of countries involved increases significantly from seven to 20. Due to its dominant position in many scientific fields, as well as to the above-mentioned bias of the SCIE database in favour of English journals (May, 1997), the USA is still the central player, being the country with most linkages (that is, the highest degree of centrality). However, the network centralization index is lower and the difference between the USA and the second most central country, France, decreases. Among the new entrants are countries such as Australia, China, Japan, Portugal and Hungary. Most of these countries enter the network and establish connections via the USA, which maintains its bridging role (that is, all countries except three are directly connected to the USA). The European countries strengthen their internal connections, though outside Europe they remain mainly connected only with the USA. In this context, the exceptions are France, linking up with Canada, and the UK and Italy, which are connected to Australia, the first New World country entering the global scientific community.

In the final period examined, corresponding to the era of consolidation of New World countries in the global wine markets, the network increases its complexity with the participation of 36 countries. Among the New World wine countries entering the international research community are Argentina, Chile and South Africa. The main features of the previous network are even more pronounced. The network centralization index decreases and the USA, though still the most central country, plays a less pivotal role. Indeed, the number of countries not directly connected to the USA increases from only three during the previous period (Greece, Denmark, Belgium) to 10, among which are Argentina, Chile and South Africa. The gap between the USA, France and Italy in terms of the number of partners narrows over time.

Overall, the most recent international scientific network of co-publication is organized around two directly connected centers: one is represented by the USA, which for many countries is the exclusive source of collaborations, and the other is Europe, represented by some Old World countries such as France, Italy and Spain. The main novelty of this new scenario is that the European leading countries have established direct collaborations with New World producers: for instance, France with Chile, and Spain with Argentina. The role of Australia is also very interesting, being well embedded in a wide network of international collaborations with several Old World countries as well as with some New World producers, such as South Africa and New Zealand.

In sum, from the analysis of the network of international collaborations it appears that overall, newcomers in the international market are also now an active part of the international scientific community, which in less than two decades has become much larger and more complex. The participation of New World countries requires further specifications because important differences persist. On the one hand, the first tier among New World countries, that is Australia, is well embedded in the international knowledge network; on the other, a second group of New World countries, namely Argentina, Chile and South Africa, have been able to tap into international knowledge only in more recent times and are still peripheral. In the next section, we explore in more detail the configuration of the research system for this latter group of countries.

6   THE STRUCTURE OF THE NATIONAL NETWORKS OF COLLABORATION

In order to provide some insights into the characteristics of the respective wine research systems in Argentina, Chile and South Africa, in this section we focus on the role that different domestic actors (that is, university, PRO and industry) play in building national and international research collaborations, measured by the network of scientific co-publications.

Taking into account the collaboration network among national organizations, Table 3.4 presents some network measures highlighting the low connectivity of the three networks and the giant component (that is, the largest connected sub-graph) that ties up the largest part of the network (from 52.4 percent in Chile to 61.3 percent in South Africa), though it

Table 3.4   Network structure properties: domestic networks

	Argentina	Chile	South Africa
National organizations	25	21	31
Domestic links	46	36	62
Density (× 100)	0.15	0.17	0.13
Giant component	15 (60.0%)	11 (52.4%)	18 (61.3%)
Isolated organizations	7	6	9
Av. degree (std dev.)	3.68 (1.59)	3.42 (1.41)	4 (2.99)

Source: Own elaboration of ISI data.

Table 3.5   Domestic networks and foreign co-publishing organizations

	Argentina	Chile	South Africa
International nodes	38	45	64
International links	54	59	84
Giant component (only domestic org.)	15	16	22
Isolated nodes	4	1	4
Av. degree* (Std dev.)	2.16 (4.01)	2.81 (4.14)	2.71 (8.33)
Network centralization	24.35	26.59	52.27

Note: * Calculated considering only the internal nodes, i.e., external links /internal nodes.

Source: Own elaboration of ISI data.

is not dominant as it often occurs in collaboration networks (Newman, 2001; Breschi et al., 2009). However, as shown in Table 3.5 the networks change when foreign organizations are considered, the number of isolated organizations sharply decreases, while the number of domestic organizations in the giant component increases, with the exception of Argentina. This last result points to the fact that the connectivity of the research system in Chile and South Africa partly depends on the presence of some foreign actors.

Figure 3.3 provides a visual representation of the structural differences among the three networks. For each country we display a graph including the national organizations (represented with a white node) and their foreign partners (black node).[10] The visual inspection suggests that the three networks differ to a large extent in terms of actors involved, international connectivity and overall structure. Note that domestic organizations play a rather different role within each network. For instance, in the Argentinean network, three different types of organizations[11] seem

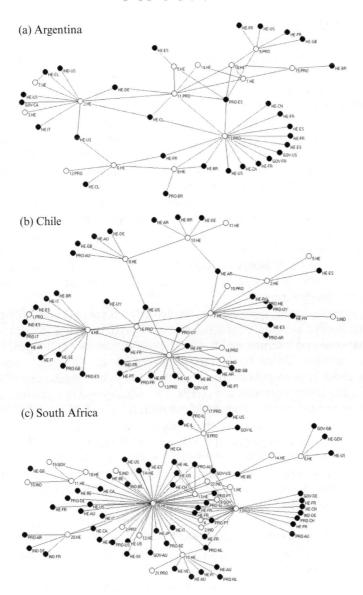

(a) Argentina

(b) Chile

(c) South Africa

Note: *Isolated nodes are not displayed.

Source: Own elaboration of ISI data.

Figure 3.3   *Collaboration networks among domestic and foreign organizations*

to be highly central: the National Scientific and Technical Research Council (CONICET, that is, node 11); the National Institute of Farming Technology (INTA, that is, node 13), in particular its local branch in the Mendoza province and the University of Buenos Aires (UBA, that is, node 2). However, the organizations that are central in terms of domestic collaborations differ from those undertaking international linkages; for example, CONICET ranks only fifth in terms of the number of international collaborations, whereas it has the highest number of domestic collaborations. Conversely, INTA is very well connected internationally.

The Chilean network displays a rather different pattern in this respect. The three most central actors, namely the University of Santiago de Chile (node 7), the Catholic University (node 9) and the University of Chile (node 4) are well connected both with national and foreign organizations. The same is true for the South African network, which is, however, by far the most centralized, with two organizations – ARC, a research institute that is part of the Ministry of Agriculture (node 7) and the University of Stellenbosch (node 16) – absorbing the quasi-totality of national and international collaborations.

A closer look at the type of actors involved is presented in Table 3.6, which reports the average number of collaborations by type of organization at both the national and international levels. The role played by the different type of organizations differs by country. In Argentina the domestic organizations involved in co-publications are public research organizations (PRO) and higher education institutions (HE). The industry and the governmental agencies are not active in scientific collaborations and this configuration might represent a weakness of the national system in its ability to bridge basic research with deployment. However, we should point out that these actors can be part of other scientific collaborations, which do not have as an output a scientific article in one of the ISI journals. In fact, using different indicators, Kunc and Tiffin (ch 5 in this book) find stronger ties between industry and university in Mendoza (Argentina) than in Talca (Chile).

The Chilean case appears to be very different because, although universities (HE) are strongly connected both internationally and locally, a few private companies (IND), which include service and input providers but not wineries, are also involved in both national and international collaborations. Therefore, the Chilean network configuration would suggest the presence of a 'triple helix' model, as would South Africa. In this country, PRO and HE show similar rates of participation and there is also a presence of governmental organizations (GOV) (for example, regional development agency and regulatory bodies). Wineries, such as Distell, one of the largest winemakers in the world, are also active in the network of collaborations. Their collaboration with research institutions is also

Table 3.6 Average degree by type of organization (national and international collaborations) (1996–2006)

Type	Argentina				Chile				South Africa			
	N	Total*	National	International	N	Total*	National	International	N	Total*	National	International
HE	18	3 (2.87)	1.5 (1.34)	1.5 (2.06)	11	6.36 (6.09)	2.28 (1.66)	4.18 (4.66)	17	5.59 (11.91)	2.0 (3.35)	3.59 (8.81)
PRO	7	6	2.14 (2.27)	3.86 (5.18)	5	2.60 (2.07)	0.8 (0.48)	1.8 (1.92)	5	6.6 (9.52)	2.2 (2.68)	4.4 (6.98)
GOV	0	–	–		1	1	1	0	3	2	2	0
IND	0	–	–		4	1.25 (1.26)	0.5 (0.58)	0.75 (0.95)	5	1.6 (1.52)	1.4 (1.14)	0.2 (0.44)

Note: Standard deviation in brackets; total = national + international average degree.

Source: Own elaboration of ISI data

facilitated by the existence of an organization such as Winetech, specifically created to finance and promote applied research in the wine sector (see Chapter 8 for more details on this).

More insights come from the analysis of the type of organizations involved in each pair of collaborations (Table 3.7). As expected, universities and PROs play a prominent role, as most collaborations are developed among these actors. However, it is interesting to note that both in South Africa and Chile, one out of 10 co-authorships concerns a collaboration involving a firm and a university/PRO. This finding further suggests that both South Africa and Chile are closer than Argentina to a configuration resembling the 'triple helix' model, in which the three pillars of the national research system interact. This result complements the investigation presented by Giuliani and Rabellotti in this book (Chapter 7) on bridging researchers, in other words on those researchers who maintain strong international linkages with their peers and at the same time are in touch with the domestic industry.

7 CONCLUDING REMARKS

Catching up is a complex process, which goes beyond simply copying foreign techniques purchased from leader countries. Rather, it entails mastering and learning about how to replicate and adapt the knowledge imported from abroad. Therefore catching up is feasible and sustainable if latecomers invest in knowledge infrastructures for building domestic scientific and technological capabilities. This seems to be more urgent today than ever as knowledge becomes more complex and has a much shorter life cycle than in the past. In such a scenario, universities and public research centers might play a central role as they provide training, general scientific inputs and specific and applied knowledge for industry. The role of research and the scientific performance of catching-up countries have recently attracted renewed attention by scholars (Mazzoleni and Nelson, 2007); nevertheless there are few empirical contributions that have tackled this issue, in particular at the sectoral level.

The aim of this chapter is to add new evidence on the scientific performance of catching-up countries in the wine sector. This is an interesting case study; over the past few decades the wine industry has been subject to remarkable changes, with the entry into the international market of several new players that in a rather short time have partially outpaced the incumbents, and some of these successful latecomers come from emerging economies.

In this chapter we have discussed the insertion of some catching-up countries in the global wine research community, presenting some stylized

Table 3.7 *Matrix of pairs of collaborations, by type of organization** *(1996–2006)*

Type	Argentina					Chile					South Africa				
	HE	PRO	GOV	IND	Total	HE	PRO	GOV	IND	Total	HE	PRO	GOV	IND	Total
HE	28 (7)	39 (13)	0	1 (0)	68 (20)	42 (9)	20 (4)	1 (0)	7 (2)	70 (15)	50 (9)	28 (5)	8 (5)	8 (5)	94 (24)
PRO		4 (1)	3 (0)	0	7 (1)		1 (0)	1 (0)	1	3 (0)		9 (1)	5 (1)	4 (2)	18 (4)
GOV			0	0	0			0	0	0			1 (1)	2	4 (2)
IND				0	0				1 (0)	1 (0)				0	0
Total					75 (21)					74 (15)					112 (28)

Note: National collaborations in brackets.

Source: Own elaboration of ISI data.

facts about their scientific performance in relation to the position of the incumbents. Overall, we show that wine is a wide and enlarging scientific field in which several scientific disciplines are involved. The number of publications in wine-related fields has grown steadily over the last two decades. Both Old and New World countries have contributed to such an increase, though we clearly observe that traditional producers, such as France, have seen their share of publications decreasing, and conversely most of the newcomers have experienced a steep increase in their publication rate. In particular, three emerging stars in the international market – Argentina, Chile and South Africa – have accompanied the growth of their exports with a radical increase of their presence in the wine scientific world.

Moreover, with the analysis of international co-publications we have been able to map the increasing complexity of the global knowledge network. We illustrate the shift from a scenario dominated during the 1990s by the Old World producers and the USA to a new setting in which New World producers, among them countries such as Argentina, Chile and South Africa, are now part of the international scientific community.

In these three countries we have also investigated which types of organization (that is, university, PRO, government, industry) are involved in domestic and international co-publications, and emphasized the differences between Argentina on the one hand and Chile and South Africa on the other. In terms of tapping into international knowledge and diffusing it within the domestic research system, both Chile and South Africa are characterized by a network in which the international and domestic leaders coincide and the industry also actively participates, thus resembling a 'triple helix' system of research. In contrast, in Argentina, only PROs and universities are involved in scientific publication and the organizations at the core of the domestic and international networks are different. This structure of the research system might represent a constraint to the local diffusion of international knowledge and hinder the effective deployment of basic research in practical applications, although this finding may be biased by the fact that we consider only scientific collaborations having an ISI article as an output. A detailed analysis of these networks, combining different sources and forms of collaboration as well as investigating their performance in terms of knowledge diffusion is an interesting topic for further research, which may provide very useful indications for policy.

Overall, we might conclude that the globalization of the wine industry has been accompanied by a similar shift in the wine research community. Emerging economies are more involved over time in international collaboration, though their presence in the scientific realm is very recent and still significantly below their role in the international wine markets.

NOTES

1. For a critical appraisal on the number of publications as an output measure of research activity, see Katz and Martin (1997).
2. We acknowledge that these arguments do not imply that catching up is a linear and uniform process; differences over time and across geographical areas and industries are marked, as exemplified by the different strategies and paths followed by catching-up countries.
3. In the analysis we have not taken into account the first period available in the dataset, from 1989 to 1992, since very few articles in our database were published in ISI journals.
4. Glänzel and Veugelers (2006) also use an additional *institutional* criterion, including all the articles that reported a name of an organization (with which the author is affili-ated) with some 'wine' reference (for example, UC–Davis Department of Viticulture and Enology). This criterion has been excluded in this chapter. Moreover, we have also excluded all the articles whose authors are affiliated to hospitals or medical schools. Differently from Glänzel and Veugelers, we included the journal *Vitis*, which is a core journal in this field of research.
5. A publication with two organizations located in two different countries is classified in the same way as a publication involving three different organizations with two of them located in the same country.
6. Large countries always tend to show a relatively lower share of co-authorships as com-pared to smaller countries. This result is well established in the literature and confirmed by some recent evidence on the evolution of the wine research community (Glänzel and Veugelers, 2006).
7. We assume that a collaboration link between two countries is in place if there are at least seven bilateral papers between these two countries. Indeed, it is reasonable to assume that two countries need to activate a certain number of collaborations in order to allow a substantial knowledge exchange. The threshold of seven co-publications has been arbitrarily fixed. We also tested different thresholds without significant changes in the results.
8. The USA is the most productive country in most of the scientific fields (Glänzel et al., 2002), so it is not surprising to find it very central also in the wine sector.
9. In order to have a star network the collaboration (that is, link) IT-FR should be removed.
10. An edge connecting two nodes represents a scientific collaboration between two organi-zations that have at least one co-publication. The direct links among foreign organiza-tions have not been included.
11. The list of organizations for each country is provided in Tables 3A.1–3 in the appendix.

REFERENCES

Agarwal, A., I. Cockburn and J. McHale (2008), 'Brain drain or brain bank: the impact of migration on poor-country innovation', National Bureau of Economic Research working paper 14592, Cambridge, MA.

Albuquerque, E.M. (2004), 'Science and technology systems in less developed countries', in H. Moed, W. Glänzel and U. Schmoch (eds), *Handbook of Quantitative Science and Technology Research*, Dordrecht the Netherlands: Kluwer Academic, pp. 759–78.

Amsden, A.H. (1989), *Asia's Next Giant: South Korea and Late Industrialization*, Oxford: Oxford University Press.

Arrow, K. (1962), 'Economic welfare and the allocation of resource for inven-
    tion', in R. Nelson (ed.), *The Rate and Direction of Inventive Activity: Economic
    and Social Factors*, NBER–University Conference, Princeton, NJ: Princeton
    University Press, pp. 609–25.
Balconi, M., S. Brusoni and L. Orsenigo (2010), 'In defence of the linear model: an
    essay', *Research Policy*, **39** (1), 1–13.
Bernardes, A. and E.M. Albuquerque (2003), 'Cross-over, thresholds and the
    interactions between science and technology: lessons for less-developed coun-
    tries', *Research Policy*, **32** (5), 867–87.
Breschi, S., L. Cassi, F. Malerba and N. Vonortas (2009), 'Networked research:
    European policy intervention in ICTs', *Technology Analysis and Strategic
    Management*, **21** (7), 833–57.
Brundenius, C., B.-A. Lundvall and J. Sutz (2009), 'The role of universities in
    innovation systems in developing countries: developmental university systems
    – empirical, analytical and normative perspectives', in B.-A. Lundvall,
    K.J. Joseph, C. Chaminade and J. Vang (eds), *Handbook of Innovation
    Systems and Developing Countries: Building Domestic Capabilities in a Global
    Setting*, Cheltenham, UK and Northampton, MA, USA: Edward Elgar, pp.
    311–33.
Bush, V. (1945), 'As we may think', *The Atlantic Monthly*, July.
D'Este, P. and P. Patel (2007), 'University–industry linkages in the UK: what
    are the factors underlying the variety of interactions with industry?', *Research
    Policy*, **36** (9), 1295–313.
Dosi, G., P. Llerena and M. Sylos Labini (2006), 'The relationships between
    science, technologies and their industrial exploitation: an illustration through
    the myths and realities of the so-called "European Paradox"', *Research Policy*,
    35 (10), 1450–64.
Etzkowitz, H. and L. Leydesdorff (2000), 'The dynamics of innovation: from
    national systems and "Mode 2" to a triple helix of university–industry–govern-
    ment relations', *Research Policy*, **29** (2), 109–23.
Fagerberg, J. and M. Godinho (2005), 'Innovation and catching up', in J.
    Fagerberg, D.C. Mowery and R.R. Nelson (eds), *The Oxford Handbook of
    Innovation*, Oxford: Oxford University Press, pp. 514–43.
Fontana, R., A. Geuna and M. Matt (2006), 'Factors affecting university–industry
    R&D projects: the importance of searching, screening and signalling', *Research
    Policy*, 35 (2), 309–23.
Glänzel, W., A. Schubert and T. Braun (2002), 'A relational charting approach to
    the world of basic research in twelve science fields at the end of the second mil-
    lennium', *Scientometrics*, 55 (3), 335–48.
Glänzel, W. and R. Veugelers (2006), 'Science for wine: a bibliometric assess-
    ment of wine and grape research for wine producing and consuming countries',
    American Journal of Enology and Viticulture, **57** (1), 23–32.
International Assessment of Agricultural Knowledge, Science and Technology for
    Development (IAASTD) (2009), Executive *Summary of the Synthesis Report*,
    accessed 20 January 2010 at www.agassessment.org.
Katz, J.S. and B.R. Martin (1997), 'What is research collaboration?', Research
    Policy, 26 (1), 1–18.
Kim, L. and R.R. Nelson (2000), *Technology, Learning, and Innovation :
    Experiences of Newly Industrializing Economies*, Cambridge: Cambridge
    University Press.

Koser, K. and J. Salt (1997), 'The geography of highly skilled international migration', *International Journal of Population Geography*, **3** (4), 285–303.

Lall, S. (1992), 'Technological capabilities and industrialization', *World Development*, 20 (2), 165–86.

May, R.M. (1997), 'The scientific wealth of nations', *Science*, 275 (7 February), 793–96.

Mazzoleni, R. (2008), 'Catching up and academic institutions: a comparative study of past national experiences', *Journal of Development Studies*, **44** (5), 678–700.

Mazzoleni, R. and R.R. Nelson (2007), 'Public research institutions and economic catch-up', *Research Policy*, **36** (10), 1512–2.

Meyer, J.B. (2001), 'Network approach versus brain drain: lessons from the diaspora', *International Migration Quarterly Issue*, **39** (5), 91–110.

Mowery, D.C. and B.N. Sampat (2005), 'Universities in national innovation systems', in J. Fagerberg, D.C. Mowery and R.R. Nelson (eds), *The Oxford Handbook of Innovation*, Oxford: Oxford University Press, pp. 209–39.

Nadvi, K. (2008), 'Global standards, global governance and the organization of global value chains', *Journal of Economic Geography*, **8** (3), 323–43.

Nelson, R.R. (1959), 'The simple economics of basic scientific research', *Journal of Political Economy*, **67** (3), 297–306.

Nelson, R.R. (ed.) (1993), *National Innovation Systems: A Comparative Analysis*, New York: Oxford University Press.

Nelson, R.R. (2008), 'What enables rapid economic progress: what are the needed institutions?', *Research Policy*, **37** (1), 1–11.

Newman, M.E.J. (2001), 'Scientific collaboration networks: I. Network construction and fundamental results', *Physical Review E*, **64**, 016131.

Nowotny, H., P. Scott and M. Gibbons (2003), '"Mode 2" revisited: the new production of knowledge', *Minerva*, **41** (3), 179–94.

Organisation for Economic Co-operation and Development (OECD) (2002), *Benchmarking Industry–Science Relationships*, Paris: OECD.

Pardey, P.G and N.M. Beintema (2001), *Slow Magic: Agricultural R&D a Century after Mendel*, Washington, DC: International Food Policy Research Institute.

Rosenberg, N. (1982), *Inside the Black Box: Technology and Economics*, Cambridge: Cambridge University Press.

Saxenian, A.L. (2006), *The New Argonauts: Regional Advantage in a Global Economy*, Cambridge, MA: Harvard University Press.

Van Leeuwen, T.N., H.F. Moed, R.J.W. Tijssen, M.S. Visser and A.F.J. Van Raan (2001), 'Language biases in the coverage of the Science Citation Index and its consequences for international comparisons of national research performance', *Scientometrics*, **51** (1), 335–46.

Vanloqueren, G. and P.V. Baret (2009), 'How agricultural research systems shape a technological regime that develops genetic engineering but locks out agroecological innovations', *Research Policy*, **38** (6), 971–83.

Vessuri, H.M.C. (1990), 'O inventamos o erramos: the power of science in Latin America', *World Development*, **18** (11), 1543–53.

Wasserman, F. and K. Faust (1994), *Social Network Analysis*, Cambridge: Cambridge University Press.

Yusuf, S. and K. Nabeshima (eds) (2007), *How Universities Promote Economic Growth*, Washington, DC: World Bank.

APPENDIX 3A

Table 3A.1   *Argentina: national organizations belonging to the external giant component*

Id	Type	Organization	Location	Degree	Internal degree	External degree
1	HE	SAN JUAN NATL UNIV	Provincia de San Juan	4	4	0
2	HE	UBA	Distrito Federal	11	3	8
3	HE	UNIV CATOLICA ARGENTINA	Distrito Federal	1	1	0
4	HE	UNIV NACL COMAHUE	Provincia de Rio Negro	4	2	2
5	HE	UNIV NACL COMAHUE	Provincia del Neuquen	4	2	2
6	HE	UNIV LUJAN CUYO	Provincia de Mendoza	6	2	4
7	HE	UNIV NACL LUJAN	Provincia de Buenos Aires	2	1	1
8	HE	UNIV NACL RIO CUARTO	Provincia de Cordoba	4	2	2
9	PRO	CERELA	Provincia de Tucuman	6	1	5
10	HE	UNIV NACL TUCUMAN	Provincia de Tucuman	5	4	1
11	PRO	CONICET	Distrito Federal	10	7	3
12	PRO	CONSEJO NACL INVEST CIENT & TECN	Provincia de Mendoza	1	1	0
13	PRO	EEA MENDOZA INTA	Provincia de Mendoza	17	2	15
14	HE	NATL UNIV SAN LUIS	Provincia de San Luis	2	2	0
15	PRO	PROIMI	Provincia de Tucuman	3	2	1

Table 3A.2 *Chile: national organizations belonging to the external giant component*

Id	Type	Organization	Location	Degree	Internal degree	External degree
1	PRO	NATL ENVIRONM CTR	Region Metropolitana (RM) de Santiago	3	1	2
2	HE	PONTIFICIA UNIV CATOLICA VALPARAISO	Region de Valparaiso	4	2	2
3	IND	SEGUIN MOREAU S AMER	RM de Santiago	1	0	1
4	HE	UNIV CHILE	RM de Santiago	14	4	10
5	HE	UNIV LA FRONTERA	Region de la Araucania	1	1	0
6	HE	UNIV LA SERENA	Region de Coquimbo	2	2	0
7	HE	UNIV SANTIAGO CHILE	RM de Santiago	12	4	8
8	HE	UNIV TALCA	Region del Maule	6	1	5
9	HE	CATHOLIC UNIV	RM de Santiago	19	5	14
10	HE	CONCEPCION UNIV	Region del Biobio	7	3	4
11	HE	CTR INFORMAC TECNOL	Region de Coquimbo	2	2	0
12	IND	DICTUC SA	RM de Santiago	3	1	2
13	IND	EXPORTADORA CHIQUITA LTD	RM de Santiago	1	1	0
14	PRO	INIA EXPT CTR	Region de Coquimbo	2	1	1
15	PRO	INIA	Region del Maule	1	1	0
16	PRO	INIA	RM de Santiago	6	1	5

68 *Innovation and technological catch-up*

Table 3A.3 *South Africa: national organizations belonging to the external giant component*

Id	Type	Organization	Location	Degree	Internal degree	External degree
1	HE	INST WINE BIOTECHNOL	Province of the Western Cape	3	3	0
2	IND	KOOPERATIEWE WIJNBOUWERS VERENIGING BEPERK	Province of the Western Cape	2	2	0
3	PRO	NATL DEPT AGR	Province of the Western Cape	1	1	0
4	*	OZ PURIFICAT	Province of North-West	2	2	0
5	IND	PROLOR TECHPROS	Province of the Western Cape	1	1	0
6	HE	RAND AFRIKAANS UNIV	Gauteng	4	0	4
7	PRO	AFR FRUIT VINE & WINE RES INST	Province of the Western Cape	23	7	16
8	PRO	AGR RES COUNCIL	Gauteng	7	1	6
9	GOV	S AFRICAN SUGAR EXPT STN	Province of KwaZulu-Natal	2	2	0
10	IND	STELLENBOSCH FARMERS WINERY	Province of the Western Cape	1	1	0
11	HE	UNIV CAPE TOWN	Province of the Western Cape	5	4	1
12	HE	UNIV DURBAN WESTVILLE	Province of KwaZulu-Natal	1	1	0
13	HE	UNIV FREE STATE	Free State	6	2	4
14	HE	UNIV JOHANNES-BURG	Gauteng	1	0	1
15	HE	UNIV PRETORIA	Gauteng	8	2	6
16	HE	UNIV STELLENBOSCH	Province of the Western Cape	51	14	37

Table 3A.3   (continued)

Id	Type	Organization	Location	Degree	Internal degree	External degree
17	PRO	ARC ROODEPLAAT VEGETABLE & ORNAMENTAL PLANT INST	Gauteng	1	1	0
18	HE	UNIV WESTERN CAPE	Province of the Western Cape	3	3	0
19	GOV	CAPE METROPOLITAN COUNCIL	Province of the Western Cape	2	2	0
20	HE	CAPE PENINSULA UNIV TECHNOL	Province of the Western Cape	5	1	4
21	PRO	CENT AGR LABS	Province of North-West	1	1	0
22	IND	DISTELL	Province of the Western Cape	4	3	1

Note: * Not classified.

4. Contributions of the innovation system to Australia's wine industry growth

Kym Anderson[1]

1 INTRODUCTION

During the past two decades Australian wines have become increasingly noticeable to the average wine consumer in the northern hemisphere, following a dramatic expansion in Australia's vineyard area, winery capacity and wine exports. The industry originated with white settlement two centuries earlier, but remained minuscule until the first exports began in the second half of the nineteenth century. Since then, efforts to innovate though trial and error on the part of producers have been increasingly enhanced by systematic investments in grape and wine research and development (R&D). Those investments were further expanded after 1955 when the Australian Wine Research Institute came into being, and even more so after the 1980s when the Grape and Wine R&D Corporation was created to coordinate the investing of grape grower and winemaker levies and matching federal government funding. Simultaneously the industry has engaged in generic promotion of exports, beginning with the formation of the Wine Overseas Marketing Board (later to become the Australian Wine Board) in 1929 but expanding considerably following its conversion to the Australian Wine and Brandy Corporation (AWBC) in 1980 and the AWBC's creation of its Australian Wine Export Council in 1992.

This chapter seeks to assess the roles that the innovation system has played in the industry's recent growth, particularly through generic promotion and R&D. It begins with a brief summary of salient features of the industry's long-run trends and cycles and especially its most recent growth spurt. It then lays out the evolving nature of the institutions that provided generic promotion and R&D outputs of relevance to the industry. The speed and success of the export take-off in the 1990s was due in no small part to the substantial prior and ongoing investments nationally in pertinent R&D and related education and extension activities. The chapter concludes by speculating on the scope for enhancing the roles of generic and firm-level promotion and R&D in the future of the Australian wine industry.

2 GROWTH OF THE AUSTRALIAN WINE INDUSTRY: A BRIEF HISTORY

It was claimed more than a hundred years ago that 'Many of the leading wine merchants of London and other important commercial centers admit that Australia promises to become a powerful rival in the world's markets with the old-established vineyards of Europe' (Irvine, 1892: 6). Even though another seven decades passed before the Australian wine industry began to fulfill that earlier promise, it has since shot into prominence. Domestic demand growth from the 1960s helped, but since 1990 Australia has trebled its share of global vine area and has raised its share of global export sales more than eightfold. Following the quadrupling of its output it is now the world's fifth-largest wine producer by volume and the fourth-largest by value (after France, Italy and Spain and ahead of Argentina – OIV, 2009).

In the decade to the mid-1980s, Australian wine exports were less than US$15 million per year and the country was a net importer of wine. By contrast, nearly two-thirds of Australia's much larger volume of wine is now sold abroad (Figure 4.1), valued at around US$2.5 to 3 billion. Wine now generates about the same export revenue for Australia as the dairy industry and is next behind the country's two biggest farm export items (beef and wheat), having recently displaced wool from that third position.

Australia's wine exports have boomed several times in the past. In each case those booms subsequently reached a plateau and the expanded acreage meant that grape growers and winemakers went back to receiving low returns. Indeed the industry's prospects were sufficiently dire as recently as 1985 as to induce the government to fund a vine-pull compensation scheme to encourage grape growers to move to alternative crops. Yet, like a phoenix, the industry has risen again and grown with renewed vigor and a strong export focus.

The long history of fluctuating fortunes gave reason to expect that Australia's latest wine boom would be followed by yet another crash, at least in wine export (and thus wine grape) prices if not in wine production and export volumes – as indeed has begun to happen (Figure 4.2), with the export volumes rising since 2002 only for the two cheapest price ranges (Figure 4.3). Each of the first four booms in the Australian wine industry finished with a plateau in vineyard area (and winery output)

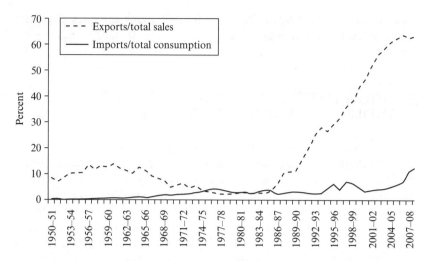

Source: Updated from Osmond and Anderson (1998), using data from http://www.awbc. com.au.

Figure 4.1   *Export share of total sales of Australian wine and import share of total consumption of wine in Australia, by volume, 1950–51 to 2008–09 (million liters)*

growth. These were periods when returns to grape growers and often also winemakers were depressed for years because of the rapid growth in new plantings during the boom. This phenomenon is of course not unique to Australia. On the contrary, it has periodically been the case in grape and wine markets elsewhere in the world for at least two millennia (Johnson, 1989).

Yet the industry's past history is also encouraging, because it shows the current boom to have several positive features that contrast with those of earlier booms. Some of these features are summarized in Table 4.1. The first boom, from the mid-1850s, was mainly driven by domestic demand growth following the gold rush that induced a trebling in Australia's white population in the 1850s. However, the wine produced from that excessive expansion could not be exported profitably, largely because of high duties on inter-colonial trade within Australasia plus poor marketing and high transport costs in exporting the rather crude product of that time to the Old World. Hence returns slumped quite quickly in that first cycle.

The second boom, from the 1880s, was due to a mixture of domestic and export demand growth, the latter involving better marketing and lower ocean transport costs for what were higher-quality but still mostly generic bulk (rather than winery bottled and branded) dry red wines. The

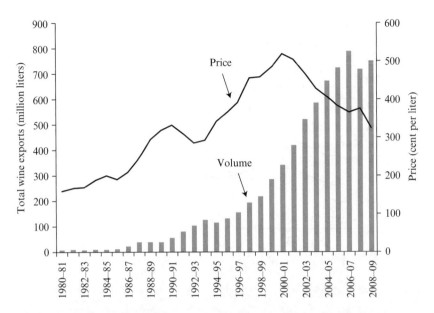

Source: Author's calculation from data retrieved from http://www.awbc.com.au.

Figure 4.2   *Volume and average price of export sales of Australian wine, 1980–81 to 2008–09 (million liters and Australian cents per liter)*

relatively open British market absorbed one-sixth of Australia's production early in the twentieth century, before the First World War intervened. That boom was part of a general internationalization of world commodity markets at that time – something that returned but in much-diminished form after that war.

The acreage boom induced by soldier settlement after the First World War provided the basis for the third boom, from the mid-1920s. That third boom was helped by irrigation and land development subsidies, a huge fortified wine export subsidy, and a new 50 percent imperial tariff preference in the British market for fortified wines. The decline in domestic consumption, induced by the export subsidy and the Great Depression, added to wine exports in the 1930s – which by then accounted for more than one-fifth of production. The subsequent removal of the export subsidy, and the huge hike in UK tariffs on fortified wine in the latter 1940s, then caused a severe decline in export orientation. As well, the return to normal beer consumption after war-induced grain rationing kept down domestic wine sales growth. From the First World War until the late 1960s, most wine grapes were destined for fortified wine or for distillation as brandy.

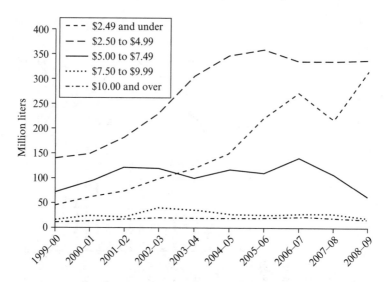

Source: Author's calculation from data retrieved from http://www.awbc.com.au.

Figure 4.3   *Volumes of wine exports by price segment, Australia, 1999–00
            to 2008–09 (A$ per liter, fob prices)*

The fourth boom, following two post-war decades of slow growth in
the industry, was entirely domestic. It emerged as Australian consumer
tastes became more Southern European, as licensing and trade practice
laws changed with income growth, as corporatization of wineries led to
more-sophisticated domestic marketing and new innovations (including
'wine-in-a-box'), and as Britain's wine import barriers rose again with
its accession to the European Community in 1973. Initially, domestic
demand grew for red table wine. Then the cask or wine-in-a-box
attracted a new clientele of white non-premium table wine drinkers,
causing Australia's per capita wine consumption to treble during the
fourth cycle (Table 4.1). The economywide recession of the early 1980s
subsequently slowed domestic demand growth and caused wine prices
to slump to the point that the Federal and South Australian governments intervened with vine-pull subsidies in the mid-1980s. As a result,
the national area of vines in 1988 was reduced to that of two decades
earlier.

The fifth and latest boom, which began in the late 1980s, differs from
the earlier booms in several respects. One difference is that the current
boom is overwhelmingly export oriented (Figure 4.1), since Australia's
per capita wine consumption has grown very little over the past two

Table 4.1 *Booms and plateaus in the development of Australia's wine industry, vintages 1854 to 2010*

Vintages	Boom/ plateau/cycle no.	No. of years	Increase in vine area (% pa)	Increase in wine production (% pa)	Increase in wine export volume (% pa)	Av. share (%) of exports in Australian wine sales(%)	Av. domestic per capita consumption (liters p.a.)
1854 to 1871	1st boom	17	15.5	18.4	14.1	1.8	na
1871 to 1881	1st plateau	10	-1.1	-0.6	-5.2	1.6	na
1854 to 1881	1st cycle	27	8.4	10.7	8.2	1.7	na
1881 to 1896	2nd boom	15	9.7	7.5	23.0	9.8	na
1896 to 1915	2nd plateau	19	-0.1	-0.4	0.4	16.5	5.1
1881 to 1915	2nd cycle	34	3.9	3.3	8.7	14.4	na
1915 to 1925	3rd boom	10	7.0	12.7	4.5	8.5	5.8
1925 to 1945	3rd plateau	20	0.9	0.1	-1.2	16.4	4.0
1915 to 1945	3rd cycle	30	2.4	3.6	4.9	14.9	4.7

Table 4.1 (continued)

Vintages	Boom/plateau/cycle no.	No. of years	Increase in vine area (% pa)	Increase in wine production (% pa)	Increase in wine export volume (% pa)	Av. share (%) of exports in Australian wine sales(%)	Av. domestic per capita consumption (liters p.a.)
1945 to 1968	Slow growth	23	0.2	2.1	0.2	5.4	6.2
1968 to 1975	4th boom	7	3.3	6.2	-1.4	2.7	10.9
1975 to 1987	4th plateau	12	-1.7	1.0	8.4	2.2	19.1
1968 to 1987	4th cycle	19	0.2	3.1	2.5	2.4	16.0
1987 to 2004	5th boom	17	18	11	22	32	20
2004 to present	5th plateau	?					

Source: Updated from Anderson (2004), using data from http://www.awbc.com.au.

decades (despite a one-fifth decline in beer consumption and a nearly 50 percent rise in spirits consumption, to 3.1, 4.6 and 2.3 liters of alcohol, respectively). This contrasts with the first and fourth booms at least, which were primarily domestic. It also differs from the inter-war boom, when exports were more a way of disposing of soldier-settlement-induced surplus low-quality wine grape production than a pre-planned development strategy.

Second, the current boom is mainly market driven, which is not unlike the first two booms but contrasts markedly with the third (inter-war) boom that evaporated once government assistance measures (the export subsidy and the preferential UK tariff) were withdrawn. What triggered the growth in export demand for Australian wine was the change in liquor licencing laws in the United Kingdom in the 1970s, allowing supermarkets to retail wine to the post-war baby boomers (by then adults). Given also Australia's close historical ties with Britain, it is not surprising that Australian companies recognized and responded to this new market opportunity. They were able to do so faster than EU suppliers because the latter had been hamstrung by myriad regulations and insulated from market forces by price supports. To exploit this rapidly growing market required large volumes of consistent, low-priced branded premium wine. Land- and capital-abundant Australia had the right factor endowments to supply precisely that. High labor costs were overcome for larger firms by adapting and adopting new techniques for mechanical pruning and harvesting, thereby generating large economies of size, especially in warm irrigated areas. That stimulated a number of mergers and acquisitions among Australia's wine firms which resulted in several large and four very large wine companies. This has provided them the opportunity to reap scale economies not only in grape growing and winemaking but also in viticultural and oenological R&D, in innovative brand promotion and related marketing investments, and in distribution including through establishing their own sales offices abroad rather than relying on distributors. It has also enhanced their bargaining power with wholesalers and retailers. The volumes of grapes grown and purchased from numerous regions by these large firms enable them to provide massive shipments of consistent, popular wines, with little variation from year to year, for the UK and now also North American and German supermarkets. Indeed some types (for example, Lindemans Bin 65 Chardonnay) were specifically developed for and only sold in those markets initially, being released in Australia several years later only after there had been a sufficient expansion in production of the required grapes.

The third major difference between now and the past is that the quality of wine output has improved hugely during the past two decades, relative to the cost of production. Moreover, for the first time, the industry is in a position to build brand, regional, and varietal images abroad to capital-ize on those improvements in the quality of its grapes and wines. That image building has been partly generic, with the help of the Australian Wine Export Council's activities in Europe and elsewhere. It has come also from the promotional activities of individual corporations and their local representatives abroad as those firms became ever larger and more multinational via mergers and takeovers during the past dozen or so years. That promotion has been helped by being able to point to the legislated wine quality standards in the Australian and New Zealand Food Standards Code, and to the fact that Australian wines overdeliv-ered in terms of value for money in Northern Hemisphere markets in the latter 1990s and the early 2000s before exports from other Southern Hemisphere and Southern European producers began to offer stiffer competition.

And the fourth feature distinguishing the current situation is the quality upgrading that has been taking place in Australia's domestic as well as export markets. As recently as 1994, two-thirds of domestic sales of Australian wine were in soft packs ('bag-in-a-box') of two to five liters, whose retail price (including the 41 percent tax) was as low as US$1.40 per liter. That share now is down to barely one-third, and the average quality of wine in soft packs is considerably greater than in previous decades. The average quality of Australia's bottled wine sold on the domestic market has also risen steadily since the 1980s. Hence even though Australia's per capita wine consumption has risen little over the past quarter-century, expenditure has gone up substantially. Australia's average export price also rose by 2.3 percent per year in US dollar terms over the period from 1990 to 2001, compared with the global average of 0.7 percent. However, that rise for Australia was exceeded by Argentina (7.3 percent), Chile (5.8 percent) and New Zealand (4.6 percent – see Anderson and Norman, 2003). Clearly, other exporters have been raising the quality of their exports at least as much as Australia, albeit from dif-ferent bases.

Since 2001 the average export price even in nominal terms has fallen for Australia, and the volume of wine exports has grown only for wines priced below A$5 a liter, free on board (fob) (Figures 4.2 and 4.3). The situation has worsened further since the global financial crisis hit in 2008, and the subsequent strengthening of the Australian dollar since then has made the exporters' task even tougher. Australia's grape growers and winemakers therefore have to strive harder than ever to maintain their competitive edge. They perceive innovation in its various forms as crucial for their economic survival, to which we now turn.

3   THE INNOVATION SYSTEM IN AUSTRALIA'S WINE INDUSTRY

The ability of a country's wineries to compete in global markets depends on the country's comparative advantage in wine, which changes over time at a rate that depends, among other things, on own- versus other-country technological and institutional innovations (see Abramovitz, 1986; Nelson, 2008; Cusmano et al., ch. 2 in this book). Standard international trade theory stresses the importance of resource endowments as the key determinant of comparative advantage at a point in time. The crucial natural resources needed for successful wine grape production include climate, land with the appropriate *terroir* and, where rain is insufficient, affordable supplemental water. Also essential are skilled viticulturalists and oenologists, and stocks of production knowledge pertinent to their country. As discussed in Chapter 1, the latter can be enhanced by investments in own-country research and development or in adapting imported technologies. For differentiated products such as wine, consumption patterns also matter. Both at home and abroad, the purchase decisions of consumers are influenced by tastes and preferences. These can be altered to some extent by advertising and through the writings of wine journalists. Hence skills in marketing, and levels of investment in market knowledge and promotion, are also important in maintaining and improving the international competitiveness of a country's wineries.

During the past two decades the Australian wine industry improved its competitiveness in no small measure by large investments not only in vineyards, wineries and wine marketing, but also in the creation and dissemination of production and market knowledge. Plenty of that is done at the firm level, but there are high rewards from supplementing it through collaboration, especially when many firms are new to the industry and when new markets abroad are being targeted.

To build and retain a competitive edge internationally, strategies are needed to obtain and make good use of available information faster and at a lower cost than do competitors, to generate new knowledge pertinent to domestic producers, and to cost-effectively disseminate that among the country's firms. The information required relates not just to consumer, retailer and distributor demands but also to appropriate new technologies as they affect all aspects of grape growing, winemaking, wine marketing and associated financing. Much of the pertinent information and knowledge has a public-good nature. It is that fact, together with the spillovers that can occur from private-firm generation of information through such activities as promotion and technical research, which ensures that collaboration between firms within the industry can have a high pay-off. We consider firm-level collaboration first, and then collaboration at the industry level and its associated institutional innovations.

Collaboration and Innovation at the Firm Level

Two levels of collaboration between wine firms are important: vertical (that is, between the grape grower, other input suppliers, the winemaker, and the wine marketer), and horizontal. The various channels through which it can occur include mergers and acquisitions, but there is also a range of other alliances.

As with so many horticultural products, processing of wine grapes and then marketing/distributing the wine is necessary before the product reaches the final consumer. Many wine grape producers have chosen to do some or all of those manufacturing and service activities themselves. But there are far more wine grape growers than there are wineries, with the former dependent on the latter to process their highly perishable and virtually non-internationally tradable product. That dependence is not a problem during boom periods, when widespread signing of long-term (up to 10-year) contracts is common so as to enhance security of supply for wineries and security of demand for grape growers. But when there is excess supply, as in recent years in Australia, the vulnerability of the non-winemaking grape grower increases. Even so, the greater emphasis on producing and promoting consistent high-quality wine (with widespread use of price bonuses and penalties according to measured grape-quality attributes), and the fact that much of that quality is determined in the vineyard, has ensured that the two-way relationships between wineries and contract grape growers is more secure now than it was before the present boom (that is, pre-1990s).

Another form of vertical integration is occurring between winemaking and wine marketing. An example is e-commerce, which is lowering the cost, especially for smaller wineries, of using email, the internet and Twitter to market their wines directly. Some Australian firms even experimented with selling their entire release by tender over the internet when prices for premium wines were rising rapidly at the turn of the century. The exemption of small wineries from the Australian government's wine sales tax for own-marketed wines has added to the incentive to explore these new options. Another example is wineries getting involved in tourism, going beyond standard cellar-door activities to restaurant and entertainment services.

Turning to horizontal collaboration, New World wineries are beginning to diversify their markets abroad as their production grows. Knowledge about the various market niches and the distributional networks in those foreign markets is expensive to acquire, however. Hence new alliances between Australian and overseas wine companies are being explored with a view to capitalizing on their complementarities in such knowledge. The purchase by the owner of Mildara Blass (Foster's Brewing Group) of Napa Valley-based Beringer, the alliance between Southcorp/Rosemount and California's Mondavi, BRL Hardy's absorption into the second-largest US wine company, Constellation Brands, and the purchase by New Zealand's biggest wine firm (Montana) of the second-largest (Corbans) and Montana's subsequent absorption into Allied Domecq – and the purchase of Allied in 2005 by Pernot Ricard (owner of Orlando Wines) – are all cases in point early this century. These may achieve the desired result much more quickly than direct foreign investment in new production facilities, although that has been happening increasingly too. As well, in this era of floating exchange rates, cross-border operations can be a form of currency hedge; and ownership abroad can also serve as a form of insurance against a major disease outbreak (for example, phylloxera or Pierce's Disease) in the home country. Horizontal mergers and acquisitions are also taking place domestically, most notably with the takeover in 2005 of Southcorp by Foster's to form perhaps the world's largest premium winemaker. A key objective is to get economies of scale and higher productivity growth not only in marketing but also in producing. This is especially important if firms wish to move beyond the boutique size and penetrate the large-scale (particularly supermarket) distribution and retail networks.

This innovation-inducing trend is occurring in many industries as part of globalization. The value of cross-border mergers and acquisitions in particular grew at 25 percent per year from 1987 to 1995, and at 50 percent in the latter 1990s (UNCTAD, 2001: 10), before slowing down somewhat in the past decade. Some left-behind wineries will be disadvantaged by the new alliances among more-progressive firms, but an alternative possibility is that even they could benefit as those merging ones improve their export performance. That could happen either by getting in the slipstream of the progressive firms' success abroad in promoting Australian wine, or in supplying a less-crowded domestic market while the merging firms focus more on markets abroad.

More worried are Australia's specialist grape growers. They are aware that the big wine corporations have valuable so-called 'knowledge capital' that is internationally mobile and hence tends to relocate to places where it can earn the highest rewards (Carr et al., 2001). During the 1990s/early 2000s Australia's grape growers enjoyed an exceptionally high proportion of the benefits of the growth in demand for commercial premium wine, in the form of high prices for their grapes. Were those high prices to continue, large wine firms (which source three-quarters of their grapes from independent growers) would have found it more profitable to expand their crushing capacity in lower-priced countries rather than in Australia, thereby causing wine grape prices to tend to equalize across countries even though the grapes themselves are not traded internationally. Such developments help to keep profits of Australian-based multinational wine companies and targeted grape growers abroad higher than they otherwise would be, while lowering profits to Australian grape growers, other things equal. However, multinational wine corporations from abroad have invested in Australia, which has an offsetting, positive effect on Australian grape growers. The demand by all such wineries for ever-better performance from their contracted growers is an ongoing stimulus for growers to seek out innovations.

Horizontal collaboration stimulated by the digital revolution is also occurring at the retail level. How are the savings from increased marketing efficiencies via supermarkets and e-commerce distributed among the consumer, marketer, winemaker and grape grower? Wittwer and Anderson (2001) explored this question with a model of the world's wine markets. They suggested that in the short run the innovative distributors would gain most but that over time, as competition among distributors and retailers drives down consumer prices, the gains would be shared among consumers and producers. Given even further time, the benefits to producers would encourage increased plantings and winemaking capacity such that consumers would end up with the lion's share (all but one-eighth) of the benefits. That prediction certainly seems to be consistent with the experiences of the past decade in Australia.

Collaboration at the Industry Level: Institutional Innovation

In addition to collaboration to improve the efficiency of grape growing, winemaking and wine marketing at the firm level, the Australian wine industry during the past two decades has enjoyed a high and envied degree of collaboration also at the industry level. The key motivations for that collaboration are to internalize externalities and to overcome the free-rider problem of collective action. Efforts traditionally have been directed in three key areas: the generic promotion and maintaining of quality standards of Australian wine sales domestically and especially overseas; investments in research, education and training, and statistical information; and lobbying governments (most notably for lower taxes on wine consumption at home and lower barriers to imports overseas). Maintaining and expanding those activities requires a non-stop flow of deliberate and skillful leadership, something that the Australian wine industry has been fortunate to have had in relative abundance compared with both other

Australian industries and the wine industry abroad. That entrepreneurial leadership was particularly noticeable during the development through the Winemakers' Federation of Australia of a shared vision for the industry set out in *Strategy 2025* (AWF, 1995). It was developed to provide a 30-year vision for the future so as to stimulate a steady flow of investment. At the time, the targets in that document were considered by many observers as rather optimistic, since they involved a threefold increase in the real value of wine production, 55 percent of it for the export market. Getting halfway to those targets required having a crush of 1,100 kt to produce 750 million liters of wine at a wholesale pre-tax value of A$3 billion (A$4/liter). Yet so convincing was that document, and so intense and rapid was the subsequent investment, that the industry was more than halfway towards most of its 30-year targets in just six vintages – and since then has had to deal with the challenge of finding new markets for that much larger output. By 2009 the national stock of unsold wine (exacerbated by the global financial crisis that began a year earlier) was so large that industry leaders began calling for up to 20 percent of vines to be pulled out. Even in that tense situation, though, the four peak industry bodies coordinated in releasing a considered report on the state of the industry and why such major adjustments are needed (WFA et al., 2009).

Long-run strategic planning by firms and the industry is made easier with an active system of producer organizations. The Australian wine industry has an excellent system involving more than 80 organizations at the national, state and regional levels, with a well-developed hierarchy of interaction between them.[2]

Among the four peak bodies is the AWBC. One of its tasks is to ensure that exported wine meets the product standards of the country of destination, so that the reputation of the industry as a whole is not jeopardized by any substandard shipments. Another is to supervise the Label Integrity Program. A third is to establish the regional boundaries for the purpose of legally registering Geographical Indications. A fourth is to lobby directly and via Australia's Department of Foreign Affairs and Trade for greater market access abroad through a lowering of tariff and non-tariff import barriers. And very important has been its role, via its Australian Wine Export Council, to invest in generic promotion. Initially that was focused broadly on 'Brand Australia' but, with the more-recent *Directions to 2025* strategy paper (AWBC and WFA, 2007), that campaign has become more refined and is now directed towards four segments of the market with an explicit objective of encouraging consumers to 'trade up' to progressively higher prices. The four are known as Brand Champions (the easy drinking commercial segment that spearheaded Australia's export drive in the 1990s), Generation Next (appealing to younger social drinkers attracted by innovative packaging and style), Regional Heroes (varietal wines that have a sense of place of origin), and Landmark Australia (high-quality, globally recognized iconic wines).

A further task for AWBC that was expanded significantly in the decade following the release of *Strategy 2025* is the systematic provision of strategic information on market developments at home and abroad. The smaller an industry, the less likely such data will be available at low cost. Yet for capital-intensive industries such as wine with long lead times and large up-front costs, information on planting intentions of others in one's own country and elsewhere is especially pertinent for those contemplating investing, given that full bearing may not occur until 5+ years after beginning to invest. The grape and wine industry recognized this and spent some of its R&D funds on commissioning the Australian Bureau of Statistics to collect more information, including on growers' planting intentions in the coming year, and the Australian Bureau of Agricultural and Resource Economics to use that information each year to project supplies several years ahead. In addition, each year the Winemakers' Federation of Australia organizes a Wine Industry Outlook Conference and the Wine Grape Growers' Council of Australia (re-constituted in 2006 as Wine Grape Growers Australia) organizes a National Wine Grape Outlook Conference, so such projections information can be shared and discussed. As well, the Australian Wine Industry Technical Conference held every third year keeps producers up to date on new technologies, as does the annual National Wine Industry Environment Conference (first held in 2000) and the annual Wine Marketing Conference (first held in 2001).

Collaboration in Research, Education and Training

At the outset of Australia's white settlement, vine experimentation was by trial and error of individual interested entrepreneurs. An early influential viticulturist was James Busby, who immigrated from near Bordeaux in France to Australia in 1824, where he was appointed to run an agricultural school which specialized in viticulture. In 1831, Busby undertook a three-month tour of Spain and France and returned with a collection of vine cuttings and started the first source block in Sydney's Botanic Gardens, along with duplicate blocks in Victoria and South Australia. By the 1850s, large areas of vineyard were being developed in Victoria, New South Wales and South Australia, but it was South Australia that became the main wine state from the 1880s onwards, largely because the other two states were hit with phylloxera (introduced to Australia on planting material after it had destroyed most of the vineyards in the United States and France). South

Australia escaped the infestation due to a far-sighted quarantine policy that is still in place.

Australia's investment in formal grape and wine education and training dates from the establishment of Roseworthy Agricultural College (now part of the University of Adelaide) in 1883. Viticulture was compulsory and oenology was an optional field of study in its Diploma in Agriculture, with a Diploma in Oenology being added in 1936. Formal wine research began in 1934 with funding to the University of Adelaide from (what soon became) the Australian Wine Board. With those funds, John Fornachon was appointed to find the cause of bacterial spoilage in fortified wines. The Board's annual reports indicated high rates of return from that and subsequent initial research investments, so when the industry was faced with the question of what to do with a fund of A\$1 million that had accumulated following the wartime suspension of wine export subsidies, it opted for a wine research facility. This eventually led in 1955 to the creation of the Australian Wine Research Institute (AWRI) adjacent to the University of Adelaide's Waite agricultural research campus, and John Fornachon became its first director (Halliday, 1994). Twenty years later a second tertiary institution in Wagga Wagga, New South Wales (now Charles Sturt University) began courses in wine science and viticulture, under the direction of Brian Croser.

It took more than another decade before the appointment of the first professor of oenology, Terry Lee, who took up his appointment at the University of Adelaide while continuing as the director of AWRI. In his inaugural lecture, he pointed out that AWRI had not had sufficient funding to undertake viticultural research. A viticulturalist was first appointed to AWRI only in 1990, and Australia's first professorial Chair in viticulture was established at the University of Adelaide in 1991. Meanwhile, the industry in 1988 established its own Grape and Wine Research and Development Corporation (GWRDC, although called a Council until 1991), and it successfully bid in 1991 for federal funding to support the establishment of a Cooperative Research Centre for Viticulture (which subsequently enjoyed a second period of seven-year funding before being wound up in 2006).

The GWRDC is funded by producer levies which the Federal government matches dollar-for-dollar up to a maximum of 0.5 percent of the gross value of output of grape growers (in the case of growers) and of the input of wine grapes (in the case of wineries). Producers initially opted for low levies, but in 1999 growers and wineries agreed to raise the research levy rates by more than one-third, to A\$2 per tonne of grapes produced and A\$3 per tonne of wine grapes crushed. In 2005 the wineries raised their rate again, to A\$5 per tonne of wine grapes crushed. Since wine grape prices averaged around A\$700 per tonne over the five vintages to 2009, and wine sold for an average of around A\$4.50 per liter (or A\$4,500 per tonne), the current rates are equivalent to less than 0.3 percent of the gross value of grape production and barely 0.1 percent of the gross value of wine production, or well under 1 percent of value added in these two activities. Wineries and even some of the larger vineyard owners also undertake their own research, and universities, state departments of agriculture and the Commonwealth Scientific and Industrial Research Organization invest funds additional to those from GWRDC in grape and wine research and the basic sciences underlying it. Even so, these research intensities represent modest investments in R&D compared with the averages for OECD (Organization for Economic Cooperation and Development) countries of around 2 percent of agricultural and 3 percent of manufacturing value added (Pardey et al., 2006).

Notwithstanding the modest level of research funding, the impact and pay-off from those investments is impressive. As shown in Chapter 3 by Cassi et al., data from the Web of Science database suggest that Australia is four times as intense in producing research papers on viticulture and oenology (exceeded only by Portugal and Spain), adjusted for the size of each economy; and was 2.8 times as intense in the mid-1990s when adjusted for the output of wine (exceeded only by the United States – Table 4.2). The latter intensity has since dropped as Australia's wine production rapidly expanded, but it may be higher if the quality of publications were to be taken into account. In terms of research pay-off, a benefit–cost study found that the 2002 portfolio of GWRDC research projects was expected to yield a 9:1 benefit/cost ratio, and that a sample of past projects yielded ratios ranging from 7:1 to 76:1 (McLeod, 2002).

Formal education in viticulture and oenology has spread from the University of Adelaide and Charles Sturt University to several other tertiary education institutions, and each has added wine marketing courses. As well, numerous technical and further education (TAFE) campuses are offering practical viticultural training both for employees and for boutique vineyard/winery proprietors and hobby farmers. And many high schools in wine areas are offering wine-oriented material in their agricultural science courses.

The pay-off from investments in R&D is higher the more readily and rapidly new information is disseminated, trialled and adopted. That requires not only education and training but also – for ongoing lifetime learning – active journal, magazine and website publications, specialized publishers/distributors, and regional, state and national associations of producers (see the comprehensive listings in Winetitles, 2009) whose culture is to share new information, ideas, and results of field experimentation.

Table 4.2   Wine research publications[a] and national shares of global wine production volume and global GDP, 1992 to 2006

	1992–1996					1997–2001					2002–2006				
	Wine prodn, %	GDP, %	Publications, %	Publics/Prodn	Publics/GDP	Wine prodn, %	GDP, %	Publications, %	Publics/Prodn	Publics/GDP	Wine prodn, %	GDP, %	Publicn cn %	Publicns/Prodn	Publicns/GDP
France	21.7	5.3	15.5	0.71	2.94	20.9	4.6	14.0	0.67	3.07	18.9	4.7	11.7	0.62	2.42
Italy	23.3	4.2	10.5	0.45	2.49	19.6	3.8	10.9	0.57	2.87	17.3	3.9	11.6	0.67	2.94
Spain	10.1	2.1	14.2	1.41	6.72	12.7	1.9	15.2	1.20	7.88	13.6	2.4	16.6	1.22	6.93
United States	6.7	25.8	25.9	3.87	1.00	8.1	29.7	21.5	2.65	0.72	8.4	28.8	18.1	2.15	0.63
Argentina	5.8	0.9	1.1	0.19	1.14	5.2	0.9	0.8	0.15	0.83	5.2	0.4	1.1	0.21	2.84
Australia	2.0	1.3	5.6	2.80	4.19	3.0	1.3	4.9	1.63	3.73	4.7	1.5	6.8	1.45	4.45
Germany	3.9	8.2	5.1	1.31	0.62	3.8	6.7	5.7	1.50	0.86	3.3	6.3	4.6	1.39	0.73
South Africa	3.2	0.5	1.3	0.41	2.47	3.6	0.4	1.2	0.33	2.75	3.3	0.5	1.7	0.52	3.48
Chile	1.3	0.2	0.4	0.27	1.63	2.0	0.2	0.7	0.36	2.97	2.6	0.2	1.3	0.50	5.42
Portugal	2.7	0.4	2.7	1.00	7.16	2.3	0.4	3.7	1.61	9.92	2.5	0.4	4.4	1.76	10.65
Others	19.3	51.0	17.7	0.92	0.35	18.8	50.1	21.4	1.14	0.43	20.2	50.9	22.1	1.09	0.44
WORLD	100.0	100.0	100.0	1.00	1.00	100.0	100.0	100.0	1.00	1.00	100.0	100.0	100.0	1.00	1.00

Note: [a] No adjustment is made for the quality or relevance of publications (as measured by, for example, citations). The source includes predominantly English-language journals and so understates the contributions of continental European and South American countries.

Sources: Author's compilation drawn from OIV wine production data, World Bank GDP data, and wine publication data compiled from the Web of Science data of the Institute for Scientific Information presented in Cassi et al. (ch. 3 in this book).

The role of grower liaison officers employed by the wineries to interact with contract growers, in disseminating new information and helping to boost and appraise grape quality, has been considerable too. Those officers now insist on the use of diaries to record irrigation, spraying and fertilizing activities, they encourage lower yields so as to intensify grape color and flavors, and they help monitor Baume (sugar) levels in the grapes to optimize harvest dates. In short, 'precision viticulture' is being continually fine-tuned as producers continue to strive for quality improvements.

While Australia has been a leader in wine R&D investments and in the rapid adoption of new technologies, Southern Hemisphere and Southern and Eastern European suppliers are rapidly catching up, including through international technology transfer. Australia is contributing to and benefiting from that in at least three ways. One is via Australian viticulturalists and winemakers exporting their services through spending time abroad as consultants (Williams, 1995; Smart, 1999). Another is via foreign investment by Australia's biggest wine companies in grape production, winemaking, and/or wine marketing and distribution in other countries. And, as shown in Chapter 3, a third way is via scientific co-publication resulting from multi-country research and development projects. Such international technology transfers are not peculiar to the wine industry of course – it is part of the general contribution by multinational corporations to globalization. That in turn has been aided by reforms to restrictions on foreign investment and by the fall in air transport costs and, thanks to the digital/information revolution, in communication costs. Smaller grape grower/winemaker firms might be affected adversely in so far as the spreading abroad of Australian expertise in viticulture, winemaking and wine marketing eventually reduces the distinctiveness of 'Australian' wine in the global marketplace. It can also lead to the exploitation of knowledge of the Australian market by those large Australian-based companies operating abroad – as with the recent flood of imports of Sauvignon Blanc from New Zealand. However, there is the offsetting prospect that internationally engaged Australians will bring back new ideas that can be exploited to good effect in Australia.

4 INNOVATION'S ROLE IN THE YEARS AHEAD

The Australian wine industry, having expanded dramatically and become (along with Chile and New Zealand) the most export focused in the world, is now facing a second generation of challenges. In addition to having to deal, like all other suppliers, with the 2008/09 global recession-driven decline in demand, the supermarket revolution and climate change impacts on production, those challenges include a strong Australian dollar because of a mining boom driven by China's rapid industrialization, a concern with the carbon imprint of shipping (especially bottled wine) long distances, and a fashion swing away from Australian wine abroad and at home (including the sudden growth in imports from New Zealand as that country too moves into a situation of excess supplies of wine).

To deal with the industry's present depressed economic conditions and return to prosperity, its producers and leaders have to place even more emphasis on innovation. The *Directions to 2025* strategy is one example of possible fresh approaches to generic promotion. That national initiative is being supplemented by regional promotion campaigns (funded entirely by regional producer levies), and by the creation of a new grouping of 'Australia's First Families of Wine'. The latter is made up of a dozen of the oldest family companies not listed on the stock exchange and hence not subject to the same financial 'short-termism' of listed companies. Emphasis needs to be given to the quality and originality of Australia's various fine wine regions and single-site labels. The need to diversify markets for Australian wine exports so as to reduce the reliance on four English-speaking countries is now evident, and generic promotion initially at least in markets such as China's is likely to have a high pay-off alongside the marketing (and possibly direct foreign investment) efforts of individual firms. Even earlier rewards are likely to be reaped from marketing into the now duty-free market of Hong Kong.

Such efforts on the demand side of the market need to be matched by equally strong initiatives on the supply side. For example, Australia's R&D investments could be expanded at least to the point of taking full advantage of the Federal government's dollar-for-dollar matching of national grower levies without lowering greatly the marginal rate of return if those funds are spent on research projects with the highest expected pay-offs, bearing in mind marketplace changes and long-term uncertainties such as climate change, water and other environmental policy reforms, and alcohol tax changes. That need has led the main producer organization to work with the industry's R&D funding body to develop a new strategy for administering research and extension activities (GWRDC and WFA, 2009).

Transgenic biotechnology offers much promise for accelerating the research discovery process, but consumer resistance to genetic engineering is limiting the exploitation of that opportunity (Pretorius and Hoj, 2005). The scope for collaboration across scientific disciplines could be exploited more, as could the scope for collaboration between scientists at the basic and applied ends of the spectrum, and between scientists in various countries. As one step towards that end, the University of Adelaide recently established its Wine 2030 research program (see www.adelaide. edu.au/wine2030), but many more such steps will be needed. Meanwhile, if producers remain attuned to the market and flexible enough to respond to exogenous shocks such as currency realignments, macroeconomic downturns, changes in consumer fashions, or disease outbreaks, as well as to try promising new technologies as soon as they become available, their long-term prospects for a return to prosperity look good. But, as anybody who has studied the history of the wine industry knows, the only thing that is really certain is that this is an industry characterized by great uncertainty, ever-fluctuating fortunes, and in particular long periods of low profits following each boom in acreage.

NOTES

1. Thanks are due to Andrea Morrison, Sakkie Pretorius and Roberta Rabellotti for helpful comments on earlier drafts.
2. For a detailed presentation, see http//www.wineaustralia.com.

REFERENCES

Abramovitz, M. (1986), 'Catching up, forging ahead, and falling behind', *Journal of Economic History*, **46** (2), 385–406.
Anderson, K. (2004), 'Australia', in K. Anderson (ed.), *The World's Wine Markets: Globalization at Work*, Cheltenham, UK and Northampton, MA, USA: Edward Elgar, pp. 252–86.
Anderson, K. and D. Norman (2003), *Global Wine Production, Consumption and Trade, 1961 to 2001: A Statistical Compendium*, Adelaide, SA: Centre for International Economic Studies.
AWBC and WFA (Australian Wine and Brandy Corporation and Winemakers' Federation of Australia) (2007), Wine Australia: Directions to 2025, An Industry Strategy for Sustainable Success, May, Adelaide, SA: AWBC and WFA.
AWF (Australian Wine Foundation) (1995), *Strategy 2025: The Australian Wine Industry*, Adelaide, SA: Winemakers' Federation of Australia for the AWF.
Carr, D.L., J.R. Markusen and K. Maskus (2001), 'Testing the knowledge-capital model of the multinational enterprise', *American Economic Review*, **91** (3), 693–708.
GWRDC and WFA (Grape and Wine Research and Development and Federation of Australia Winemakers) (2009), *National Primary Industries Research, Development and Extension (R,D&E) Framework: Wine Sector Strategy*, August, Adelaide, SA:GWRDC and WFA.
Halliday, J. (1994), *A History of the Australian Wine Industry: 1949–1994*, Adelaide, SA: Winetitles for the Australian Wine and Brandy Corporation.

Irvine, H.W.H. (1892), *Report on the Australian Wine Trade*, Melbourne, NSW: R.S. Brain, Government Printer for the Victorian Minister of Agriculture.

Johnson, H. (1989), *The Story of Wine*, London: Mitchell Beasley.

McLeod, R. (2002), *Ex Ante and Ex Post Cost Benefit Analysis of the GWRDC's Project Portfolio*, Adelaide, SA: Grape and Wine Research and Development Corporation.

Nelson, R.R. (2008), 'What enables rapid economic progress: what are the needed institutions?', *Research Policy*, **37** (1), 1–11.

OIV (International Organization of Vine and Wine) (2009), *State of the Vitiviniculture World Report*, Paris: OIV.

Osmond, R. and K. Anderson (1998), *Trends and Cycles in the Australian Wine Industry, 1850 to 2000*, Adelaide, SA: Centre for International Economic Studies.

Pardey, P.G., N.M. Beintema, S. Dehmer and S. Wood (2006), *Agricultural Research: A Growing Global Divide?*, International Food Policy Research Institute. Food Policy report, Washington, DC: IFPRI.

Pretorius, I.S. and P.B. Hoj (2005), 'Grape and wine biotechnology: challenges, opportunities and potential benefits', *Australia Journal of Grape and Wine Research*, **11** (2), 83–108.

Smart, R. (1999), 'Overseas consulting: selling the family silver, or earning export income?', *Australian and New Zealand Wine Industry Journal*, **14** (4), 64–67.

UNCTAD (United Nations Conference on Trade and Development) (2001), *World Investment Report 2001: Promoting Linkages*, New York and Geneva: United Nations.

WFA, WGGA, AWBC and GWRDC (Winemakers' Federation of Australia, Wine Grape Growers Australia, Australian Wine and Brandy Corporation, and Grape and Wine Research and Development Corporation) (2009), *Wine Restructuring Action Agenda* (statement and supporting report), November, Adelaide, NS: WFA, WGGA, AWBC and GWRDC.

Williams, A. (1995), *Flying Winemakers: The New World of Wine*, Adelaide, SA: Winetitles.

Winetitles (2009), *Australian and New Zealand Wine Industry Directory 2009*, Adelaide, SA: Winetitles (and earlier years) accessed at http//:www.winetitles.com.au.

Wittwer, G. and K. Anderson (2001), 'How increased EU import barriers and reduced retail margins affect the world wine market', *Australian and New Zealand Wine Industry Journal*, **16** (3), 69–74.

PART II

Drivers of technological catch-up in the wine industry: universities, public–private institutions, researchers and firms

5. University involvement in wine region development: a comparative case study between Universidad de Talca (Chile) and Universidad de Cuyo (Argentina)

Martin Kunc and Scott Tiffin

1 INTRODUCTION

Since the 1980s, the concept of a 'national system of innovation' to study the linkages between firms, organizations and knowledge creation institutions has emerged (Freeman, 1987; Lundvall, 1992, 2002). This concept is based on several assumptions: one considers that key elements of the knowledge base are highly localized; another is that the interactive nature of the innovation process means that it is socially embedded. As a consequence of both these assumptions, systems of innovation differ significantly in terms of their capacity for capitalizing on new sources of knowledge and their productive capabilities (Feldman et al., 2006). Cooke (1992, 2001) coined the term 'regional system of innovation' to describe the systems of innovation localized in a region, a level below the national system of innovation that might have cultural or historical homogeneity and where localized economic development can be identified. However, regional systems of innovation differ in their level of development.

Schiller (2006) suggests that in nascent innovation systems in developing countries such as Argentina and Chile it is more important to learn how to assimilate and improve existing technologies than to generate new ones, since many technologies are often only new to local firms. In this situation, universities can become important actors in emerging regional innovation systems (Giuliani and Arza, 2009). In this role, universities provide a qualified workforce, locally adapted research, appropriate services and technologies for their regional stakeholders. Thus, universities are simultaneously enhancing the absorptive capacity of the regional system of innovation and directly supporting technological change and development for less resourceful small to medium-sized enterprises (SMEs), which may not have technological capabilities that are as developed as those in large firms. Thus, universities can have an important role in the economic development of their regions through networking processes that connect university with industry. However, there is relatively little awareness by university managers and regulators of the specific roles and techniques that universities employ to participate in regional economies and promote their development; what universities are actually doing in this regard; and how to manage their involvement better (Rowley et al., 1997; Gray, 1999). Our goal is to address this gap between general public expectation and detailed management techniques of university involvement with regional industries. We focus on definition and measurement of linkages between universities and industries, following Cano (1998) and Lang and Zha (2004), to propose indicators aimed at measuring the existence of these links that can be comparable across countries and regions. The goal of this chapter is to contribute to the literature on management of the involvement of universities in regional development through linkages and to provide policy implications for university managers, higher education policy makers, local government officials and regional industry associations.

This chapter applies the proposed measurement framework to two universities located in wine-producing regions in Argentina and Chile. In the case of Argentina, the chapter assesses the role of the Universidad de Cuyo, located in the heart of Mendoza, the largest Argentinean wine-producing region. In the case of Chile, the chapter reviews the role of the Universidad de Talca, located in the Maule Valley, one of the largest wine-producing regions in Chile. The universities were chosen because they are regional universities embedded in the wine region, which is one of the conditions for localized regional systems of innovation. The chapter is structured as follows. First, a conceptual design of the measurement framework is presented. Second, the context of comparative case studies is examined. Third, methodology and resulting indicators are discussed. Finally, conclusions and policy implications are provided.

2   A MEASUREMENT FRAMEWORK FOR LINKAGES BETWEEN INDUSTRY AND UNIVERSITY

Godin (2005) points out in his comprehensive study of the history of science and technology indicators that measurement systems are intimately tied to social values and political objectives, in their design, operation and interpretation. They are not neutral or entirely objective, and never wholly accurate. Sometimes they invent and define issues that have not necessarily existed before, and stakeholders use them to advance their own social or economic agendas. For example, using indicators to create systems of ranking against 'leaders' or 'best practice' is an exceptionally powerful application, as in the case of the business school rankings developed by the media. Unfortunately, this comes at the price of significant and often misleading oversimplification (Rappoport et al., 2004) and can cause very negative distortions to university strategy. The benchmarking and quality improvement literature is much more sophisticated in its application of indicators than the media, of course, and its focus on alignment and process helps overcome many of these criticisms (Phipps, 2000; Bender and Schuh, 2002). Doerfel and Ruben (2002) show that performance measurement and benchmarking applied to higher education is an emerging field and most feasible for mature areas such as teaching, research and employee management but it is still problematic for new areas such as university–industry linkages and regional development involvement.

The Role of Universities in Regional Systems of Innovation

In recent years the traditional research and teaching missions of universities have been extended to direct interactions with regional stakeholders (Etzkowitz, 2001). Universities and public research organizations have become important knowledge sources in regional innovation systems and partners in industrial innovation processes. The essence of this process resides in the linkages that are being built between universities and industry (Giuliani and Arza, 2009). There are two models of university involvement in regional development. First, the generative role serves regional needs directly by providing boundary-spanning activities such as incubators and science parks (Schiller, 2006). Second, a developmental role consists of adjusting research and teaching activities to regional needs (Etzkowitz, 2001; Lundvall, 2002). In any case, universities can take over a broader developmental role at the regional level since academic or even administrative autonomy of universities allows them to respond to regional needs more efficiently through long-term relationships with local actors (Boucher et al., 2003). University–industry linkages vary in their degree of institutionalization, which may range from the informal hiring of professors and *ad hoc* services, to long-term partnerships and joint research centers (Giuliani and Arza, 2009). In this exploratory study, we concentrate on defining the performance measures of the following activities related to the level of engagement of universities in the development of their regions:

- *Training* The Organisation for Economic Co-operation and Development (OECD, 1999) has recommended that new universities should be created with the explicit, central mandate to promote regional development through training people (Boucher et al., 2003; Karlsson and Johansson, 2006). In the case of the wine industry, the increasing complexity of winemaking processes implies the need to train people in sophisticated processes. Similarly, the use of diverse grape varieties, in many cases exogenous to those regions, also implies more sophisticated viticulture practices, including the knowledge of new varieties from different countries. Therefore training activity is key to enhancing the capability of the region to absorb new knowledge and generate solutions to production problems.

- *Research* The role of developing and transferring knowledge is the subject of intense ongoing research. Gibbons et al. (1993) claim that the university is no longer the dominant institution developing knowledge. Nevertheless, Godin and Gingras (2000) show that the university is still a major source of economically important knowledge produced through research and development (R&D). The university's engagement in research should be considered in the context of the industry. For example, R&D processes in natural resource-based industries may follow two paths (Coenen et al., 2006): R&D processes that occur inside large multinational corporations, or research institutes with close ties to industry that are established in regions where the natural resources are exploited. In the first case, regional universities can be powerful engines for attracting R&D activities from multinationals. In the second, regional universities can offer their facilities and faculty for establishing research institutes to investigate local specific problems in wine production, which in turn may generate patents related to solutions to wine production issues in different regions. For example, universities can perform research in fermentation and enzyme technology (Fleet, 1993) as well as controlling grape vine growth rates.

- *Consulting/servicing* Mowery (2007) stresses that faculty consulting, although undocumented and underemphasized by universities, is generally regarded by industry as significantly more important for knowledge transfer than patents. In this case, the motivation of the industry is to solve immediate problems or realize opportunities (Arvanitis et al., 2005). Looking at the relationships between universities and industry from this point of view, there is another activity that is similar to consulting: laboratory and testing services (Lester, 2003; Arvanitis et al., 2005). Laboratory services are examples of outsourcing functions strongly based on knowledge, which require investments that exceed the available resources of SMEs. In the case of the wine industry, winemaking activities require numerous tests, and it makes economic sense to perform them in a central location with specialized people such as those in universities.

- *Facilitating linkages* Lester (2003) and Lawton-Smith (2006) examine different forms by which interaction takes place between universities and industry, stressing, among others, commercial ventures by universities and commercial activities by academics, technicians and students. Karlsson and Johansson (2006) find that entrepreneurship is an essential input to the growth of regions and, in turn, dynamic functional regions develop a number of entrepreneurs. Universities can play the role of a multidisciplinary 'honest broker' to build social capital in a region (Cooke, 2002). Yusuf and Nabeshima (2007) assert that universities should consider building local innovation systems as central to their missions to promote the development of the region. The formation of linkages also depends on the strength of a firm's knowledge base (Giuliani and Arza, 2009), so the formation of linkages strongly depends on the fulfillment of the training and research roles of the regional universities. In a wine region, universities can support the development of communities of practice around specific issues such as soil conservation.

The Measurement Framework

There is always a difficult trade-off between accuracy and the feasibility of obtaining information, and completeness and parsimony that can be used for theory testing (Arthurs et al., 2009). However, the starting point for designing a measurement framework should be the functionality desired. The literature discussed above has suggested many actions (for example, selling licenses, teaching entrepreneurship). For each activity selected for the framework, we have one or more indicators that are the items measured (for example, number of licenses, number of entrepreneurship courses in current year). We have grouped the actions into broader categories, called activities, and the resulting activity level determines the general level of involvement of the universities and the fulfillment of their role in regional development. For the indicators, we have been inclusive rather than exclusive in order to see which measures are more feasible and meaningful.

We note three significant design decisions that define a set of limitations to our framework. First, the framework focuses only on the university itself and does not measure anything about the main regional industry with which the university is involved. This places certain limitations on what kind of analysis can be made, but is necessary to keep the complexity of data gathering within a limit. Second, we measure direct, numerical variables as opposed to opinions on a sliding numerical scale. Thorn and Soo (2006) do the latter in their study of quality indicators for Peruvian universities. We hope that our choice results in more accurate and objective data than gathering expert opinion, although it presents other problems such as comparability if the indicators are not clearly explained or there are different standards for similar activities across regions or countries. Third, the framework measures how universities relate to a particular industrial sector in a region. This requires that all measurements refer only to the regional industry in question, which adds a methodological difficulty of determining what activities are directly related to the development of the industry. For example, when we measure the number of courses, we mean only those courses that have a significant, explicit, or complete, focus on the industry. We would not count a general accounting course, but we would count a course such as 'accounting in wine companies'. Obviously there will be some imprecision and judgment involved. Therefore our study aims not only to measure the intensity of the universities in the four activities described with respect to the most important industry in a region, but also to explore the methodological considerations on implementing a system of performance measures[1] that allow policy makers to define policies to engage in higher levels of interaction between industry and university.

3   THE CONTEXT

Knowledge Stocks and Flows in Wine Regions

Coenen et al. (2006) suggest that agro-food industry knowledge originates from agricultural practices. The knowledge in this industry has largely drawn upon empirical and experimental upscaling of artisan processes, as well as substitution processes to replace specific raw materials by means of chemical or biological synthesis. This type of knowledge is related to activities that work as solutions to practical problems. Thus innovation in agricultural industries refers to the application or novel combination of existing knowledge to solve practical problems during the growing or processing of agricultural products.

In this respect, there are two main issues related to the flow of knowledge from generators to users. One is the capacity of the user to understand the new knowledge, and the second is the connection between the generators of knowledge and the users of this knowledge. Therefore the existence of learning patterns within a region depends on the knowledge accumulated by local firms and their different contributions to the enhancement of the local knowledge base (Giuliani and Bell, 2005). However, these patterns are not homogeneous since firms have heterogeneous capacities to absorb knowledge flows. Thus, regional universities can act to strengthen the knowledge base of weaker firms by providing knowledge workers or training workers of less resourceful firms, which increases the stock of knowledge.

The wine industry, like any agribusiness industry, involves two main processes: growing and manufacturing. Small producers are mainly specialized in grape growing, and backwards-integrated wine producers, which have direct control on viticulture and winemaking processes, integrate both grape growing and wine producing. Two professions are the most appropriate for conducting knowledge generation, transference and application on all the phases of the productive chain in wine firms: oenologists and agronomists. There are also other actors who can transfer knowledge, such as researchers from public research institutes, people who have worked in other firms with similar technologies, or consultants. Therefore the capacity of a winery to absorb and generate knowledge is mainly determined by the employment of these workers and the linkages with these experts.

There is no assurance that having an oenologist and/or an agronomist will generate or apply new knowledge, since it is necessary that they engage in processes of knowledge exchange with peers in the region through communities/networks of professionals. Oenologists and agronomists may be able to produce and internalize shared understandings through collaborative problem-solving activities embedded in interorganizational relations (Håkanson, 2005; Malmberg and Power, 2005; Coenen et al., 2006).

In conclusion, the main actors in a wine region are connected professionals who have the capabilities to understand R&D advances and transform them into applied knowledge to solve problems in grape growing and wine producing. While these actors may act autonomously, they nevertheless need to be connected to receive and exchange knowledge. A critical institution in the development and connection of these professionals can be a regional university if it has a prominent role and is respected in its region.

The Universities in Our Study

Table 5.1 provides a summary of the universities studied and their regions.

Table 5.1   Summary of wine regions and university characteristics

	Universidad de Talca, Chile	Universidad de Cuyo, Argentina
Urban District Population (est.)	190,000	540,000
City and location	Talca, 250 km south of Santiago	Mendoza, 1,000 km west of Buenos Aires
Ownership	Public	Public
Date of founding	1981	1939
Total number of students	6,900	31,500
Total number of FTE faculty	236	498
Local GDP per capita US$ (estimated)	7,200	9,000
Vine planted area – ha. (estimated)	30,000	140,000
Wine exports from the region (2006)	US$150 million	US$360 million

Sources: UNC (2006) and Tiffin (2008).

Universidad de Cuyo (Argentina)

The School of Agricultural Sciences in the Universidad Nacional de Cuyo is located 18 km from the city of Mendoza, in Lujan de Cuyo. Mendoza and the greater urban region have a combined population of 540,000. In Lujan de Cuyo there are 94 well-known wineries, such as Chandon and Norton, specializing in premium varietals and sparkling wines. Mendoza has always been at the center of the Argentinean wine industry (see McDermott and Corredoira, ch. 6 in this book for a detailed discussion of the evolution of the Argentinean wine industry). The School has 1,300 students and 103 hectares of occupied land with a farm, an experimental winery, and an experimental factory of olive oil and preserves. There are a number of institutes in the School: the Institute of Animal Biology, the Institute of Soil and Irrigation, the Institute of Vine and Wine and the Institute of Food Science. There are two specific programs aimed at the wine industry: a Bachelor of Science (BSc) in oenology and viticulture and a Master of Science (MSC) in viticulture and oenology, where students can obtain a double diploma with the École Nationale Supérieure Agronomique de Montpellier (AGRO-Montpellier) and INRA-Montpellier (Institut National de la Recherche Agronomique).

In addition, wine studies are part of common undergraduate courses such as Agricultural Engineering and Food Safety.

Universidad de Talca (Chile)

Only the Universidad de Talca and the Universidad Catolica del Maule are located in the heart of Maule Valley wine region. The Pontificia Universidad Catolica de Chile and the Universidad de Chile are located in Santiago, Chile's capital, which is close to the large wine region of Maipo Valley. The Universidad Catolica del Maule has a very small involvement with the wine industry through a wine-testing laboratory. The Universidad de Talca has more-developed connections with the wine industry so it matches our criteria of location in the region and involvement with the industry. While the Universidad de Talca is situated in a wine area, its strategies relate only vaguely to the regional industry, although it maintains a different level of engagement at country level through a research consortium with the wine industry and other universities in Chile (Cusmano et al., ch. 2 in this book). In engaging with the industry, there is a specific intent to decentralize operational decisions to particular specialized centers. This is the approach taken with regard to the wine industry when CTVV (Centro Tecnólogico de la Vid y el Vino) was established. In the Universidad de Talca there are no specialized degrees in wine. Fifty percent of students with a degree in agriculture obtain jobs in the wine region: 30 percent of students work in activities related directly to the wine industry (vineyards and cellars), and 20 percent work in activities indirectly associated with the wine industry (irrigation, selling inputs from distributors, fertilizer companies, and so on). In the area, there is also a strong production of apples, kiwi fruit, corn seeds and rice, which competes for students' attention and final job location. Some students move to other wine regions for employment.

4   ANALYSIS OF UNIVERSITY INVOLVEMENT IN WINE REGIONS: A COMPARATIVE STUDY BETWEEN UNIVERSIDAD DE TALCA (CHILE) AND UNIVERSIDAD DE CUYO (ARGENTINA)

Data Collection

The research methodology consisted of data-gathering processes, which occurred between September 2006 and September 2007. Our interviews were with deans and directors of different departments in each university. The interviews were mainly structured around the set of indicators that

Table 5.2   Training indicators

Activity	Indicators	Talca	Cuyo
Degrees and courses	Specialized degrees in wine industry	0	2
	Average number of students currently enrolled in specialized degrees per year	0	30
	Courses related to wine industry outside specialized degrees per year	5	0
	Average number of students taking these courses outside specialized degrees per year	100	0
Post-degree diplomas	Courses per year	1	3
	Students per course	20	25
Continuing corporate education	Courses related to wine industry per year	5	10/15
Industry scholarships	Scholarships paid by wine industry per year	0	5/6
Management of continuing corporate education	Executive education staff responsible for supporting corporate education in general	1	1

we developed to measure the involvement of local universities in their regional context in terms of training, research, consultancy and facilitators of linkages discussed in Section 2. We preferred to collect the values for our indicators through interviews to explain their use and avoid ambiguous interpretations by the interviewees. The use of structured interviews with performance indicators also helped us to realize the differences in terms of focus pursued by each university. Interviews were complemented with open questions and secondary data to triangulate and interpret the results. The information presented refers to the year 2007.

In the following subsection, we present the comparative measures[2] obtained from our review of the Universidad de Talca and the Universidad de Cuyo. All measurements refer to the regional wine industry (see Section 2 for the methodological challenges involved).

Training Activity

The indicators in Table 5.2 measure the intensity of the university–industry linkages through the process of educating and training the workers required by the industry. These linkages can be formal, such as degrees and postgraduate programs accredited by higher education agencies, or informal such as specialized courses aimed at specific issues or scholarships paid for by the industry for students to attend diverse courses in the university. While these activities are not directly generating knowledge, they are necessary to develop the absorptive capabilities of the firms to use new knowledge (Giuliani and Bell, 2005). Therefore, measures capturing the intensity of these activities will be leading indicators of future development in firms and in the regional industry.

In Talca, students can obtain a generalist degree in Agronomist Engineering (undergraduate) and a Master's in International Agribusiness with Göetingen University (Germany), but wine education does not have a specific degree. Nevertheless, there are courses in viticulture, oenology and vinification as part of the undergraduate degrees. In terms of Diploma[3] courses, one center offers a course in irrigation, in which at least a third of the students come from the wine industry. In Talca it is felt that the local market for companies is limited, so few courses are related to corporate education. The Universidad de Cuyo emphasizes its training role. As said above, there are two courses related directly to wine: a BSc in oenology and viticulture and an MSc in viticulture and oenology in conjunction with AGRO-Montpellier and INRA-Montpellier. Moreover, there are a variety of diploma courses related to every aspect of vine growing such as water management and soil conservation. There is a strong market for in-company programs as well as technical support. Training that is related to the wine industry is dispersed among many departments in the School of Agribusiness, which have longstanding linkages with the sector. Every year, at least 5–6 students attend the MSc course funded through industry scholarships.

The Universidad de Talca does not develop its training function as intensively as the Universidad de Cuyo, when measured by the number of courses and activities related to education specifically directed to the wine industry, as Table 5.2 shows. Since most graduates in wine-related degrees come from the Pontificia Universidad Catolica and the Universidad de Chile in Santiago (Kunc and Bas, 2009), training in wine seems to be centralized in the capital city rather than localized at the regional level as in Argentina. Among the many reasons for this situation is the closeness of Santiago to Talca, the reputation and relative size of the Pontificia Universidad Catolica and the Universidad de Chile with respect to Talca in terms of researchers (see Giuliani and Rabellotti, ch. 7 in this book for more information on the Pontificia Universidad Catolica and the Universidad de Chile).

Research Activity

Table 5.3 presents the data related to research activity. The set of indicators presented in the table aims to measure the intensity of formal

Table 5.3   Research indicators

Activity	Indicators	Talca	Cuyo
Research aimed at wine industry in formal units	Research units	3	40
	Number of academic staff involved in research units	5	120
	% academic staff involved in research units with PhD	66	15
Formal research Diffusion mechanisms	Research diffusion mechanisms such as trade fairs, open courses, newsletters per year related to the wine industry	4	4
Technology transfer	Licenses negotiated in the wine industry per year	1	3
Funding related to wine industry (all values are in thousand US dollars)	Total value of grants to research units from public sources per year	2017	300
	Total value of grants to research units from private sources per year	30	0
	Total value of research grants to individual professors from public sources per year	88	5
Research management (related to wine industry)	Management staff in each individual research unit	1	0
	Research management office staff	2	8

knowledge-generation activities directly related to the wine industry in each university. Indicators include most of the activities taken into account in the literature from research units to research outputs, including mechanisms for diffusing and transferring knowledge. Indicators also capture the corresponding responses from the industry and government through funding levels, and the amount of interaction is measured through an indirect indicator related to the administrative effort to manage these linkages.

Talca has three specific research units dedicated to research in the wine industry: the Centro Tecnologico de la Vid y el Vino, founded in 1996; a consortia named Tecnovid with the Universidad de Chile, the Universidad Federico Santa Maria, the two main industry associations (Chilevid and Corporacion Chilena del Vino) and a company, Toneleria Nacional; and CITRA, related to irrigation and climate. In each of these centers, there are on average 1.5 full-time equivalent (FTE) faculty engaged who have PhDs or are studying for a PhD. On the other hand, Cuyo has 40 research units specialized in each subject area taught, for example irrigation, soil management, vine growing, and so on, but there are no specific funded research centers as in Talca. The high number of research units in Cuyo, which may seem to indicate a more-intensive research activity compared with Talca, is determined by the requirement of Argentinean higher education national law[4] that faculties should be actively engaged in research. However, only 15 percent of academic staff in Cuyo actually have a PhD and 35 percent have an MSc. The main reason for Talca's better research performance is related to changes in the Chilean higher education system which have recently encouraged professors not only to engage in internationally relevant research, as measured by the journal citation systems such as the Institute for Scientific Information (ISI), but also to obtain their PhD from international universities (Tiffin and Kunc, 2009), while Argentinean public universities have not moved in this direction.

In Chile the government has been very active in providing funds for research to the wine industry as well as to regional universities. The two research units of Talca (CTVV and CITRA) and the technological consortium (Tecnovid) have been financed using government funds. In Argentina there is no specific funding for research units from the government and most of the funding is assigned on a project basis to individual faculties. Therefore the funding available is clearly different between Talca and Cuyo. Unfortunately the funding from industry is almost zero when compared to public funding.

In terms of outputs, the situation is less clear. Talca produces four annual events related to the diffusion of its research within the wine industry, such as seminars and conferences, and has generated one technology license related to the wine industry per year. Cuyo produced a similar number of events to Talca, such as conferences and four newsletters, and has transferred technology in three instances (relating to yeast, vine management and irrigation efficiency) during the year under consideration. While there is infrastructure supporting the development of research in both universities, there are no established fundraising activities.

The research indicators present a conflicting picture. While there seems to be higher levels of research activity in Talca compared to Cuyo in terms of research funding, Cuyo seems to have more people doing research and there are more instances of technology transfer. One explanation for this difference is related to the size of Cuyo compared to Talca in terms of faculty and the faculty performance review existing in Cuyo (see note 4), implemented by a national law, which measures faculty engagement with industry through agreements with firms and intellectual contributions. However, the faculty activity in Cuyo is not supported by grants or measured in terms of peer review publications. With regard to the impact of these activities, Cuyo may also be more active than Talca as it has more

Table 5.4   Consulting/servicing indicators

Activity	Indicators	Talca	Cuyo
Research extension office	Number of people in this office	0	5
	Number of research contracts oriented to the industry	1	25
University consulting corporation	Number of units devoted to consulting	2	1
	Number of consulting contracts	20	+10
Individual faculty consulting	Number of professors who consult	7	100
	Total number of contracts per year	33	100
Laboratory services	Average number of laboratory contracts per year (in the case of Talca includes legal product quality certifications)	1000	60
Management	Laboratory staff, excluding technicians and non-office operational people	7	50
	Consulting office staff	0	15
	Staff in the R & D extension office	0	5

technology transfer licenses with industry. While most of Talca's faculties are staffed by PhD holders (66 percent), which is in line with recent trends in the Chilean higher education system (Tiffin and Kunc, 2009), Cuyo has very few PhDs in its faculties, which may be affecting its research output although we have no information to confirm this. Undoubtedly the larger size (see Table 5.1) of Cuyo compared to Talca plays an important role in explaining the differences in levels of intensity obtained for the measures.

Consulting/Servicing Activity

Table 5.4 presents a measurement of the informal linkages in knowledge transfer, such as consultancy contracts or instances where the industry can outsource some of its knowledge-intensive requirements to universities, for example laboratory services for testing products. While the level of activities diverges significantly, a set of indicators measuring the quality of the intensity of these activities can provide clearer information.

The R&D Extension Office is not actively looking for R&D contracts and grants. The consulting processes for the university consulting corporation are run by the research units in Talca (Table 5.3) and by a cooperative in Cuyo (Table 5.4). The faculty of the Universidad de Cuyo has set up a cooperative which organizes all the consulting contracts with the industry since faculty cannot be hired directly by firms. The cooperative manages the relationship with the industry and the money that is paid to the faculty. We perceive that there is no clear separation between the activities of the R&D extension office, the units engaged in the consulting company and the private consulting projects of individual faculty members of both universities. The indicators do not seem to capture the high level of engagement with the industry according to the resources existing in each university.

In terms of laboratory services, the Universidad de Cuyo has six laboratories for diverse subjects: molecular biology, soil, nematology, viticulture/ oenology, cold weather and waste management. Thus, the Cuyo laboratories provide full services to different actors in the local wine industry as well as projects in other areas of Argentina (60 projects). In the case of Talca, most of the laboratory contracts come from the wine industry located not only in the Maule Valley but also in the nearby Colchagua Valley. The Universidad de Talca operates numerous laboratory service contracts (1,000 services per year) dealing with issues such as appellation control and evaluation of virus-free vine clones (the main task of CTVV). Therefore the high volume of activity is driven mainly by legal requirements rather than by the intention to exploit unique and sophisticated knowledge. However, the laboratory services' activities seem to be a good way of engaging with industry in providing value-added services in areas where the industry has neither skills nor sufficient economies of scale.

Developing Linkages Activities

Indicators in Table 5.5 quantify the level of activities related to building linkages between industry and university. For example, student internships are seen as valuable for putting theory into practice and fostering the connections between firms and university. The development of alumni networks is important to establish permanent linkages between industry and university, as well as role exchange between academic staff and professionals.

All students in the Universidad de Cuyo undertake *practicum* (short-term professional practice) in small, medium and large wineries as a requirement to obtain their degree, as Table 5.5 shows. In Cuyo most of the students come from wine companies or have connections with local wineries/farms. Cuyo also runs a College of Agriculture with an Agricultural Technician's diploma/qualification for those who do not intend to obtain a university degree. College students usually work in small family-owned wineries and they may not undertake a university degree. Therefore technical qualifications are important for the development of basic absorptive capabilities in small firms. The large size of the

Table 5.5   Developing linkages indicators

Activity	Indicators	Talca	Cuyo
Practicum	Students getting term jobs in the industry per year	24	60
Graduate placement	% students who get permanent jobs in the wine industry per cohort	50	100
Alumni	University alumni in firms related to the wine industry	49	500
Agreements with technical schools	Formal links established	1	1
Faculty industry placements	Full-time faculty on industrial placements	0	10
Faculty employment	Full-time professors who have left the university to take up wine industry jobs, over the past 3 years.	1	5
	Full-time professors who have held full-time employment in wine industry organizations before	0	4
Professionals teaching	Wine industry professionals teaching full courses	0	100
Research collaboration	Outputs co-authored with people from the wine industry	1	na
Internships	Scholarships for students to spend time in the industry	0	5
Management of industry development	Public awareness infrastructure or activity staff	4	na
Management of students in the workplace	*Practicum* staff	2	8
	Alumni staff	1	0

wine industry, as well as the large city – Mendoza – implies a high volume of new students and a high retention rate of graduates in the region and the wine industry (100 percent of students obtained jobs in the wine industry either because the size of the wine industry is large enough to absorb them or because these students have already come from wine firms (see McDermott and Corredoira, ch. 6 in this book). Therefore the Universidad de Cuyo seems to be strongly connected with the industry either through the alumni network or through professors who have previously worked for wineries or are professionally engaged in the wine industry (100 out of

120 faculty members in the School of Agricultural Sciences). Cuyo appears to be an active member of the regional economic system since through its graduates it is connected with different institutions, such as the regional food safety institute (ISCAMEN), the local branch of the national agricultural institute (INTA) or the national association established by the industry (Fondo Viti).

On the other hand, the Universidad de Talca does not have a strong influence on the development of linkages with the wine industry at the regional level, either through the development of knowledge workers or through the movement of professionals from the industry to the university and vice versa. In the case of Talca, there seem to be more contractual relationships between the university and the industry, for example the use of laboratory services (Table 5.4). The small number of students in Talca, due to its location in a low population area and the competition from the universities located in Santiago such as the Pontificia Universidad Catolica, may be affecting the low numbers shown in the indicators appearing in Table 5.5.

5   CONCLUDING REMARKS

Our chapter explains the level of intensity in university–industry linkages using a set of indicators. We measure the intensity of the these linkages at regional level in two wine regions located in Argentina and Chile. Our study is exploratory due to lack of data for some indicators and owing to the methodological challenges (see Section 2) faced during the development and data gathering. Nevertheless, the findings are interesting in terms of lessons for measuring and managing university–industry linkages and the development path taken by the two regions in our study. Our concluding remarks can be categorized in three areas: lessons from our cases, lessons on the development and management of measures for university–industry linkages, and policy implications.

First, Table 5.6 summarizes our findings in terms of our two cases. We have grouped our findings in the four dimensions by which we measured the intensity of university involvement in regional wine development: training, research, consulting and service providers to local industry, and facilitating future linkages.

The highest level of university involvement in regional wine development differs between Cuyo and Talca. In the case of the Universidad de Cuyo, training activities such as undergraduate courses and an international MSc in wine represent its highest commitment to the industry. In the case of the Universidad de Talca, laboratory services for certification

Table 5.6   Level of intensity in university–industry linkages

Linkage	Talca	Cuyo
Training	Low intensity without specific courses	High intensity with undergraduate and master's courses
Research	High intensity in funding	High intensity in resources committed but low funding
Consulting/ servicing	High intensity in laboratory services	High intensity in evaluation services
Facilitating future linkages	Low intensity in network development	High intensity in network development

purposes are the main linkage with the wine industry located in the region. In terms of university–industry linkages to develop local knowledge through research, our review showed that the two universities are actively engaged in combining existing knowledge to solve practical problems through their research units, such as adaptation and calibration of weather and irrigation systems to local characteristics. In the case of Talca, several centers that had been created with significant funding from the industry to provide laboratory services, have grown, diversified, and are largely self-supporting. However, the centers are not linked to academic research. Part of the reason is the need to generate operational funding, part is the lack of interest by industry in supporting research and part the lack of support from the university to free the faculty involved from teaching obligations. The role of academics as consultants seems to be well developed in both universities but there is no evidence of long-term relationships with firms. The level of activities facilitating linkages between universities and industry is still low, and although informal comments from our interviewees hinted at the intention to develop science parks or even incubators, these ideas are still in the design phase. More involvement of global and local wineries or even suppliers to the wine industry with these local universities may help to develop their involvement with regional development.

We conclude from the analysis of our measures that the Chilean wine region of Maule and Argentina's largest wine region are following two different paths in regional development. The Chilean wine region seems to focus on exogenous knowledge sources, such as graduates from centrally located universities like the Pontificia Universidad Catolica de Chile, identified in micro-level studies by Giuliani and Bell (2005), combined with more-intensive local university–industry linkages related to knowledge-based services such as laboratory services. University involvement is mainly managed through the provision of knowledge-based services. Argentina's largest wine region development seems to be more endogenously driven through local university–industry linkages (albeit the recent establishment of foreign firms is changing this situation). The high intensity of training activities and facilitating linkages, such as professors in the industry, leads to the existence of strong networks formed by graduates and professors embedded in diverse institutions, also found in McDermott and Corredoira (Chapter 6) about networks and institutions in the Argentinean wine industry. The Universidad de Cuyo shows good interaction at the regional level but it is not clear what value is generated for the industry and regional development, an aspect that needs further research. In this case, there is active management of university–industry linkages through the development of networks.

Second, our exploration of university–industry linkages measurement gave rise to a number of suggestions to develop measurement systems in higher education, more specifically the management of university–industry linkages. The importance of clear measurement systems cannot be overstated since they are not neutral as they define issues that have not necessarily existed before and can cause distortions to university strategy, especially in their interactions with industry. For example:

- Differences related to university degrees and diplomas reduce the meaning of standard categories for graduates and knowledge worker development.
- There is no standardized definition of university functions since most administrative offices have multiple functions (for example, research management, research extension and technology transfer) and it is sometimes difficult to measure the intensity of the engagement of universities with their regional industry.
- Within a single indicator there can be a great deal of variability of the phenomenon measured; courses can vary from full semester and focused entirely on the industry, to an optional, very short workshop or seminar; research publications can be very different in their importance with respect to patents and licenses. Therefore counting events such as courses and seminars or publications and patents as equal is convenient and widely practiced, but it may be misleading.
- Some data are not gathered by universities in activities related to their role as promoter of the region, as in the case of consulting activities, or it is impossible to tell from databases exactly where alumni are working.

To conclude, only the combination of micro-level analysis, such as in Giuliani and Arza (2009), together with network analysis such as in McDermott and Corredoira (Chapter 6), can shed light on the issues and problems that macro-level analysis, like the set of measures presented in this chapter, has highlighted. Only multilevel analysis will be able to identify the forces affecting the process of catch-up in emerging industries such as wine.

Third, both the Chilean and the Argentinean wine regions have infrastructure issues such as lack of private and public finance support for research. Although wineries can acquire extra-regional knowledge directly through their relationships with their foreign owners or through foreign consultants (Giuliani and Bell, 2005), universities need support to bring extra-regional knowledge through alliances with foreign universities in certain programs (especially at postgraduate level) and foreign research centers. It is encouraging to see efforts to develop a qualified workforce and appropriate services and technologies for regional firms, especially those firms that do not have the resources to hire or bring in foreign consultants, but universities need public support to intensify their activities. It is clear that the university is an important contributor to regional development by providing trained people, advanced knowledge, technical problem solving and opportunity realizing. But perhaps its most important role is networking to encourage industry and government to work with the university to develop the region. All universities can play this role, not just the large, metropolitan ones. For resource-based industry development it is critical that small, peripheral universities become aware of their potential to link with their main regional industries on multiple levels and be supported by government regulation to do so. Jacob et al. (2003) suggest that public regulators have an obligation to structure the system so that the burden of creating this linkage does not fall solely on the universities; otherwise, the universities will undertake only those components that generate revenue, such as laboratory services or individual faculty engaging in consulting projects.

NOTES

1. Performance measurement systems represent a balance between output measures – the performance and impact of an organization – and the measures that will drive future organizational performance – input measures (Kunc, 2008).
2. A detailed explanation of each measure can be obtained from the authors.
3. 'Diploma' is the generic name given in the Chilean higher education system to courses aimed directly at practitioners where the content is mainly practical.

4. Argentinean Law No 24521 establishes the obligation for staff to be active in research as part of their performance evaluation every five years in order to retain their post, which has to be subject to public evaluation. However, the definition of research is not clear and does not imply an obligation to publish in ISI or English-language journals.

REFERENCES

Arthurs, D., E. Cassidy, C. Davis and D. Wolfe (2009), 'Indicators to support innovation cluster policy', *International Journal of Technology Management*, **46** (3–4), 263–79.

Arvanitis, S., U. Kubli, N. Sydow and M. Woerter (2005), 'University–industry knowledge and technology transfer in Switzerland: the university view', Swiss Federal Institute of Technology Zurich working paper 119.

Bender, B. and J. Schuh (eds) (2002), *Using Benchmarking to Inform Practice in Higher Education, New Directions for Higher Education, No. 118*, San Francisco, CA: Jossey-Bass.

Boucher, G., C. Conway and E. Van Der Meer (2003), 'Tiers of engagement by universities in their region's development', *Regional Studies*, **37** (9), 887–97.

Cano, E. (1998), *Evaluación de la calidad educativa [Evaluation of Education Quality]*, Madrid: Editorial La Muralla.

Coenen, L., J. Moodysson, C. Ryan, B. Asheim and P. Phillips (2006), 'Comparing a pharmaceutical and an agro-food bioregion: on the importance of knowledge bases for socio-spatial patterns of innovation', *Industry and Innovation*, **13** (4), 393–414.

Cooke, P. (1992), 'Regional innovation systems: competitive regulation in new Europe', *Geoforum*, **23** (3), 365–82.

Cooke, P. (2001), 'Regional innovation systems, clusters and the knowledge economy', *Industrial and Corporate Change*, **10** (4), 945–74.

Cooke, P. (2002), *Knowledge Economies: Clusters, Learning and Cooperative Advantage*, London: Routledge.

Doerfel, M. and B. Ruben (2002), 'Developing more adaptive, innovative, and interactive organizations', in B. Bender and J. Schuh (eds), *Using Benchmarking to Inform Practice in Higher Education – New Directions for Higher Education, No. 118*, San Francisco: Jossey-Bass, pp. 5–28.

Etzkowitz, H. (2001), 'The second academic revolution and the rise of entrepreneurial science', *IEEE Technology and Society Magazine*, **20** (2), 18–29.

Fleet, G.H. (1993), *Wine Microbiology and Biotechnology*, London: Taylor & Francis.

Feldman, M., M. Gertler and D. Wolfe (2006), 'University technology transfer and national systems of innovation', *Industry and Innovation*, **13** (4), 359–70.

Freeman, C. (1987), *Technology Policy and Economic Performance: Lessons from Japan*, London: Pinter.

Gibbons, M., C. Limoges, H. Nowotny, S. Schawartzman, P. Scott and M. Trow (1993), *The New Production of Knowledge: The Dynamics of Science and Research in Contemporary Societies*, London: Sage.

Giuliani, E. and V. Arza (2009), 'What drives the formation of "valuable" university–industry linkages? Insights from the wine industry', *Research Policy*, **38** (6), 906–21.

Giuliani, E. and M. Bell (2005), 'The micro-determinants of meso-level learning and innovation: evidence from a Chilean wine cluster', *Research Policy*, **34** (1), 47–68.

Godin, B. (2005), *Measurement and Statistics on Science and Technology: 1920 to the Present*, New York: Routledge.

Godin, B. and Y. Gingras (2000), 'The place of universities in the system of knowledge production', *Research Policy*, **29** (2), 273–8.

Gray, H. (1999), 'Re-scoping the university', in H. Gray (ed.), *Universities and the Creation of Wealth*, Buckingham: The Society for Research into Higher Education and Open University Press, pp. 3–17.

Håkanson, L. (2005), 'Epistemic communities and cluster dynamics: on the role of knowledge in industrial districts', *Industry and Innovation*, **12** (4), 433–63.

Jacob, M., M. Lundqvist and H. Hellsmark (2003), 'Entrepreneurial transformations in the Swedish university system: the case of Chalmers University of Technology', *Research Policy*, **32** (9), 1555–68.

Karlsson, C. and B. Johansson (2006), 'Dynamics and entrepreneurship in a knowledge-based economy', in C. Karlsson, B. Johansson and R. Stough (eds), *Entrepreneurship and Dynamics in the Knowledge Economy*, New York: Routledge, pp. 12–46.

Kunc, M. (2008), 'Using systems thinking to enhance strategy maps', *Management Decision*, **46** (5), 761–78.

Kunc, M. and T. Bas (2009), 'Innovation in the Chilean wine industry: the impact of foreign direct investments and entrepreneurship on competitiveness', American Association of Wine Economists (AAWE) working paper, 46, September, accessed at www.wine-economics.org.

Lang, D. and Q. Zha (2004), 'Comparing universities: a case study between Canada and China', *Higher Education Policy*, **17** (4), 339–54.

Lawton-Smith, H. (2006), *Universities, Innovation and the Economy*, London: Routledge.

Lester, R. (2003), 'Universities and local systems of innovation: a strategic approach', presentation at workshop on high tech business, Robinson College, Cambridge, 28 May.

Lundvall, B.-A. (1992), *National Systems of Innovation: Towards a Theory of Innovation and Interactive Learning*, London: Pinter.

Lundvall, B.-A. (2002), 'The university in the learning economy', DRUID working paper, 02-06, University of Aalborg, Denmark.

Malmberg, A. and D. Power (2005), '(How) do (firms in) clusters create knowledge?', *Industry and Innovation*, **12** (4), 409–31.

Mowery, D. (2007), 'University–industry research collaboration and technology transfer in the United States since 1980', in S. Yusuf and K. Nabeshima (eds), *How Universities Promote Economic Growth*, Washington DC: The World Bank, pp. 163–82.

OECD (Organisation for Economic Co-operation and Development) (1999), *The Response of Higher Education Institutions to Regional Needs*, Paris: OECD.

Phipps, R. (2000), 'Measuring quality in internet-based higher education: benchmarks for success', *International Higher Education*, **20** (summer), Boston College Center for International Higher Education, Boston, MA.

Rappoport, D., J. Benavente and P. Meller (2004), 'Rankings de universidades chilenas segun los ingresos de sus titulados' ['Chilean universities' ranking according to graduates' salaries'], Central Bank of Chile working paper 306, December, Banco Central de Chile.

Rowley, D., H. Lujan and M. Dolence (1997), *Strategic Change in Colleges and Universities*, San Francisco, CA: Jossey-Bass.

Schiller, D. (2006), 'Nascent innovation systems in developing countries: university responses to regional needs in Thailand', *Industry and Innovation*, **13** (4), 481–504.

Thorn, K. and M. Soo (2006), 'Latin American universities and the third mission: trends, challenges and policy options', World Bank Policy Research working paper 4002, Washington, DC.

Tiffin, S. and M. Kunc (2009), 'A survey of management PhD programmes in Latin America', *International Journal of Management in Education*, **3** (1), 82–103.

Tiffin, S. (2008), 'Measuring university involvement with industrial clusters: a comparison of natural resource sectors in Chile and Canada', final report KEA-21, accessed at www.kawax.cl.

UNC (Universidad de Cuyo) (2006), report of activity 2006, Mendoza.

Yusuf, S. and K. Nabeshima (eds) (2007), *How Universities Promote Economic Growth*, Washington, DC: World Bank.

6. Recombining to compete: public–private institutions, shifting networks and the remaking of the Argentine wine sector

Gerald A. McDermott and
Rafael A. Corredoira

1 INTRODUCTION

How can developing countries upgrade their industries to compete in the world? Scholars of international management and economic development have increasingly argued that the attendant ability of local firms to upgrade – combine existing resources in new ways to create new higher-value products – depends in large part on their access to a variety of knowledge resources (Moran and Ghoshal, 1999; Giuliani et al., 2005). But it is less clear what types of institutional infrastructure facilitate such access.

A growing current in the innovation literature argues that access to knowledge often depends on whether firms are embedded in rich inter-firm networks, which enable them to build collaborative relationships, gain resources, learn and coordinate experiments (Powell et al., 1996). However, scholars also note how firm practices, social structures and institutions are slow to change and can constrain one's access to new knowledge resources (Uzzi, 1996). This enabling and constraining nature of embeddedness resonates strongly in emerging market countries (Spicer et al., 2000), and especially in Latin America, where societies are often noted for their weak institutions and social capital (Schneider, 2004).

Unfortunately much of the research on development has misinterpreted this dual nature of embeddedness as a function of a society's immutable stock or endowment of social capital and 'right' institutions. For instance, researchers tend to argue that firms fail to learn and adapt because they are trapped in societies with long histories of weak associationalism and low densities of economic and social organizations (Putnam et al., 1993).

In contrast, this chapter understands embeddedness, and in turn the innovative capacities of a region, in terms of the structure and composition of organizational networks (Granovetter, 2002). At the macro level although a society may contain a plethora of associations and dense inter-firm networks, this diversity can thwart broad-based upgrading and concerted action. The social ties and norms that promote cohesion within certain communities can also lead to fragmentation and isolation between them (Locke, 1995; Ostrom, 1999; Safford, 2007). At the micro level, the very inter-organizational network that may facilitate collaboration among particular firms can equally restrict their access to a variety of new resources and information beyond the network (Uzzi, 1996; Lin, 2001).

Conversely, researchers have also illustrated how particular institutional characteristics of an industry or a region can relieve these constraints. For instance, Zuckerman and Sgourev (2006) and Safford (2007) show how certain voluntary civic and industry associations facilitate learning because of their ability to create horizontal or cross-cutting ties between firms from different social and geographic communities. McEvily and Zaheer (1999) and Owen-Smith and Powell (2004) have found similar characteristics in government support institutions (GSIs), such as public research institutes and training centers. Because of their public mandate to provide collective resources and broadly disseminate their findings, GSIs, be they fully or partially funded by the government, can help firms access different sources of knowledge and innovate.

This chapter argues that product upgrading depends on a firm being tied not simply to any or many organizations and GSIs, but rather to those that act as social and knowledge bridges across distinct producer communities and in turn offer firms access to a variety of knowledge resources. In particular, we highlight the ways in which governments can alter the trajectory of product upgrading not simply through largess or market liberalization but by constructing a new set of GSIs with a variety of previously isolated, even antagonistic, stakeholder groups. To the extent that GSIs are constituted with rules of inclusion and participatory governance for relevant public and private actors, they can anchor new multiplex, cross-cutting ties between producer communities that underpin their ability to provide firms with a new scale and scope of services and facilitate new problem-solving relationships between them. That is, governments can reshape the structure and composition of organizational fields, and in turn, knowledge flows, by instigating the creation of new public–private institutions that recombine existing social and knowledge resources in new ways and at different levels of society (Locke, 1995; Stark and Bruszt, 1998).

We advance this argument through a quantitative analysis of the transformation of the Argentine wine sector in the two neighboring, dominant winemaking provinces of Mendoza and San Juan. On the one hand, Argentina is a country better known for its dysfunctional social capital and institutions, while its wine industry has a long history of backwardness and virtually no international presence. On the other hand, the Argentine wine sector witnessed a dramatic turnaround in the 1990s and now accounts for over 3 percent of the $16 billion global wine market. This revival has been based on significant innovations in quality control and design of new wines and grapes (McDermott, 2007). Mendoza has led this change as the dominant exporter and innovator, pioneering a new constellation of institutions and inter-firm networks that appears to have facilitated widespread product upgrading. San Juan, in contrast, remained a laggard, despite its numerous firms, high density of associations, and policies that ushered in new investment. In turn, by identifying how Mendoza created a new path of innovation so different from its own past and from its neighbor, we can highlight the types of institutional mechanisms that help firms access a variety of knowledge resources and learn.

2. NETWORKS, INSTITUTIONS AND THE CHALLENGE OF UPGRADING

Following Schumpeterian and evolutionary theories of the firm, we view product upgrading as a particular form of innovation, in which firms focus on the creation of new products for higher value by incrementally and iteratively experimenting with new combinations of existing material and natural inputs (Moran and Ghoshal, 1999; Giuliani et al., 2005). As Fleming (2001) has argued, this process of recombination is fraught with technological and market uncertainties, demanding that firms gain knowledge and expertise to convert different types of inputs into specific products, to assess the reliability of suppliers, and to learn which types of products can gain traction in different market niches in the short and long runs. While firms gain experience from their own in-house activities and human capital, they access a variety of raw and applied knowledge through their peers, customers and suppliers as well as via non-market actors, such as trade associations and GSIs that provide training or research and development (R&D) services (McEvily and Zaheer, 1999; Owen-Smith and Powell, 2004).

Such a view of product upgrading is widely embraced in studies of developing countries in general and wine in particular (Roberts and Ingram, 2002; Giuliani and Bell, 2005; Perez-Aleman, 2005). Upgrading in wine takes several years, beginning with transforming the middle segments of the value chain: state-of-the-art quality control and product development running from careful vineyard maintenance to flawless harvests to fermentation and blending. Oenologists work closely with agronomists and growers to introduce, evaluate, and document experiments with new methods of growing and fermentation for different types of varietals and clones. Because of the variation in climates and soils, experimentation is contextualized and knowledge is often tacit, posing barriers to dissemination and application elsewhere. In turn, to accelerate product upgrading, wineries gain a variety of market and applied technical knowledge from other firms as well as collective resources housed in industry associations, schools and GSIs.

Such coordination and relational-based upgrading is not necessarily forthcoming, however, especially for firms embedded in volatile environments with limited resources and potentially fragmented industry structures. Developing countries, such as Argentina, are widely known for their lack of collective knowledge resources, weak markets and limited state capacities (Schneider, 2004). Moreover, although diversity and a decentralized industry structure can be sources of innovation, they can also exacerbate the problems of concerted action and block the widespread diffusion of new practices (Jacobs, 1984). Mendoza and San Juan have over 100 microclimates supporting a wide variety of high-value grapes and thousands of small vineyards, which typically supply 30–50 percent of a winery's needs. Both provinces still have over 680 and 170 wineries, respectively, which range from many small and medium-sized family firms to some cooperatives and a few large diversified corporations.[1] Over three hundred wineries export, with relatively low concentration ratios by international standards.

Given the coordination problems associated with product upgrading, our comparison of the two transformation paths focuses on two related questions that link the mechanisms of upgrading with broader policy problems of development. How was a broad set of firms able to upgrade their products and exploit variety rather than being paralyzed by it? What types of new institutional mechanisms did Mendoza create to help firms access a variety of knowledge resources and learn?

Elsewhere, McDermott (2007) has offered a detailed qualitative comparison of the two provinces during the 1980s and 1990s. The study suggested that the variance in performance was not based on inherited economic and social endowments of the two provinces. While the two provinces had similar indicators of associationalism and business–government relationships through the 1980s, a key problem for knowledge creation was the fragmented nature of social and political life between producer communities or *Zonas* within the provinces. The need for more-specific applied knowledge and skills, coupled with regional prejudices and resource inequalities, can create barriers to the processes of aggregation and joint action vital for a sustainable base of innovation. Public policy can remedy this problem by initiating a process in which public and private actors create new institutions with governance principles that anchor new horizontal ties between previously isolated producer communities. Such a view shifts the comparative lens of upgrading paths away from the existing economic and social endowments of regions and towards their institution-building processes.

Variance in upgrading paths emerged from the contrasting policies towards resolving a common crisis in the late 1980s in the two regions. Mendoza's policies led to new organizational and institutional arrangements in the 1990s. While San Juan sought to impose arm's-length economic incentives on the market, Mendoza gradually built a new set of GSIs with agricultural, especially wine and grape sectoral associations, to provide a variety of new support services and resources in agriculture and especially the winemaking value chain (for example, hazard insurance, training, R&D, export promotion and so on). We call these new GSIs 'public private institutions' (PPIs).

Table 6.1 gives an abridged description of the most prominent PPIs, their different support activities and shared governance traits. They are public–private in their legal form, governance structures, resources and membership, which includes representatives from the government and associations of a variety of zones and subsectors. As a subgroup of GSIs, they too received at least partial public funding, had state representatives on their boards, and had a public mandate. The PPIs were distinct from the pre-existing GSIs, since the latter were state/bureaucratic centered in their governance and had only *ad hoc* contact with a few elite groups instead of having governance and resource ties to a variety of associations. They were also distinct from the pre-existing sectoral and zonal associations, since the latter were voluntary organizations with no government representation or resources, were narrow in membership and mission, and had few services other than to lobby the government, as mentioned above.

Our particular interest is how the distinct governance rules of PPIs anchored their ability to act as multiplex bridges (Padgett and Ansell, 1993; Burt, 2000) between the public and private domains as well as between the relevant producer communities, and in turn create mechanisms to improve firm access to a variety of knowledge resources. The combination of these governance rules and network qualities in PPIs fostered three mechanisms to transmit a new variety of applied knowledge to firms. First, in combining the material and informational contributions of the public and private participants, the PPIs gradually built up knowledge

Table 6.1 Public-private institutions in Mendoza created in the 1990s

Institution	Year of creation or restructuring	Governing members	Activities	Resources	Legal form
INTA EEAs	1991; INTA San Juan reformed in 1996	Mza govt, 15 agro assns, natl and provl institutes and univs	R&D (inputs, plants, tech), extension training, consulting	50% – govt budget (salaries & overheads); 50% – services, alliances, *cooperadoras*	Part of INTA Cuyo; 4 in Mza, 1 in SJ; public, non-state, non-profit entity
Fondo Vitivinicola	1993–94	Mza govt, 11 wine/grape assns	Oversees new wine regulations, promotes wine industry/marketing	Tax on firms from overproducn of wine	Public, non-state, non-profit entity
Fondo para la Transformacion y el Crecimiento (FTC)	1993–94	Mza govt, regional advisory councils, assns	Subsidized loans and credit guarantees to SMEs for tech. against extreme weather & for grape conversion	Self-financing; initial capital from govt	Independent legal entity under authority of governor

Table 6.1 (continued)

Institution	Year of creation or restructuring	Governing members	Activities	Resources	Legal form
Instituto Desarrollo Rural (IDR)	1994–95	36 founders – INTA Cuyo, Mza govt, 2 peak assns, various agro sectoral assns	Technical info collection & dissemination; database mgmt; R&D, training, consulting	Mza govt; services; gradual increase of fees from member assns	Non-profit foundation, with oversight by Min of Economy
Instituto Tecnologico Universitario (ITU)	1994	Founders – Mza govt, Univ Nacional Cuyo, UTN, 2 peak assns	Continuing education for managers and some R&D in mgmt and technology	Founders; fees for services	Non-profit foundation
Pro Mendoza	1995–96	Mza govt, 3 peak business associations	Export promotion – organize fairs, delegations, strategic information, training	Mza govt; peak assns; services	Non-profit foundation

Note: INTA – Instituto Nacional de Tecnología Agropecuaria; EEA – Estaciones Experimentales (Sub-regional centers); Mza – Mendoza; *Cooperadoras* – Non-profit NGOs.

Source: Adapted from McDermott (2007: 123).

124

resources at a scale, scope and cost that the government and the associations could not have provided individually and did not exist before or in other provinces.

Second, PPIs produced services that integrated the needs of their different constituencies with international standards. The leverage of each participant came from its ability to provide or withhold resources as well as its ability to voice proposals and grievances through the board. Third, the PPIs built programs to help firms learn from one another and create new relationships. Both firm managers and directors of these institutions repeatedly told us that one of the most-valued qualities of services was the way they helped to diffuse standards, practices and experiences from one zone or sector to another.

By the end of the 1990s the overlapping ties and demonstration effects of the new institutions channeled spillovers across to the pre-existing GSIs, policy domains and provinces. Mendoza's approach to building new GSIs appears to have helped induce upgrading by improving the access firms had to a variety of knowledge resources and functioning akin to the 'network facilitator' role discussed by McEvily and Zaheer (2004). The rules of inclusion and multi-party governance helped representatives of previously isolated producer communities gradually forge common strategies and a coherent, dynamic set of support policies with the state. Consequently the programs and services of the relevant institutions helped firms learn how to apply new knowledge with existing natural inputs and build new relationships with one another. With statistical techniques, we now explore the degree to which this new constellation of organizational and institutional ties, once it had taken root, improved a firm's product upgrading.

3   NETWORK COMPOSITION AND PRODUCT UPGRADING

The cross-sectional nature of our quantitative data impedes us from statistically tracking the changes in a firm's network and product upgrading. It does, however, allow us to evaluate how the composition and structure of a firm's ego-network impact its product upgrading, and the plausibility of our key claim that Mendoza's policy approach facilitated firm access to a new variety of knowledge resources by creating new institutions with multiplex bridging qualities that fostered cross-cutting ties between producer communities.

The baseline view in the network literature is that a firm's access to a variety of knowledge resources depends on being highly embedded in an inter-organizational network, as indicated by the degree centrality of one's ego-network (Wasserman and Faust, 1994; Uzzi, 1996). The more ties a firm has to all types of organizations ('alters'), the more likely it is able to access a greater volume, and potentially variety, of information.

Although this claim may in general be valid, it can blur the way Mendoza's approach created new actors and mechanisms for transferring knowledge. That is, it assumes a certain level of homogeneity about the members of an organizational field and the types of information and resources they can afford one another. The recent work on networks and innovation has increasingly sought to differentiate a firm's network composition, emphasizing that only certain types of alters, be they firms or non-firm organizations, lend valuable information and resources for the task at hand (Lin, 2001; Fleming and Waguespack, 2007; McDermott and Corredoira, 2010).

Our previous discussions argued that the alters which appeared most valuable to firms, were those offering a new variety of applied knowledge resources and cross-cutting channels of information and professional contacts between different producer communities, especially the different zones. Mendoza's approach appeared to improve access for firms to a variety of knowledge resources by creating a new set of GSIs, the PPIs, and then reforming the old GSIs to offer new services directly to firms and foster new types of relationships between them. Our qualitative analysis further suggested that wineries benefited most from their interactions with other firms and the GSIs, because these alters, as opposed to the other types, offered the combination of new knowledge resources and interactive relationships for solving ongoing problems of product development. In contrast, pre-existing organizations, such as schools, banks, associations and cooperatives were not the repeated recipients of policies of new knowledge resources and continued to focus their membership, clientele and orientation towards their locality or zone. In turn, the broader claim is that firms will benefit from ties to organizations and institutions whose activities and governance principles underpin access to different applied knowledge and cross-cutting professional relationships. But firms will not necessarily benefit from ties to organizations that offer limited knowledge resources and rather local professional relationships. We operationalize this view in the following hypotheses:

Hypothesis 1a: The greater number of ties the focal firm has to other firms, the higher will be its level of product upgrading.

Hypothesis 1b: The greater number of ties the focal firm has to GSIs, the higher will be its level of product upgrading.

Hypothesis 2: The greater number of ties a focal firm has to associations, banks, cooperatives and schools, the lower will be its level of product upgrading.

We can further distinguish the impact of different types of GSIs on product upgrading. Although we suggested that the overlapping ties between the PPIs and the old GSIs facilitated recent changes in the mission and programs of the latter, one would likely expect that firms would find greater relative value in the former. First, the PPIs were *created* with distinct governance rules and network qualities, while the old GSIs were not. Our qualitative analysis emphasized that the rules of inclusion and participatory governance fostered multiplex, bridging qualities in the PPIs, which in turn anchored their ability to deliver a new variety of applied knowledge resources to firms in different zones and facilitate the development of new inter-firm relationships. Recent research has shown that the institutionalization of cross-cutting ties between previously isolated groups of firms can greatly improve support services, the diffusion of standards and the access to diverse sources of information (McEvily and Zaheer, 2004; Zuckerman and Sgourev, 2006). Second, research in economic sociology and historical institutionalism notes that older institutions and their attendant stakeholders are often slower to change than newer ones, especially if they have longer histories of being unresponsive or were built for particular aims in one period but of lesser value in subsequent periods (DiMaggio and Powell, 1983; Knoke, 2001). The policy of Mendoza emphasized first the construction of new institutions, not reforming the existing ones, and then spinning off new operations as demands from a greater variety of programs grew. For instance, IDR and ProMendoza grew out of initiatives within INTA Mendoza and the Fondo Vitivinicola.

The broader claim, in turn, is that firms will gain access to a variety of knowledge resources, and thus relatively high levels of product upgrading, to the extent that they have many ties to GSIs that were created *de novo* with rules of inclusion and participatory governance.

Hypothesis 3: The greater number of ties the focal firm has to the PPIs, the higher will be its level of product upgrading.

The foregoing makes indirect inferences about the mechanisms for knowledge transfer from the Mendoza policies and the governance histories of GSIs. Given our previous claims about the importance of ties to other firms and GSIs being positively associated with higher levels of product upgrading, we focus here directly on cross-cutting qualities of these alters in facilitating access to a variety of knowledge resources. A key aspect of

Mendoza's approach was to infuse GSIs with governance principles that helped overcome prior problems of socio-economic fragmentation by being *both* more encompassing than existing associations *and* gradually functioning as social bridges between producer communities. Moreover, one could infer that certain firms developed these network qualities because of their participation in training, R&D and export programs that fostered new professional relationships between firms from different zones. According to recent research on networks, those mediators with diverse knowledge resources are particularly those that are the most central or those that act as the most important bridges (Burt, 2000; Fleming and Waguespack, 2007). The two traits are not necessarily exclusive, and both serve as key tests about one's access to diversity.

Firms might learn more rapidly when they are linked with organizations and institutions that are the most central or encompassing in the region, because they would have access to a great number of other associated firms and in turn a variety of information and resources (Safford, 2007). Being linked to a highly central organization or institution can also convey on the firm a particular level of legitimacy, which can act as a positive signal for its products and practices to other potential collaborators (Provan and Milward, 1995; Knoke, 2001). In contrast, being linked to less central mediators would not provide access to a variety of knowledge resources.

Hypothesis 4a: The greater number of ties a focal firm has to firms with high levels of network centrality, the higher will be its level of product upgrading.

Hypothesis 4b: The greater number of ties a focal firm has to GSIs with high levels of network centrality, the higher will be its level of product upgrading.

One can also emphasize the ability of Mendoza's GSIs to act as social and knowledge bridges among the distinct, previously isolated communities, particularly those bounded by the aforementioned zones. Centrality may reflect simply the most dominant organizations and offer redundant knowledge (Burt, 2000). That is, to the extent that variety is key for developing new product upgrading capabilities, then the relative importance in intermediating organizations and institutions is the geographical diversity, not the quantity, of actors associated with them. While bridging traits are known to enhance access to variety, structures to help bring together previously unconnected actors can improve product innovation (Obstfeld, 2005), industry adaptation (Zuckerman and Sgourev, 2006), and regional development (Safford, 2007). McEvily and Zaheer (1999) also find that government technology centers improved firm performance by giving firms access to a variety of information from different geographic locations. In contrast, having numerous ties to mediators that have relatively few bridging qualities would not give a firm access to a variety of knowledge resources. Given the limitations of our data, we cannot estimate which firms and institutions bridge structural holes in the conventional manner. However, given the literature on localities creating search costs for the pursuit of variety and our previous discussion about the ways in which social fragmentation occurred in the provinces according to subregional zones, a reasonable proxy for an intermediating organization's bridging role is the geographic diversity of the firms associated with it. We operationalize the relative value for a firm being tied to intermediaries with strong bridging qualities in the following hypotheses:

Hypothesis 5a: The greater number of ties a focal firm has to firms with high geographic diversity, the higher will be its level of product upgrading.

Hypothesis 5b: The greater number of ties a focal firm has to GSIs with high geographic diversity, the higher will be its level of product upgrading.

4 DATA AND METHODOLOGY

The design of the sample and survey was based largely on the aforementioned field interviews in Mendoza and San Juan. We developed and administered our survey instrument during 2004–05. Our survey captured a focal firm's level of product upgrading, demographics, location, as well as its ties to firms, publicly supported institutions and other organizations.

A simple random sample (SRS) of 115 firms was selected from a roster of the wineries in Mendoza and San Juan. We undertook several measures to increase participation and response rates, including gaining the enthusiastic approval of the project by the relevant sectoral associations, inviting firm owners/directors by mail and telephone to participate in the survey (Buse, 1973), and replacing 15 firms that declined to participate with 15 similar firms randomly selected. A total of 112 firms completed our surveys (97 percent response rate).[2] We compared our sample data with data of wineries from relevant government sources and found no significant differences between them in geographic distribution, age, size and foreign direct investment (FDI). For instance, about 60 percent of the firms are less than 20 years old, about 70 percent have fewer than 25 employees, and 50 percent have less than $330,000 in sales. Roughly 10 percent have foreign investment.

We divided the questionnaire into two parts. The owner or general manager filled out the part covering firm demographics and general strategies. The chief oenologist filled out the part covering production, product development and ego-networks. We designed and implemented the survey in collaboration with a leading agro-extension center in the region, whose field consultants interviewed each informant in person for about one hour, using the questionnaire.

Our dependent variable, *Product Upgrading*, captures a firm's focus on the creation of new products for higher value by incrementally experimenting with new combinations of knowledge, materials and natural resources (Fleming, 2001; Giuliani et al., 2005). Following a well-established research stream in the strategy and organizations literatures, we measured it by asking respondents to assess the extent to which the firm implemented the relevant practices associated with product upgrading in this particular context using a five-point Likert scale (MacDuffie, 1995). Such practices are the regular introduction of new and higher-value wines, emphasis of quality over cost, experimentation with new blends, varietals and clones, and monitoring domestic and overseas markets.

In order to assess the validity of our instrument we conducted an exploratory factor analysis with oblimin rotation (PROC FACTOR, SAS v.9) on 22 questions that extracted five factors. Questions that loaded in more than one factor were dropped. Two of the five factors are associated with distinct aspects of product upgrading and each contains four items. The items in each of these two factors, respectively, address directly the extent to which the firm overcomes technological and market uncertainties, which, as discussed earlier, are present in product upgrading for the wine industry. Our dependent variable is created by adding the responses to the eight questions loading in the factors associated with product upgrading (the index has a Cronbach's alpha of 0.78). A third factor is associated with *Upgrading Intent*, which we use as a control for the underlying motivation of the focal firm to engage in product upgrading (see below).

Our explanatory network variables were created from our survey, which asked oenologists to identify firms (up to seven) and non-firm entities (up to five) with which they regularly interact, collaborate, or exchange information regarding specific strategic areas, such as product development, production methods, technology acquisition, training, marketing and exports. We validated and classified these firms and non-firm alters into six categories: associations (trade, peak level, and so on), banks, cooperatives, firms (wineries, independent grape growers, technology suppliers, and so on), GSIs (such as those discussed above) and schools (universities, technical schools, and so on). As noted above, most GSIs are provincial and, hence, firms have access to them mainly within their own respective jurisdictions. Following the preceding discussions, we also decomposed GSIs into two subcategories – PPIs and Old GSIs.[3]

We constructed a two-mode network consisting, on the one hand, of focal firms, and, on the other, of alters (firm and non-firm). Ties were defined as any relationship between the focal firm and the alter. All the measures based on ties are generated from the total count of mentions to the alter, which include repeated counts of the same alter if they were identified by the focal firm as providing useful information or services in multiple operational areas of firm management and winemaking.

Ties to All Alters and *Ties to Different Types of Alters* measure the degree centrality (Wasserman and Faust, 1994) that captures a focal firm's exposure to the knowledge and immediate influence of others (alters) by counting the focal firm's total number of ties to other organizations and institutions. It is based on the ego-network and lacks any dyadic characteristic. The variable, *Ties to All Alters*, is the total count of ties a focal firm has to all types organizations and institutions mentioned above, capturing the overall embeddedness of the firm assuming homogeneity across alter types in terms of their knowledge resources afforded to focal firms. We relax this assumption and emphasize heterogeneity by decomposing this variable, following standard methods (Lin, 2001; Owen-Smith and Powell, 2004), into six variables that capture the composition and structure of the focal firm's ego-network. The variables, *Ties to Firms*, *Ties to Associations*, *Ties to Banks*, *Ties to Cooperatives*, *Ties to Schools*, and *Ties to GSIs*, are each constructed by counting the number of ties between the focal firm and the given type of alter, as classified above. We follow the same method, when decomposing *Ties to GSIs* and constructing *Ties to PPIs* and *Ties to Old GSIs*. We discuss our second method of decomposition and aggregation of network ties below.

Ties to Top Central Firms and *Ties to Top Central GSIs* capture the benefits that a firm can obtain indirectly from being connected to alters with high centrality, and therefore, exposure to influence and resources of a large number of actors in the network (Burt, 2000). We first identified all the firm and GSI alters and ranked them separately by the total number of ties from the focal firms. Firms and GSIs with in-degree centrality in the top decile were considered to be highly central alters. Then, for each focal firm, we calculated the total number of ties to these high network centrality alters.

Ties to Top Geo Div Firms and *Ties to Top Geo Div GSIs* capture the diversity of knowledge accessed through network ties by considering geographic zones as proxies of different knowledge. High network heterogeneity is associated with increased opportunities to innovate (Burt, 1983). We calculated the geographic diversity of network ties by examining the alter's direct ties to firms in different zones of the region. Even lacking information about the complete network, our random sample of firms provides the information to generate unbiased estimations of such a measure (Frank, 2005). We calculated the total number of ties for each alter and assigned the ties to zones based on the geographic location of the surveyed firms that identified the relationship. These zone counts were then used to derive a Herfindahl Index score for each alter, based on the number of ties in each zone. Alters were ranked from highest to lowest based on their diversity score, and the top decile was selected.[4] We generated the variables by counting the number of ties that the focal firm has to these most geographically diversified alter firms and GSIs.

Our control variables include location variables that are dichotomous and associated with different zones that experts identified (Grand Mendoza, East, Valle Uco, South, San Juan). We control for superior resources with *Foreign Ownership*, a dummy variable taking the value of 1 for firms with foreign investment greater than 10 percent of equity and 0 otherwise, and *Total Sales*, an interval variable with five levels. Using sales instead of employment provides a measure of resources that is consistent across technologies and scale. To control for differences in absorptive capacity (Cohen and Levinthal, 1990) and learning capabilities, we introduced *Education* and *Oenologist*. The former is measured as an index based on the education levels of general managers and oenologists. The latter is a dummy variable that takes a value of 1 when the firm has at least one full-time oenologist. Both are common indicators in emerging markets and winemaking of a firm's capabilities to incorporate new practices (Giuliani and Bell, 2005). To control for the effects of a firm's demand structure and positioning choice (Kaplan, 2008), we introduce *Upgrading Intent*, a perceptual variable derived from the factor analysis that captures the firm's unobserved intention to upgrade by its commitment to activities and assets that support upgrading (that is, technology agreements, wine R&D agreements, and investment in micro-fermentation).

In order to test our hypotheses, we estimated two sets of linear regression models that regressed product upgrading on control variables and three groups of explanatory network variables with the firm as the unit of analysis. To correct skewness of our network variables we applied the Box–Cox transformation (Box and Cox, 1964) to each of our network measures. To address the problem of outliers, we report the results from robust regression (proc robustreg, SAS v.9) with least trimmed squared (LTS) estimation (Rousseeuw, 1984), which generates ordinary least squared (OLS) estimates robust to the presence of outliers.

The first set of models explores the relative impact of being tied to distinct types of alters on the firm's level of product upgrading (see Table 6.3a). Model 1 is the baseline, which includes only the control variables. Model 2 introduces our overall measure of embeddedness, *Ties to All Alters.* Model 3 decomposes this variable into the degree centrality for each one of the six networks based on the type of alter (*Ties to Associations, Banks, Cooperatives, Schools, Firms,* and *GSIs,* respectively). Model 4 decomposes *Ties to GSIs* into *Ties to PPIs* and *Ties to Old GSIs.*

The second set of models explores the relative impact on product upgrading of being tied to alters that are, respectively, the most central and most geographically diversified, in terms of their own connections (see Table 6.3b). We limit this analysis to firms and GSIs – the only types of alters that show significant impact on *Product Upgrading* in the first series of models. To provide consistency between the two sets of models and to account for our limited degrees of freedom, we modify our method of decomposition and aggregation in three systematic ways. First, in Models 5–8, we continue to include the ties to associations, banks, cooperatives, and schools by collapsing them into the variable *Ties to All Alters Except Firms and GSIs.* Second, Model 7 explores Hypotheses 4a and 4b by decomposing *Ties to Firms* and *Ties to GSIs* into, respectively, *Ties to Top Central Firms* and *Ties to All Firms Except Top Central Firms,* and *Ties to Top Central GSIs* and *Ties to All GSIs Except Top Central GSIs.* Third, Model 8 explores Hypotheses 5a and 5b by decomposing *Ties to Firms* and *Ties to GSIs* into, respectively, *Ties to Top Geo Div Firms* and *Ties to All Firms Except Top Geo Div Firms,* and *Ties to Top Geo Div GSIs* and *Ties to All GSIs Except Top Geo Div GSIs.*

The differences between models reflect decomposing the variable *Ties to All Alters* in different ways rather than adding new variables. In every case the sum of the decomposing variables is equal to the decomposed variable. In this way, we are able to show the distinct impact of alters that possess the characteristic of interest and those that do not.[5]

5   DEDUCTIVE ANALYSIS: RESULTS AND DISCUSSION

Table 6.2 presents descriptive and correlation statistics. Tables 6.3a and 6.3b present the results.

We focus here on our explanatory variables and related hypotheses. With regard to the network variables, Model 2 shows that there is a positive and significant effect from *Ties to All Alters* ($\beta = 0.20$). This serves as a baseline model as we decompose the networks. Following Fleming (2001), Lin (2001), and Owen-Smith and Powell (2004), we have argued that Mendoza's approach helped improve product upgrading because it offered wineries access to new knowledge resources via specific types of organizations and institutions. This view gains support from the increase

Table 6.2   Descriptive statistics and correlation table

		Obs	Mean	SD	1	2	3	4	5	6
1	Product Upgrading	97	19.20	0.68	1.00					
2	Total Sales	97	3.06	0.19	0.12	1.00				
3	Foreign Ownership	97	0.09	0.03	0.24	*0.23	*1.00			
4	Education	97	4.14	0.25	0.24	*0.17	0.34	*1.00		
5	Oenologist	97	0.71	0.04	0.18	0.17	0.03	0.09	1.00	
6	Upgrading Intent	97	4.76	0.32	0.39	*0.12	0.25	*0.38	*0.05	1.00
7	East	97	0.31	0.04	−0.06	0.01	−0.21	*−0.18	0.15	−0.26
8	South	97	0.15	0.03	−0.21	*0.20	*−0.05	−0.05	−0.03	−0.09
9	Valle Uco	97	0.13	0.03	0.05	−0.16	0.16	0.31	*−0.26	*0.49
10	San Juan	97	0.20	0.04	0.01	−0.15	−0.15	−0.07	0.10	−0.07
11	Ties to All Alters	97	21.28	1.32	0.20	0.19	−0.08	0.21	*−0.08	0.24
12	Ties to All Alters Except Firms & GSIs	97	4.42	0.43	0.07	0.18	−0.01	0.31	*−0.05	0.31
13	Ties to Associations	97	1.39	0.19	0.26	*0.23	*0.28	*0.57	*0.12	0.43
14	Ties to Banks	97	1.08	0.12	−0.03	0.18	−0.09	0.19	−0.31	*0.20
15	Ties to Cooperatives	97	0.84	0.16	−0.05	0.11	−0.06	0.04	−0.07	0.20
16	Ties to Firms	97	12.02	0.76	0.19	*0.25	*−0.11	−0.04	0.06	−0.04
17	Ties to GSIs	97	4.84	0.51	0.19	0.03	0.06	0.32	*−0.11	0.42
18	Ties to Schools	97	1.11	0.15	0.30	*0.21	*−0.03	0.09	−0.03	0.25
19	Ties to Old GSIs	97	2.11	0.26	0.02	−0.08	−0.09	0.19	0.00	
20	Ties to PPIs	97	2.72	0.31	0.20	*0.10	0.11	0.24	*−0.15	0.37
21	Ties to All Firms Except Top Geo Div Firms	97	8.62	0.57	0.09	0.25	*−0.19	−0.09	0.04	−0.14
22	Ties to All GSIs Except Top Geo Div GSIs	97	3.29	0.39	0.15	0.00	−0.09	0.22	*−0.02	0.36
23	Ties to All Firms Except Top Central Firms	97	6.09	0.42	0.20	*0.32	*−0.12	−0.10	0.17	−0.14
24	Ties to All GSIs Except Top Central GSIs	97	2.25	0.28	0.11	−0.07	0.03	0.21	*−0.15	0.32
25	Ties to Top Central Firms	97	5.93	0.44	0.06	0.14	−0.07	−0.01	−0.03	0.00
26	Ties to Top Central GSIs	97	2.59	0.28	0.17	0.13	0.07	0.22	*−0.05	0.32
27	Ties to Top Geo Div Firms	97	3.40	0.28	0.26	*0.14	0.05	0.02	0.10	0.09
28	Ties to Top Geo Div GSIs	97	1.54	0.16	0.17	0.05	0.17	0.12	−0.13	0.28

in the R^2 values for the subsequent models, and it is magnified when we consider the effects of the different network variables, to which we now turn.

As discussed in the previous section, we created two sets of models to allow for consistency in the way we decompose the network variables. We found support for our Hypotheses 1a and 1b in Model 3 (Table 6.3a) and Model 5 (Table 6.3b). Model 3 shows that higher levels of product upgrading are positively and very significantly associated with the number of ties a focal firm has to other firms ($\beta = 0.41$) and to GSIs ($\beta = 1.12$), both with significance at the 0.01 level. Model 5 shows similar results. We

7	8	9	10	11	12	13	14	15	16	17	18	19
*1.00												
−0.31	*1.00											
*−0.29	*−0.20	1.00										
−0.31	*−0.21	*−0.20	1.00									
*0.04	−0.10	0.52	*−0.35	*1.00								
*−0.23	*0.08	0.41	*−0.12	0.63	*1.00							
*−0.26	*−0.03	0.37	*−0.04	0.52	*0.59	*1.00						
−0.29	*0.25	*0.41	*−0.12	0.53	*0.64	*0.29	*					
0.00	−0.02	0.44	*−0.21	0.48	*0.48	*0.17	0.49	*1.00				
0.37	*−0.15	0.06	−0.36	0.77	*0.20	0.17	0.14	0.19	1.00			
*−0.29	*0.01	0.60	*−0.21	0.59	*0.54	*0.50	*0.46	*0.36	*0.09	1.00		
*−0.19	−0.10	0.15	0.03	0.46	0.56	*0.32	*0.37	*0.25	*0.19	0.35	*1.00	
*−0.19	−0.01	0.39	*0.09	0.36	0.48	*0.39	*0.29	*0.26	*−0.07	0.72	*0.21	*1.00
*−0.21	*0.08	0.56	*−0.51	0.62	*0.43	*0.38	*0.42	*0.34	*0.25	*0.85	*0.31	*0.38
0.38	*−0.08	0.01	−0.29	0.68	*0.14	0.07	0.13	0.20	0.93	*0.00	0.15	−0.09
*−0.17	−0.08	0.43	*0.00	0.45	0.48	*0.40	*0.31	*0.24	*0.05	0.82	*0.30	*0.87
0.21	*0.04	−0.23	*−0.16	0.49	0.05	0.01	0.02	0.06	0.82	*−0.12	0.13	−0.18
*−0.34	*−0.15	0.45	*0.15	0.37	0.46	*0.44	*0.36	*0.21	*−0.09	0.72	*0.37	*0.72
0.39	*−0.24	*0.25	*−0.42	0.72	*0.24	*0.22	*0.15	0.22	*0.80	*0.25	*0.16	0.08
*−0.11	0.20	*0.41	*−0.57	0.57	*0.39	*0.33	*0.34	*0.31	*0.28	*0.78	*0.22	*0.39
0.22	*−0.14	0.09	−0.32	0.58	*0.28	*0.28	*0.10	0.16	0.68	*0.18	0.19	0.04
*−0.22	*0.17	0.42	*−0.53	0.51	*0.35	*0.29	*0.35	0.29	*0.22	0.74	*0.24	*0.31

found support for Hypothesis 2 in Models 3 and 4 of Table 6.3a. In both models the variables for the number of ties a focal firm has to associations, schools, banks, cooperatives and schools were either negative or insignificant. These types of organizations could be beneficial to the extent that they promote support services and cross-cutting ties that provide access to a variety of knowledge resources (Zuckerman and Sgourev, 2006; Safford, 2007). Rather, the results suggest that in this context these organizations do not have such traits, while wineries access new applied knowledge mainly through ties to other firms and to GSIs. Our qualitative analysis showed that Mendoza's policy approach helped firms gain such access

Table 6.2　(continued)

		20	21	22	23	24	25	26	27	28
1	Product Upgrading									
2	Total Sales									
3	Foreign Ownership									
4	Education									
5	Oenologist									
6	Upgrading Intent									
7	East									
8	South									
9	Valle Uco									
10	San Juan									
11	Ties to All Alters									
12	Ties to All Alters Except Firms & GSIs									
13	Ties to Associations									
14	Ties to Banks									
15	Ties to Cooperatives									
16	Ties to Firms									
17	Ties to GSIs									
18	Ties to Schools									
19	Ties to Old GSIs									
20	Ties to PPIs	*1.00								
21	Ties to All Firms Except Top Geo Div Firms	0.17	1.00							
22	Ties to All GSIs Except Top Geo Div GSIs	*0.54	*−0.02	1.00						
23	Ties to All Firms Except Top Central Firms	0.07	0.86	*−0.10	1.00					
24	Ties to All GSIs Except Top Central GSIs	*0.45	*−0.16	0.73	*−0.21	*1.00				
25	Ties to Top Central Firms	0.35	*0.66	*0.19	0.40	*0.05	1.00			
26	Ties to Top Central GSIs	*0.89	*0.21	*0.55	*0.11	0.25	*0.38	*1.00		
27	Ties to Top Geo Div Firms	0.24	*0.42	*0.14	0.41	*0.06	0.71	*0.26	*1.00	
28	Ties to Top Geo Div GSIs	*0.88	*0.14	0.39	*0.08	0.41	*0.29	*0.81	*0.23	*1.00

Notes:
Descriptive statistics are based on nominal values.
Network variables are transformed in correlation table.
* Significant at *p-value* < 0.05.

because of the new scale and scope of resources available in GSIs and the way that their programs helped firms learn from one another.

The effect of GSIs is further clarified from the supporting evidence for Hypothesis 3 found in Model 4 (Table 6.3a) and Model 6 (Table 6.3b), which decompose the GSI variable into two parts – *Ties to PPIs* and *Ties to Old GSIs* – while holding all other variables the same. Both models show

Table 6.3a   *Regression results with product upgrading as dependent variable (Models 1–4)*

	Model 1		Model 2		Model 3		Model 4	
	Coeff.	Std err.	Coeff.	Std err.	Coeff.	Std err.	Coeff.	Std err.
Intercept	14.30	2.15	11.84	2.49	9.25	2.43***	9.24	2.32
Total Sales	0.33	0.36	−0.13	0.40	−0.04	0.37	−0.12	0.34
Foreign Ownership	1.80	2.32	4.26	2.57†	4.20	2.28†	2.26	2.23
Education	0.34	0.28	0.20	0.29	0.45	0.27	0.44	0.25
Oenologist	1.93	1.46	1.09	1.50	−0.46	1.43	0.98	1.36
Upgrading Intent	0.74	0.23**	0.83	0.23***	0.54	0.22*	0.53	0.20**
East	−2.74	1.86	−2.04	1.93	−0.76	1.85	−1.57	1.84
South	−7.05	2.09***	−5.36	2.17*	−3.70	2.14†	−4.90	2.07
Valle Uco	−4.59	2.29*	−8.42	2.71**	−3.30	2.73	−2.11	2.51
San Juan	−1.79	2.05	−0.19	2.22	2.60	2.16	4.98	2.39*
Ties to All Alters			0.20	0.07**				
Ties to Associations					−9.68	5.16†	1.32	5.12
Ties to Banks					−11.85	7.53	−19.33	7.00**
Ties to Cooperatives					−64.25	32.86†	−27.86	30.61
Ties to Schools					13.14	9.47	12.39	8.76
Ties to Firms					0.41	0.12***	0.36	0.12**
Ties to GSIs					1.11	0.40**		
Ties to Old GSIs							−2.04	2.11
Ties to PPIs							3.03	1.28*
N	97		97		97		97	
R-Squared	0.53		0.59		0.63		0.62	

Notes: The Grand Mendoza Zone is the omitted location.
† *p*-value < 0.10; * *p*-value < 0.05; ** *p*-value < 0.01; *** *p*-value < 0.001.

that higher levels of product upgrading are positively and significantly (at the 0.05 level) associated with the number of ties the focal firm has to PPIs, but not significantly associated with the ties to the old GSIs. These results support our qualitative analysis that wineries found value mostly in the PPIs, because they were the initiators of the new participatory governance mechanism that anchored their ability to create and deliver a new variety of knowledge resources to firms.

Hypotheses 4–5 sought to explore further the different mechanisms

Table 6.3b   *Regression results with product upgrading as dependent variable (Models 5–8)*

	Model 5		Model 6		Model 7		Model 8	
	Coeff.	Std err.	Coeff.	Std err.	Coeff.	Std err.	Coeff.	Std err.
Intercept	11.12	2.48***	10.55	2.54***	12.45	2.50***	11.26	2.53***
Total Sales	−0.01	0.38	−0.06	0.38	−0.01	0.39	0.16	0.39
Foreign Ownership	3.86	2.43	3.90	2.44	3.83	2.47	2.56	2.52
Education	0.37	0.28	0.41	0.28	0.40	0.29	0.53	0.29†
Oenologist	0.60	1.44	0.71	1.45	0.29	1.48	0.39	1.45
Upgrading Intent	0.70	0.23**	0.70	0.23**	0.68	0.24**	0.66	0.24**
East	−1.98	1.91	−1.11	2.03	−1.24	2.02	−1.17	2.06
South	−5.73	2.13**	−5.41	2.16*	−6.54	2.21**	−5.70	2.14**
Valle Uco	−6.89	2.52**	−6.59	2.53**	−5.23	2.61*	−5.31	2.50*
San Juan	0.92	2.17	3.23	2.61	2.58	2.59	2.90	2.62
Ties to All Alters Except Firms & GSIs	−0.71	0.45	−0.53	0.46	−0.50	0.46	−0.77	0.46†
Ties to Firms	0.34	0.12**	0.29	0.13*				
Ties to GSIs	0.97	0.41*						
Ties to Old GSIs			−0.21	2.34				
Ties to PPIs			3.53	1.46*				
Ties to All Firms Except Top Central Firms					0.42	0.24†		
Ties to All GSIs Except Top Central GSIs					0.55	2.45		
Ties to Top Central Firms					0.22	0.43		
Ties To Top Central GSIs					3.59	1.59*		

Table 6.3b   (continued)

	Model 5		Model 6		Model 7		Model 8	
	Coeff.	Std err.	Coeff.	Std err.	Coeff.	Std err.	Coeff.	Std err.
Ties to All Firms Except Top Geo Div Firms							0.18	0.19
Ties to All GSIs Except Top Geo Div GSIs							0.72	1.22
Ties to Top Geo Div Firms							1.53	0.73*
Ties to Top Geo Div GSIs							5.44	2.75*
N	97		97		97		97	
R-Squared	0.61		0.63		0.62		0.62	

Notes: The Grand Mendoza Zone is the omitted location.
† p-value < 0.10; * p-value < 0.05; ** p-value < 0.01; *** p-value < 0.001.

through which mediating firms and GSIs provide access to a variety of knowledge resources. As discussed in the previous section, to test these hypotheses we decomposed *Ties to Firms* and *Ties to GSIs* by isolating the ties to the most central firms and GSIs, respectively (Model 7), and the ties to the firms and GSIs, respectively, with the most geographically diverse networks (Model 8).

Model 7 (Table 6.3b) does not lend support to Hypothesis 4a, as the number of ties to the most central firms was not significant. It does support Hypothesis 4b, showing that higher levels of product upgrading are positively and significantly associated with the number of ties a focal firm has to the most central GSIs ($\beta = 3.59$, at the 0.05 level). We also found support for Hypotheses 5a and 5b in Model 8 (Table 6.3b). Higher levels of product upgrading are positively and significantly associated with the number of ties a focal firm has to other firms and GSIs with the most geographically diverse pattern of connections ($\beta = 1.53$ and 5.44, respectively, both at the 0.05 level). Models 7 and 8 also reveal that the effects of the other network variables are negative or not significant, with the exception of *Ties to All Firms Except Top Central Firms*, which was positive and marginally significant.

The qualitative analysis sought to illuminate the institutional mechanisms that could reshape network ties and knowledge diffusion between firms by examining how the policy divergences between San Juan and Mendoza could account for differences in product upgrading. The evidence suggested that while pre-existing socio-economic relationships could impede broad-based collective action and knowledge diffusion, Mendoza's approach to constructing PPIs helped firms improve their access to new knowledge resources by providing a new scale and scope of services and by facilitating new relationships between firms themselves. In particular, the resulting PPIs had governance rules that allowed them to develop multiplex, bridging relationships between different producer communities as well as to facilitate collective problem solving among their representatives which governed the PPIs. The combination of these rules and network qualities helped the PPIs, and later some older GSIs, to solve two major barriers to product upgrading and learning for firms in emerging markets – weak institutional resources and socio-economic fragmentation.

The statistical analysis then tested the relationship between product upgrading and a focal firm's ties to other firms, GSIs, and PPIs as well as explored more fully the mechanisms that facilitate one's access to a variety of knowledge resources via these intermediating firms and institutions. The statistical evidence appeared to support our claims about the role of Mendoza's approach to improving access for firms to a variety of new applied knowledge resources, in turn their product upgrading, particularly given the positive and significant impact of such variables as the ones capturing ties to the PPIs and those capturing ties to the alters that have the highest centrality and bridging traits. This reinforces the view that access to a variety of knowledge resources depends not simply on whether the alters are public or private *per se* but whether the alters are constituted in ways that provide cross-cutting ties between producer communities (Zuckerman and Sgourev, 2006; Safford, 2007). Indeed, if we limit analysis to only market and non-state actors, we might miss two key ways in which the institutional qualities of regional clusters and government policy can improve innovative capacities in general.

First, to the extent that access to a variety of knowledge resources is vital for firm upgrading, the qualitative and quantitative evidence reframes our notion about which types of alters may facilitate such access. Prior research on innovation has emphasized the importance of firms and associations providing cross-cutting relationships between previously isolated groups of firms (Fleming, 2001; Zuckerman and Sgourev,

2006; Safford, 2007) and the role of GSIs helping to diffuse knowledge in providing collective resources and having a public mission to share new knowledge (Owen-Smith and Powell, 2004; Breznitz, 2007). The evidence here supports a blending of the two views in that the effectiveness of government programs is rooted in the institutionalization of their network qualities. The innovation in Mendoza's approach was constructing a new set of GSIs, the PPIs, with rules of inclusion and participatory governance. These rules anchored the multiplex bridging qualities of PPIs that underpinned their ability to provide a new scale and scope of knowledge resources to firms and mold new relationships between them. Hence, this research suggests that firms can improve their access to a variety of knowledge resources and their attendant 'combinatory capacities' (Moran and Ghoshal, 1999: 409) if they participate in structures that are constituted with the aforementioned institutional and network qualities.

Second, the evidence in its entirety suggests that organizational fields can be reshaped in different ways, primarily because one component – GSIs – is highly responsive to government policy. This is consistent with growing work on issues ranging from technology diffusion to healthcare to industrial policy, which shows the impact of government policy in structuring inter-organizational networks (Provan and Milward, 1995; Knoke, 2001; Owen-Smith and Powell, 2004). Hence, a long-term consequence of Mendoza's policy has been to reshape the organizational field in ways that differed significantly from the province's past and from San Juan.

6 CONCLUDING REMARKS

This chapter has sought to explain how firms upgrade products in a society seemingly trapped in a history of dysfunctional institutions and social capital. In building on research emphasizing how the composition of networks can impede and facilitate knowledge transfer, we have argued that a firm's access to a variety of knowledge resources depends on its ties not simply to any or many organizations or institutions but especially to those that excel in their bridging qualities. In particular, we have highlighted the distinct governance principles that can anchor multiplex bridging traits in GSIs and, in turn, underpin their ability to provide to firms a new scale and scope of diverse services and foster new learning relationships between firms from previously isolated producer communities. Rules of inclusion and participatory governance for relevant public and private actors institutionalize mechanisms that can facilitate a recombination of knowledge resources and create new cross-cutting professional ties between actors engaged in public policy and firm strategy. Our inter-disciplinary approach suggests two related directions for further research at the inter-section of institutional and network theory.

First, the results suggest further research on the ways in which firms can access a variety of knowledge resources via intermediaries with different institutional and network qualities. While much of the research on knowledge transfer and innovation has focused on the types of relationships between firms and individuals (Fleming and Waguespack, 2007), students of public policy tend to focus on the stock of collective knowledge resources provided by non-market actors, such as GSIs and associations (Breznitz, 2007). In contrast to both, this chapter supports an increasingly salient stream of research, which emphasizes how public and private actors can construct new institutions that improve firm access to a variety of knowledge resources because of the underlying network properties of these non-market intermediaries (McEvily and Zaheer, 1999; Zuckerman and Sgourev, 2006).

Second, our research calls for further analysis of the relationship between the governance principles of intermediating organizations, namely GSIs, and their ability to alter the flow of knowledge in industries. While such scholars as Owen-Smith and Powell (2004) have studied how the institutional demography of networks shapes the content of information, they have stressed how GSIs and non-profit organizations are distinct because of their rules guiding the dissemination of proprietary information. We do not deny the importance of this institutional trait. But our research also emphasizes that the governance principles of GSIs can help institutionalize distinct network qualities, such as the multiplex bridging qualities of the PPIs in Mendoza. Such principles as empowered inclusion and participatory governance for a diverse set of relevant public and private actors can enable GSIs to provide more effective knowledge resources to firms as well as to reshape the relationships between firms themselves. Naturally, we have not exhausted the relevant governance principles or the types of institutions. Rather, this research is but one contribution to a growing effort in management and policy studies to identify how the construction of institutions in a variety of industries can recast or reify the diffusion of information and resources between firms (Knoke, 2001).

As societies debate ways to improve their industries, their governments have alternatives to pure state or market coordination by constructing new institutions that are governed by a wider variety of public and private actors than previously considered. Inclusive, participatory governance can institutionalize problem-solving mechanisms that help such actors build new horizontal professional ties and graft broader strategic considerations onto their past mutual hold-up instincts. In turn, such an institutional approach, be it for new regulatory bodies or agencies that provide R&D and training, has the opportunity to facilitate a recombination of different knowledge resources and aid constituent firms to learn from one another.

NOTES

1. On the variety and decentralized structure of wine and grape production, see Cetrangolo et al. (2002) and Ruiz and Vila (2003). According to the data from the Instituto Nacional Vitivinicoltura (INV), there were still over 16,000 vineyards in Mendoza and 6,000 in San Juan; vineyards in both provinces with less than 25 has still accounted for about 92 percent of the total number and 60 percent of surface area. According to the 2003 agricultural survey of vineyards in Mendoza, the largest 18 vineyard owners control only 5 percent of vineyard surface area, and about 1,100 owners control 50 percent. (Authors' calculations for both sets of figures.)
2. Of the 112 wineries, 22 are from San Juan and 90 are from Mendoza, of which 26 are from Gran Mendoza, 32 from the East Zone, 15 from Valle de Uco, and 17 from the South Zone. Due to missing variables, our models include data from 97 firms (an effective response rate of 84 percent).
3. PPIs include: Fondo de Vitivincola, Fondo para la Transformacion y Crecimiento, IDR, Promendoza, INTA Mendoza, INTA San Juan, and ITU. Old GSIs include all other GSIs, which pre-date PPIs and differ in terms of the governance rules discussed above.
4. We subtracted this Herfindahl Index from one so that a higher score represented greater geographic diversity in the ties of the organization.
5. Multicollinearity problems were limited to our measures of ties to the most central and geographically diversified alters, which had variance inflation factors between 3.2 and 4 and correlations ranging from 0.78 to 0.85 (see Table 6.3). For this reason, and for lack of better solutions (Wooldridge, 2002), we only report models introducing those variables one group at a time instead of combining them.

REFERENCES

Box, G.E.P. and D.R. Cox (1964), 'An analysis of transformations', *Journal of the Royal Statistical Society, Series B (Methodological)*, **26** (2), 211–52.

Breznitz, D. (2007), *Innovation and the State: Political Choice and Strategies for Growth in Israel, Taiwan, and Ireland*, New Haven, CT: Yale University Press.

Burt, R.S. (1983), 'Range', in R.S. Burt and M.J. Minor (eds), *Applied Network Analysis*, Beverly Hills, CA: Sage, pp. 176–94.

Burt, R.S. (2000), 'The network structure of social capital', in R. Sutton and B. Staw (eds), *Research in Organizational Behavior*, Vol. 22, Greenwich, CT: JAI Press, pp. 345–423.

Buse, R.C. (1973), 'Increasing response rates in mailed questionnaires', *American Journal of Agricultural Economics*, **55** (3), 503–8.

Cetrangolo, H., S. Fernandez, J. Quagliano, V. Zelenay, N. Muratore and F. Lettier (2002), *El negocio de los vinos en la Argentina* [*The Business of Wines in Argentina*], Buenos Aires: FAUBA.

Cohen, W.M. and D.A. Levinthal (1990), 'Absorptive capacity: a new perspective on learning and innovation', *Administrative Science Quarterly*, **35** (1), 128–52.

DiMaggio, P. and W. Powell (1983), 'The iron cage revisited: institutional isomorphism and collective rationality in organizational fields', *American Sociological Review*, **48** (2), 147–60.

Fleming, L. (2001), 'Recombinant uncertainty in technological search', *Management Science*, **47** (1), 117–32.

Fleming, L. and D.M. Waguespack (2007), 'Brokerage, boundary spanning, and leadership in open innovation communities', *Organization Science*, **18** (2), 165–80.

Frank, O. (2005), 'Network sampling and model fitting', in P.J. Carrington, J. Scott and S. Wasserman (eds), *Models and Methods in Social Network Analysis*, Cambridge: Cambridge University Press, pp. 31–56.

Giuliani, E. and M. Bell (2005), 'The micro-determinants of meso-level learning and innovation: evidence from a Chilean wine cluster', *Research Policy*, **34** (1), 47–68.

Giuliani, E., C. Pietrobelli and R. Rabellotti (2005), 'Upgrading in global value chains: lessons from Latin American clusters', *World Development*, **33** (4), 549–73.

Granovetter, M. (2002), 'A theoretical agenda for economic sociology', in M.F. Guillen, R. Collins, P. England and M. Meyer (eds), *The New Economic Sociology*, New York: Russell Sage Foundation, pp. 35–60.

Jacobs, J. (1984), *Cities and the Wealth of Nations: Principles of Economic Life*, New York: Random House.

Kaplan, S. (2008), 'Cognition, capabilities, and incentives: assessing firm response to the fiber-optic revolution', *Academy of Management Journal*, **51** (4), 672–95.

Knoke, D. (2001), *Changing Organizations: Business Networks in the New Political Economy*, Boulder, CO: Westview Press.

Lin, N. (2001), *Social Capital*, New York: Cambridge University Press.

Locke, R.M. (1995), *Remaking the Italian Economy: Local Politics and Industrial Change in Contemporary Italy*, Ithaca, NY: Cornell University Press.

MacDuffie, J.P. (1995), 'Human resource bundles and manufacturing performance: organizational logic and flexible production systems in the world auto industry', *Industrial and Labor Relations Review*, **48** (2), 197–221.

McDermott, G.A. (2007), 'The politics of institutional renovation and economic upgrading: recombining the vines that bind in Argentina', *Politics & Society*, **35** (1), 103–43.

McDermott, G.A. and R.A. Corredoira (2010), 'Network composition, collaborative ties, and upgrading in emerging market firms: lessons from the Argentine autoparts sector', *Journal of International Business Studies*, **41** (2), 308–29.

McEvily, B. and A. Zaheer (1999), 'Bridging ties: a source of firm heterogeneity in competitive capabilities', *Strategic Management Journal*, **20** (12), 1133–56.

McEvily, B. and A. Zaheer (2004), 'Architects of trust: the role of network facilitators in geographical clusters', in R. Kramer and K. Cook (eds), *Trust and Distrust in Organizations*, New York: Russell Sage, pp. 189–213.

Moran, P. and S. Ghoshal (1999), 'Markets, firms, and the process of economic development', *Academy of Management Review*, **24** (3), 390–412.

Obstfeld, D. (2005), 'Social networks, the tertius iungens orientation, and involvement in innovation', *Administrative Science Quarterly*, **50** (1), 100–130.

Ostrom, E. (1999), 'Coping with tragedies of the commons', *Annual Review of Political Science*, **2**, 493–535.

Owen-Smith, J. and W.W. Powell (2004), 'Knowledge networks as channels and conduits: the effects of spillovers in the Boston biotechnology community', *Organization Science*, **15** (1), 5–21.

Padgett, J.F. and C.K. Ansell (1993), 'Robust action and the rise of the Medici, 1400–1434', *American Journal of Sociology*, **98** (6), 1259–320.

Perez-Aleman, P. (2005), 'Cluster formation, institutions and learning: the emergence of clusters and development in Chile', *Industrial and Corporate Change*, **14** (4), 651–77.

Powell, W.W., K.W. Koput and L. Smith-Doerr (1996), 'Interorganizational collaboration and the locus of innovation: networks of learning in biotechnology', *Administrative Science Quarterly*, **41** (1), 116–45.

Provan, K.G. and H.B. Milward (1995), 'A preliminary theory of interorganizational network effectiveness: a comparative study of four community mental health systems', *Administrative Science Quarterly*, **40** (1), 1–33.

Putnam, R.D., R. Leopardi and R.Y. Nanetti (1993), *Making Democracy Work*, Princeton, NJ: Princeton University Press.

Roberts, P. and P. Ingram (2002), 'Vertical linkages, knowledge transfer and export performance: the Australian and New Zealand wine industries, 1987–1999', unpublished manuscript, Emory University, Atlanta, GA.

Rousseeuw, P.J. (1984), 'Least median of squares regression', *Journal of the American Statistical Association*, **79**, 871–80.

Ruiz, A.M. and H. Vila (2003), 'Structural changes and strategies of the Argentinean wine chain actors', in S. Gatti, E. Giraud-Heraud and S. Mili (eds), *Wine in the Old World: New Risks and Opportunities*, Milan, Italy: FrancoAngeli, pp. 215–28.

Safford, S. (2007), *Why the Garden Club Couldn't Save Youngstown: Social Networks and the Transformation of the Rust Belt*, Cambridge, MA: Harvard University Press.

Schneider, B. (2004*), Business Politics and the State in Twentieth-Century Latin America*, Cambridge and New York: Cambridge University Press.

Spicer, A., G.A. McDermott and B. Kogut (2000), 'Entrepreneurship and privatization in Central Europe', *Academy of Management Review*, **25** (3), 630–49.

Stark, D. and L. Bruszt (1998), *Postsocialist Pathways: Transforming Politics and Property in Eastern Europe*, Cambridge and New York: Cambridge University Press.

Uzzi, B. (1996), 'The sources and consequences of embeddedness for the performance of organizations: the network effect', *American Sociological Review*, **61** (4), 674–98.

Wasserman, S. and K. Faust (1994), *Social Network Analysis: Methods and Applications*, Cambridge: Cambridge University Press.

Wooldridge, J.M. (2002), *Econometric Analysis of Cross Section and Panel Data*, Cambridge, MA: MIT Press.

Zuckerman, E. and S. Sgourev (2006), 'Peer capitalism: parallel relationships in the U.S. economy', *American Journal of Sociology*, **111** (5), 1327–66.

7. Bridging researchers and the openness of wine innovation systems in Chile and South Africa

Elisa Giuliani and Roberta Rabellotti[1]

---

1. INTRODUCTION

Nobody would now disagree with the contention that access to globally available technology and knowledge is a key determinant of learning and innovation in countries, regions, industries and firms. In the literature, a lot of attention has been focused on foreign firms as major channels to exchange and diffuse knowledge and innovation through mechanisms based on 'learning from exports' (Wagner, 2007) as well as through knowledge spillovers from foreign direct investment (FDI) (Barba Navaretti and Venables, 2004) and from leading buyers in global value chains (Gereffi et al., 2005).

As clearly stated in the literature on national innovation systems (Lundvall, 1992; Freeman, 1995), firms are important actors in the innovation and learning process. However, they are not the only ones, given the role played by the institutions (the rules of the game) and the organizations that systemically interact with and affect the creation and diffusion of innovations in any national economic system. Other key actors are universities and public research organizations (PROs), which have recently increasingly attracted the attention of the literature, due to the strengthening of ties between science, technology and innovation in many industries, and also beyond those sectors traditionally defined as knowledge intensive.

In less developed countries, the role played by universities as channels to tap into the international knowledge base has been the focus of a small number of recent studies (Mazzoleni and Nelson, 2007; Yusuf and Nabeshima, 2007; Mazzoleni, 2008; Brundenius et al., 2009). Within universities and PROs, the links of individual researchers with international research networks are interesting channels for accessing external knowledge which has not yet been investigated. This chapter is aimed at addressing this gap in the literature with an investigation into the existence and the characteristics of a particular category of scholars, which we call 'bridging researchers' and define as those who are well connected both with their international peers and with the domestic industry. As far as we know, this type of researcher has not yet been investigated in the literature but it deserves attention given its potential key role in bridging foreign-generated knowledge and technology with the national industry. Therefore the research questions addressed in the chapter are: what characteristics identify bridging researchers and how special are bridging researchers as opposed to other researchers?

These questions are explored with reference to Chile and South Africa, using a new original database on researchers specialized in scientific disciplines related to wine. Chile and South Africa are two emerging countries that have recently increased their presence in the international wine market. The wine industry is a particularly appropriate context for investigating bridging researchers because of two key aspects: first, the increasing importance of innovation and scientific research for the upgrading of the industry, as has been documented in a number of recent studies (Giuliani, 2007; Morrison and Rabellotti, 2007; Smith, 2007; Cassi et al., ch. 3 in this book); and second, the global explosion of demand for easily identifiable and pleasant-tasting international varietal wines – such as Cabernet, Merlot and Chardonnay – which has generally increased the industry's need to access external knowledge (Cusmano et al., ch. 2 in this book).

The chapter is organized as follows. Section 2 develops the conceptual framework, reviewing the literature on innovation systems and investigating the role of universities and researchers in this context. Section 3 provides an overview of the wine industry in the two specific contexts in which the empirical exercise is conducted. Section 4 presents the data and the method of analysis and Section 5 the empirical results. Section 6 concludes.

2   CONCEPTUAL FRAMEWORK

Innovation Systems (IS) in Developing Countries

The idea that innovation occurs in a 'system' – a set of interacting enterprises, institutions, research bodies and policy-making agencies that share knowledge and both jointly and individually contribute to the development and diffusion of new technologies – is by now widely accepted.[2]

Although the IS concept was originally conceived and applied to advanced countries, it has rapidly diffused to less developed countries

(LDCs). This follows the acknowledgment of the need for a conscious and purposive innovation effort and capacity building in LDCs, even if they rely primarily on imported technology. Similarly to developed countries, systemic elements affect LDCs' ability to innovate and to access, master, adapt, and improve upon, imported technologies (Freeman, 1995), and to build the required competences (Lundvall, 1992). Nevertheless, the application of the IS concept in a developing country context is not at all straightforward. It is widely agreed in the literature that in LDCs there is a need to adopt a broader notion of innovation systems that also includes economic, social, educational and political institutions that can affect learning and technology and knowledge diffusion (Gu, 1999; Arocena and Sutz, 2000; Edquist, 2001; Intarakumnerd et al., 2002; Cassiolato et al., 2003; Chaminade and Vang, 2008).

Moreover, in LDCs the inflows of knowledge and technology from external sources are essential components in the innovation and learning processes. From this it follows that it is particularly important to provide the innovation system approach with an international dimension.[3] The most widely analyzed external channels in the process of innovation and learning are the links with foreign markets and foreign firms; these range from the exploration of the learning and efficiency-improving potential offered by exports ('learning from exporting', see Wagner, 2007 for a survey), to the focusing on the role of FDI through spillovers, imitation and direct innovation efforts (Barba Navaretti and Venables, 2004; UNCTAD, various years). Another increasingly important channel to access knowledge and enhance learning and innovation in firms located in LDCs is the participation in global value chains (GVCs) (Gereffi et al., 2005; Giuliani et al., 2005).

Nonetheless, within IS, firms are not the only actor through which external knowledge may be accessed. Universities and other PROs can play a key role in the internationalization of IS. The role of universities and PROs in innovation systems has received greater attention in the literature and several studies have highlighted their increasing contribution to the industry. This literature is the focus of the next subsection.

Universities and the Role of Bridging Researchers

It is widely agreed that universities and other research organizations have a central role in innovation systems. Their function in creating and transmitting knowledge has become ever more crucial in recent times, where the basis of production globally has become increasingly knowledge intensive and the connection between science and technology has been growing considerably. The attention in the literature to the linkages between universities and industry has consequently increased, with analyses of the 'entrepreneurial' role of universities and the reduction in their historical 'ivorytowerism' (Gibbons et al., 1994; Etzkowitz, 1998; Mowery and Sampat, 2004). At the policy level, national and subnational governments have sought to increase the rate of transfer of academic research advances to industry through a set of different mechanisms and channels of interaction (Bonaccorsi and Piccaluga, 1994; Geuna, 2001; Mowery et al., 2001; Van Looy et al., 2003).

Developing countries have also been paying increasing attention to universities and PROs as key institutions in the process of acquisition of technological capabilities (Arocena and Sutz, 2000). In 2007, *World Development* dedicated a special issue (Erschberg et al., 2007) to the contribution of universities to the diffusion of knowledge-intensive economic activity in a number of Asian cities, and two World Bank economists, Yusuf and Nabeshima (2007), edited a book, *How Universities Promote Economic Growth*, which is entirely focused on how universities may serve industry through direct flows of information from ongoing research.

Adopting a historical approach, two recent papers by Mazzoleni and Nelson (2007) and Mazzoleni (2008) investigated the role played by academic institutions in the catching-up process, providing examples of countries and sectors in which universities and PROs have contributed effectively to economic progress at different times. In developing countries there is a need to stimulate innovation in low-tech sectors (Srinivas and Sutz, 2008) as well as to develop indigenous research capabilities for solving idiosyncratic issues in fields such as agriculture and medicine. Moreover, according to Mazzoleni and Nelson (2007), there are reasons to believe that the importance of having the capability to carry out research and development locally will be even greater in the future due to the increasingly stringent health and quality standards that have to be satisfied in the international markets and to intellectual property right-related issues.

In addition to their role in creating and transferring knowledge to the domestic industry, universities may also play a key bridging role in connecting the national IS with foreign science and technology, as stressed by Mazzoleni and Nelson (p. 1515), 'having a domestic base of good scientists provides the basis for breaking into the international networks where new technologies are being hatched'. Traditionally the main channel of foreign technology and science has been the flow of students from developing countries studying abroad and then returning home, as well documented in the case of Korea (Kim, 1999) and Taiwan (Hou and Gee, 1993). Zucker and Darby (2007) investigated the migration of 'star scientists' and found that in some emerging countries (for example, Brazil, China, India and Taiwan) their return is an increasingly common phenomenon. Also, Saxenian (2006) stressed the importance of the 'New Argonauts', highly skilled migrants from developing countries, in the creation of new technological businesses in Silicon Valley and then back in their home country. Inspired by the increasing importance of return migration in emerging countries, Mayr and Peri (2008) show that for regions such as Eastern Europe and Asia, return migration may imply that 20 to 30 percent of highly educated emigrants return home when they are still productive and contribute importantly to the average income and wages of the sending country.

Another important gateway to foreign discoveries and scientific advancement is the participation of scholars in international research networks. During the last decade, as shown in bibliometric studies, co-authorship relations have grown both in number as well as in the countries involved (Leydesdorff and Wagner, 2008; Frenken et al., 2009; Cassi et al., ch.3 in this book). Given that the involvement of researchers with their peers may represent an increasingly important channel to tap into the international knowledge pool, we shall investigate who these researchers are and examine their characteristics – the focus on individual scientists being justified by the fact that an important part of the knowledge is embodied in individuals as tacit knowledge (Polanyi, 1967).

In this work, focusing on the wine industry in two emerging stars in the international market – Chile and South Africa – we shall investigate a particular category of researcher – bridging researchers – who are at the same time well connected internationally with their peers and maintain strong links with the domestic industry. The research questions addressed are: what are the main characteristics of bridging researchers and how do they differ from other researchers in the system? Our interest in this type of researcher is motivated by their potentially important role in connecting the local innovation system with the global knowledge base. They could provide a key contribution to the achievement of a 'developmental university system', as advocated by Brundenius at al. (2009), open to global knowledge and at the same time contributing to economic and social development.

3   THE CONTEXT

The Wine Industry in Chile and South Africa

The wine industry has been undergoing radical changes over the last couple of decades, namely a seismic shift in production methods, research intensity and organization, global competitiveness and producer ranking. Until the end of the 1980s the international market for wine was dominated by European countries, and particularly by France and Italy. But since the beginning of the 1990s this supremacy started to falter due to the spectacular performance, in terms of both exported volumes and values, of new international players. Among the New World countries eroding the long-established position of the Old World producers are Chile and South Africa, which are the focus of this study. In both countries the tradition of winemaking is centuries old but their entry into the international market is very recent and has followed their adaptation to the international demand pattern by planting noble international vine varieties and adopting advanced oenological and viticulture techniques. The quality upgrading of their wine exports is shown by the increase in unit value, which has gradually been converging towards the world average, although is still below countries such as France, Italy and Australia (see Table 2.4 in Chapter 2).

In spite of the sustained growth of the wine industries in both Chile and South Africa, there are some differences between the two countries: as stated above, the unit value of exports has gradually been increasing, but Chile has made more progress than South Africa in this respect. As a consequence of quality upgrading and volume expansion, the value of exports has increased in Chile from about US$100 million in the first half of the 1990s to more than US$1,400 million in 2007, and in South Africa from less than US$40 million in the second half of the 1990s to almost US$600 million (FAOSTAT, 2009). Their difference in generating value is also confirmed by some sketchy evidence coming from the specialized journal, *Wine Spectator*. In its Wine Ratings' Database there are 26 South African wines with an average rating of 82 and average release price of US$9 and 68 Chilean wines with an average rating of 84 and an average price of almost double that of South African wines – that is, US$16.

The gap between the two countries and international leading exporters such as Australia, Italy and France is due to a number of factors stemming from differences in marketing strategies, to the more recent liberalization and opening of the South African economy, to differences in the industry and institutional structures and, more broadly, to the macroeconomic characteristics of each economy. In their analysis of sectoral wine systems, Cusmano et al. (Chapter 2) illustrate that Chile and South Africa represent two different stages of the catching-up process undertaken in the international market by New World wine producers, which have been heading towards a certain degree of convergence in recent years.

In this chapter our focus is on access to international knowledge and technology and their diffusion within the national industry, which may represent a key factor for bridging the quality gap, given the preference for international wine varieties in the international market. Our empirical analysis identifies and investigates the bridging researchers who, given their strong academic international connections and their domestic links with the industry, may play a significant role in the catching-up process.

Science and Research Institutions in the Wine Industry

One aspect that makes the wine industry an appropriate context for exploring our research questions is the importance of university research for introducing improvements in the industry. As reported by Paul (1996), scientists have played a key innovative role in the wine industry since the 1860s' phylloxera outbreak, when 'science played a large role in the constitution of the devastated vineyards, and especially in the preservation of quality wines from *vinifera* vines' (pp. 10–11). Most of the advances in agronomic, chemical or engineering research in the wine industry are based on applied science, carried out in PROs or universities and leading to directly applicable solutions for the industry. For example, there are great benefits from discoveries such as the relationship between the incidence of certain viral pathogens and the decrease in grape yields, a greater understanding of the relationship between different types of yeast and the sensory attributes of wines, or about changes in irrigation due to climate change. Hence universities and PROs are seen as a source of skills and knowledge, with which firms engage in joint research activities.

For New World wine countries like South Africa and Chile, the access to foreign scientific knowledge is very important. First, because these countries have traditionally drawn from the scientific base and discoveries of Old World countries, especially France, which have a longstanding tradition in applied research in wine-related fields. Second, although these countries have set up their own research agendas,[4] these require constant interactions and collaborations with other countries – both from the New World like Australia and the USA and from the Old World, because of the diffusion of international vine varieties and techniques for wine production which are favoured by the market (see Chapter 2 for a discussion on demand changes).

In the two countries under investigation, there are a number of institutions with a tradition in research on wine-related issues. In Chile the two main universities of the country, both based in Santiago, the Pontificia Universidad Católica and the Universidad de Chile, have by far the largest number of researchers (see Table 7.1). Among the other universities involved, the Universidad de Talca is the only one located in a wine region in the South, a region that has recently increased its participation in the export market (Bell and Giuliani, 2007). Apart from universities,

Table 7.1   Characteristics and affiliations of researchers

		Indicator	Chile	South Africa
Sex	Female	%	17.5	23.81
	Male	%	82.5	76.19
Age		Average	48.27	43.02
Years of experience in research		Average	21.40	15.66
Education	Only undergraduate degree	%	17.5	4.76
	Postgraduate degree (MSc/PhD)	%	82.5	95.24
	Foreign degree (undergrad/MSc/PhD)	%	60	19.05
Position as full professor or associate professor (university) or senior researcher (other PRO)		%	55	36
Researchers working at universities:		%	90	57.14
Affiliations in Chile:				
Universidad de Chile (Santiago)		%	40	
Universidad Católica (Santiago)		%	34	
Universidad de Santiago de Chile (USACH)		%	5	
Universidad de Talca		%	5	
Universidad Federico Santa Maria (Santiago)		%	5	
Instituto Nacional Investigacion Agropecuaria (INIA)		%	5	
Centro de Informacion de Recursos Naturales (CIREN)		%	3	
Universidad de Concepción		%	3	
Affiliations in South Africa:				
Stellenbosch University		%		55
Agricultural Research Council (ARC) Infruitec Nietvoorbij		%		41
Agricultural Research Council (ARC) Plant Protection		%		2
Pretoria University		%		2
Total number of researchers		N°	40	42

there are also two PROs involved in wine research: the Instituto Nacional de Investigación Agropecuaria (INIA) and the Centro de Información de Recursos Naturales (CIREN) both affiliated to the Ministry of Agriculture. To strengthen the collaboration between universities, PROs and the industry, in 2006 two consortia, Vinnova and Tecnovid, were established with the support of the Chilean Economic Development Agency (CORFO) through the *Innova Chile* programme. Both consortia are aimed at promoting investments in innovation and research in wine-related areas and better orientating researchers' efforts towards issues relevant for the domestic producers.

In South Africa the research system is dominated by two institutions, both located in Stellenbosch, in the heart of the main wine region of the country. The University of Stellenbosch has several departments involved in research projects relevant for the domestic wine industry. Among them, the Institute for Wine Biotechnology is a world-leading institution in this field. The other leading institution in the country is ARC Infruitec-Nietvoorbij, a member of the Agricultural Research Council and affiliated to the Ministry of Agriculture. In South Africa most of the research funds come from a levy from exports and are distributed, on the basis of a competitive process, by the Wine Industry Network of Expertise and Technology (Winetech), which is an association involving all the main stakeholders in the industry. Winetech's role is to orient domestic research towards those issues that are identified as key by the industry representatives.

4 METHODOLOGY

Data

The study is based on original survey data collected in Chile and South Africa in the period from October 2005 to October 2006. With the assistance of key scholars and by contacting the heads of the university departments and of the research institutes involved in the wine field spanning a number of disciplines (that is, viticulture, oenology, agronomy, agriculture, microbiology, genetics, chemistry and engineering), we have been able to identify the population of researchers,[5] whose main research interest is wine-related issues. We have personally interviewed 40 researchers in Chile, and 42 in South Africa. Through the interviews we have been able to collect data that are not usually available from secondary sources.

The questionnaire covers many aspects related to the researchers' background and their personal collaborations with other researchers and people in the industry. The background information on researchers' personal profiles also includes details on their education and work experience (that is, age, sex, years of experience in research, position, affiliations, level of education achieved). Table 7.1 presents some descriptive statistics.

Further, for each respondent, we have obtained his/her academic curriculum vitae (CV), including additional information about publications (books, book chapters, journal articles, working papers, conference papers and so on), as well as prizes and awards gained as a result of academic excellence (that is, prizes for best paper, best dissertation, best teacher of the year). Given that CVs are likely to be structured differently by each researcher, we have carefully checked the consistency of all of them and controlled for missing or heterogeneous information.[6]

An important part of the questionnaire is designed to collect relational data on the linkages between the respondents and (i) other researchers, both in the country and abroad; and (ii) professionals working in the domestic wine industry.[7] Given that the population of possible contacts of each researcher could not be identified beforehand, relational data were gathered through a free recall method (Wasserman and Faust, 1994), asking each respondent to name his/her contacts without a predetermined list. In line with much of the established literature in this field (Marsden, 2005), respondents were asked to provide answers for a maximum of 10 individuals (researchers or professionals). The relational data collected are as follows:

1. Data on *academic linkages* between the researcher interviewed and other researchers. Respondents were asked whether they had collaborated with researcher(s) located in their country or abroad, specifying the name of each researcher, his/her affiliation (department, university), and the country (if foreign). The question asked was: 'Please indicate names and affiliations of academic researchers with whom you carried out research on wine-related fields in the past 5 years'.[8] In the face-to-face interviews, respondents were informed that they should report connections with other researchers with whom they were involved in some form of collaboration for research activity or for a project (irrespective of whether this was based on a formal or informal agreement or contract). They were also asked to indicate the strength of the relationship, although this information is not used in this chapter.

2. Data on *university–industry linkages* between the respondent and professionals in the domestic wine industry,[9] based on the following question: 'Please indicate the name of professionals/researchers with whom you have interacted through at least one of the different activities listed below, in the past 5 years'. The activities considered were: (i) joint research agreements (involving research undertaken by both parties); (ii) contract research agreements (research commissioned by industry and undertaken by researchers only); (iii) consultancy work (commissioned by industry, not involving original research); (iv) informal contacts (technical advice not based on a market transaction); (v) attendance at conferences with industry and university participation; (vi) participation in electronic networks (for example, mailing lists); (vii) setting up of spin-off companies; (viii) training of company employees (through enrolment in courses, or personnel exchanges); and (ix) student internships in firms.

On the basis of these relational data, two types of networks were constructed:

- The *academic network*, reporting the existence of a research linkage between the respondent and other researchers in the country and abroad. These network data are pooled in two matrices (one for Chile and one for South Africa), composed of x rows and x columns corresponding to the number x of researchers in the network, derived from summing the researchers interviewed and the researchers named by them. Therefore each cell in the matrix reports the existence of a relationship between researcher i in the row and researcher j in the column. In other words, in cell (i, j) there is 1 if there is at least one linkage between i and j, and 0 otherwise.[10]
- The *university–industry network*, reporting the existence of a linkage (through any of the nine possible channels listed above) between the respondent and the wine industry professionals he/she named. These network data are also pooled in matrices, following the same methodology described above, used for building the academic network. This network, however, only contains national linkages.

The Operational Definition of Bridging Researchers

The aim of the chapter is to identify and explore the characteristics and nature of bridging researchers, defined as those researchers who are simultaneously well connected with both the domestic industry and the international academic community and therefore are an important channel for the openness of the innovation system and the catching up of the industry. Hence, from an operational point of view, bridging researchers are defined as those having the following three features.

First, higher than average number of *international academic linkages* formed by each researcher to other scholars working in a *foreign* country. This is measured through the academic network and it simply counts the number of declared collaboration linkages formed by each respondent with foreign academics.

Second, higher than average *international scientific openness*. This is an indicator that captures the degree to which a researcher is involved in collaborations with foreign academics versus domestic collaborations, on the basis of Gould and Fernandez's (1989) measure of brokerage. According to Gould and Fernandez, when actors a and b belong to different groups (in this case they are affiliated to domestic or foreign institutions), three types of brokerage are possible in undirected networks (in our case academic collaboration is considered a bidirectional relationship).[11]

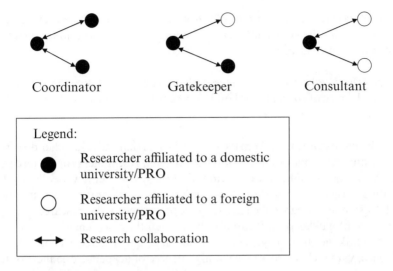

Coordinator   Gatekeeper   Consultant

Legend:

● Researcher affiliated to a domestic university/PRO

○ Researcher affiliated to a foreign university/PRO

◄─► Research collaboration

Source: Gould and Fernandez (1989).

Figure 7.1   Brokerage roles

The three types are named using social role terminology (Figure 7.1):

- *Coordinators*: respondents and their direct contacts belong to the same group. In our case, given that the measure is calculated only for the respondents, this occurs when the researchers are all from the country under investigation.
- *Consultants*: brokers who belong to one group (that is, the country under investigation), while their two direct contacts belong to a different group (in our case, they are foreign).
- *Gatekeepers*: a broker and one of the direct contacts belong to one group (that is, the country under investigation), and the second direct contact to another group (therefore affiliated to a foreign institution).

Assuming that academic knowledge flows through collaboration, gatekeepers and consultants are those who are in contact with the international knowledge base, because of their linkages with researchers affiliated to foreign institutions. However, each researcher has a limited number of different academic collaborations[12] and may take on these different roles at various times. Given that we are interested in identifying those researchers who are more oriented to international research collaborations, we calculate an indicator taking into account the number of times they play the role of gatekeeper and/or consultant vis à vis those in which they act as a coordinator. Hence, we introduce an indicator of 'international scientific openness', measured as:

International scientific openness = 1 – (Number of times the researcher plays the role of *coordinator*/Total number of times in which the researcher has a *brokering* role of any kind)

The indicator ranges from 0 to 1: 0 indicates that the researcher does not have any academic collaboration with foreign researchers (or no research collaborations at all) and 1 indicates that the researcher never collaborates with another domestic researcher unless the collaboration also involves at least one foreign colleague (this happens when the researcher plays the role of gatekeeper). It can also be 1 when the researcher has only academic linkages to foreign scholars (that is, he/she just acts as consultant). Hence, values closer to 1 reveal a high degree of academic openness of the researcher and, consequently, a low degree of engagement in collaborations with domestic scholars.

Third, higher than average number of *university–industry linkages* formed by each researcher with professionals in the wine industry. As explained above, these linkages may be formed through any of the nine channels including joint research agreements, contract research agreements and consultancy work.

We also tried alternative measures of bridging researchers, that is, by using the median and the top 75 percent threshold as cut-off values, instead of the mean values. To account for international academic openness, we also excluded the indicator of 'international scientific openness' and just focused on the number of international academic linkages. The statistical results do not change substantially, hence we decided to present the results based on the methodology presented above.

5   EMPIRICAL RESULTS

Researchers as a Channel to 'Open' the Innovation System

In this subsection we explore the extent to which the two countries under investigation differ in terms of openness to foreign science of their academic systems on the basis of domestic scientists' research collaborations with their foreign colleagues. Table 7.2 shows the average number of linkages that each researcher has established with other colleagues affiliated to foreign universities. The value for both countries is

Table 7.2   Linkages to foreign researchers

	Chile	South Africa
Number of linkages by researcher	1.65	1.61
Distribution of linkages (%) by country:		
United States	25.0	6.90
Spain	23.33	6.90
Italy	11.67	20.69
France	13.33	13.80
Australia	1.67	13.80
Germany	6.66	12.07
The Netherlands	0	6.90
Portugal	5	3.45
Slovenia	0	3.45
Canada	3.33	1.72
Switzerland	0	1.72
Chile	0	1.72
Argentina	3.33	0
South Africa	0	0
Rest of the world	6.68	13.88
Total	100	100

Table 7.3   Degree of international scientific openness

	Chile	South Africa	Sig.
Mean	0.30	0.20	10%
SD	0.28	0.28	
No of obs.	40	42	

almost the same – 1.65 for Chile and 1.61 for South Africa – although there are differences in terms of preferential partners. Most of the connections of South African researchers are with Italian (20 percent of all foreign linkages), French, Australian (both 14 percent) and German (13 percent) researchers, while Chilean researchers are primarily connected with US and Spanish researchers (25 and 23 percent, respectively) and less with French and Italian researchers (13 and 12 percent, respectively).

In spite of a rather similar openness in undertaking linkages with foreign researchers, there are differences in the degree of scientific openness of researchers. Table 7.3 reports the mean value of the indicator, which shows that in Chile the average value is 0.30, significantly higher

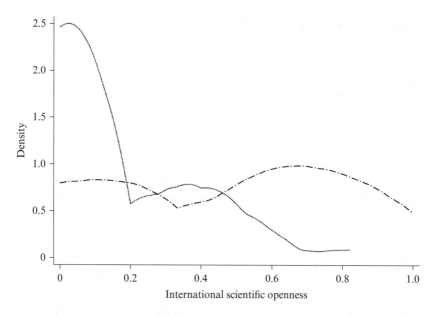

Note: The plot reports Kernel density distributions. Dotted line refers to Chile, straight line to South Africa.

Figure 7.2   Distribution of researchers' international scientific openness: South Africa and Chile

than the South African value of 0.20. The ANOVA test also confirms that the differences are statistically significant, although only at 10 percent. In order to understand the implication of this result, Figure 7.2 presents an overlaid plot of kernel density distributions of the indicator of scientific openness in the two countries. The Chilean case (dotted line) displays a denser tail for high values of the indicator, as highlighted by the fatter tail, as compared to the South African case in the figure. This result suggests that although South African and Chilean researchers are on average similarly connected to foreign scientists, among Chilean researchers there is a rather large group more involved in foreign collaborations than in domestic ones.

University–Industry Linkages

This subsection illustrates the differences across the two countries with respect to the propensity of academic researchers to undertake linkages with the industry. Table 7.4 shows that the average number of

Table 7.4   Different types of linkages with the industry

	Indicator	Chile	South Africa
(a) Number of university–industry linkages per researcher	Average (SD)	3.825 (2.551)	2.762 (2.428)
	ANOVA (Sig.)		0.057
(b) Types of linkages			
(i) Joint research agreements	Number of ties (% on total links)	64 (36)	25 (19)
(ii) Contract research agreements	Number of ties (% on total links)	36 (20)	31 (24)
(iii) Consultancy work	Number of ties (% on total links)	31 (18)	24 (19)
(iv) Informal contacts	Number of ties (% on total links)	19 (11)	31 (24)
(v) Attendance at conferences	Number of ties (% on total links)	10 (06)	5 (4)
(vi) Participation in electronic networks	Number of ties (% on total links)	0 (0)	0 (0)
(vii) Setting up of spin-off companies	Number of ties (% on total links)	0 (0)	3 (2)
(viii) Training of company employees	Number of ties (% on total links)	11 (6)	6 (5)
(ix) Student internship in firms	Number of ties (% on total links)	6 (3)	4 (3)
Total links	Number of ties	177	129

ties formed by each researcher with professionals in the industry is slightly higher in Chile than in South Africa, although differences are statistically significant only at 10 percent (p-value is 0.057). In the same table we present the breakdown by type of linkages, reporting the total number of ties for each type of relationship and their percentage on total university–industry (U–I) linkages. In Chile, the most frequent type of linkage is a joint research agreement, while in South Africa research contracted by the industry and undertaken by the researchers plus informal contacts are the two most frequent types of relationships. Finally, both Chilean and South African researchers are significantly involved in consultancy.

In Table 7.5 we present the characteristics of the U–I networks formed by the academic researchers in the two countries. The Chilean network is

Table 7.5   Statistics about university–industry networks

Indicator		Statistics by country	
		Chile	South Africa
Size	Number of nodes present in the network (including universities and professionals in the industry)	163	125
Density	Proportion of possible linkages that are actually present in a network. Ranges from 0 (total disconnection) to 1 (maximum connection)	0.0100	0.0084
Number of components	Components are separate subsets within a network	12	10
Proportion of nodes in the largest component	Percentage of nodes that form part of the largest component	30.7%	38.4%
Fragmentation index	Number of components divided by number of nodes	0.846	0.777

larger and slightly denser (164 nodes and 0.01 in density) than the South African one (125 nodes and 0.0084 in density). Moreover, it is also more fragmented, as reflected by the greater number of components (12 versus 10 in the South African network) and by the higher fragmentation index (0.846 versus 0.777 in South Africa).

These differences are reflected in Figures 7.3 and 7.4, which depict the U–I networks in Chile and South Africa, respectively. Figure 7.3 shows that in Chile, researchers from the two leading institutions (that is, the University of Chile and Catholic University) are strongly connected with the industry, but researchers from other institutions such as the University of Talca and INIA are also well linked with the industry. In contrast, in South Africa (Figure 7.4), as described in Section 3 and presented in Table 7.1, in terms of affiliations of the researchers interviewed, there are two main research institutions – the ARC Institute and the University of Stellenbosch – and of course, they emerge as dominant in the linkages with the industry.

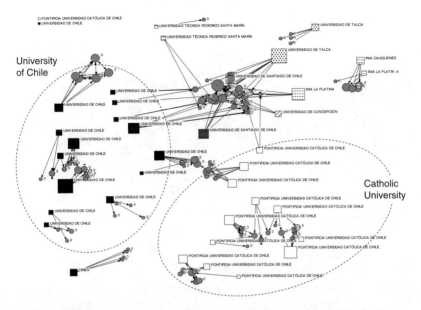

Note: Square nodes indicate the researchers working in universities or PROs; circles indicate professionals. The size of the nodes is proportional to the number of linkages each node has established.

Figure 7.3   University–Industry network in Chile

Bridging Researchers: What's So Special about Them?

As defined in Section 4, 'bridging researchers' are those who have a higher than average (i) number of collaborations with foreign academics, (ii) scientific openness, and (iii) domestic U–I linkages. On the basis of these criteria, six bridging researchers in Chile and seven in South Africa are identified. As illustrated by Table 7.6, in Chile bridging researchers represent 35 percent of the researchers with higher than average scientific openness and 40 percent of the researchers with a higher than average number of linkages to foreign academics. This means that around 60 percent of researchers with strong international connections are not strongly connected with the domestic industry. In contrast, we observe that only 30 percent of researchers with higher than average U–I linkages are also connected to a significant degree with foreign scientists. Similar features are found for South Africa, with the only difference that in this case the proportion of bridging researchers among those with higher than average scientific openness and linkages to foreign scientists is higher (46 and 54 percent, respectively).

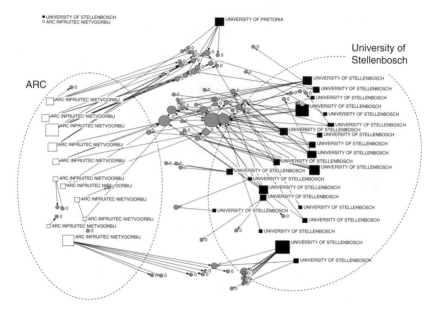

Note: Square nodes indicate the researchers working in universities or PROs; circles indicate professionals. The size of the nodes is proportional to the number of linkages each node has established.

Figure 7.4   University–Industry network in South Africa

Table 7.7 explores the differences between bridging and non-bridging researchers, based on a set of researchers' characteristics, available through the questionnaire and the detailed CVs. It is interesting to note that there are no differences across these two groups, either in their demographic characteristics (sex and age), or in their level of training and experience (years of experience and having studied abroad as a degree or postgrad student).

However, when we turn to indicators of scientific merit, we find that bridging researchers have higher scientific productivity in indexed journals (ISI publications) and have been awarded more prizes during their academic career. In particular, we find that Chilean bridging researchers have more than three times the level of ISI publications, discounted by the years of experience of each researcher, than the rest of their Chilean colleagues (1.10 versus 0.33). In South Africa we have quite similar features: 0.93 versus 0.47 (significant at 10 percent) for ISI publications and 2.35 versus 0.83 (significant at 1 percent) for non-indexed publications, which include book chapters, books and publications in journals that are

Table 7.6   Bridging researchers: frequency distributions

		Number of researchers	Of which bridging researchers (%)
Chile			
1.	Higher than average collaborations with foreign researchers	15	40%
2.	Higher than average international scientific openness	17	35%
3.	Higher than average U–I links	20	30%
	Bridging researchers	6	
South Africa			
1.	Higher than average collaborations with foreign researchers	13	54%
2.	Higher than average international scientific openness	15	46%
3.	Higher than average U–I links	20	35%
	Bridging researchers	7	

not in the ISI list. When considering the cumulative number of prizes awarded, both in South Africa and in Chile, bridging researchers have three to five times more prizes than the other researchers in their own country.

The systematic result of higher scientific merit of bridging researchers is also more striking if we take into account the results presented in Table 7.7 and those presented in Tables 7A.1–3 in the appendix, in which we compare the characteristics of those researchers having (i) higher than average scientific openness (Table 7A.1), (ii) higher than average collaborations with foreign researchers (Table 7A.2) and (iii) higher than average U–I linkages with domestic professionals (Table 7A.3), with the other researchers. The comparison reveals that bridging researchers are indeed different from other researchers in terms of scientific merit, while these differences are less prominent when we take into consideration their colleagues with similar high openness to foreign science or high linkages with the domestic industry.

These results suggest two things. First, in both of the investigated wine innovation systems there is a small number of researchers who at the same time have a prominent scientific openness as well as a significant degree of connection with the domestic industry, thus behaving as bridging researchers. Second, these researchers are significantly more 'talented' than the other researchers who were investigated in this study, both

Table 7.7 Statistics on bridging researchers

	Indicator	Chile			South Africa		
		Bridging researchers	All other researchers	Sig.	Bridging researchers	All other researchers	Sig.
Number of researchers	Count	6	34		7	35	
Collaborations with foreign researchers	Avg.	5.00	0.970	***	6.571	0.247	***
International scientific openness	Avg.	0.638	0.240	***	0.477	0.274	***
U–I links	Avg.	1.156	0.380	***	2.437	1.038	***
Characteristics of researchers:							
Sex							
Female	Count (%)	1 (14%)[a]	6	n.s.	4 (40%)	6	n.s.
Male	Count (%)	5 (25%)	28		3 (10%)	28	
Age	Avg.	46.61	48.62	n.s.	38.57	43.88	n.s.
Years of experience	Avg.	19.83	21.63	n.s.	12.42	16.35	n.s.
Any study abroad	Count (%)	4 (67%)[b]	21 (61%)	n.s.	2 (29%)	6 (34%)	n.s.
Holding a postgrad abroad	Count (%)	4 (67%)	20 (59%)	n.s.	1 (14%)	5 (15%)	n.s.

Type of institutional affiliation:						
University	Count	5	31	n.s.	5	18	n.s.
Public research organization	Count	1	3		2	16	
Scientific output:						
1. ISI publications per year of experience (up to 2006)	Avg.	1.10	0.33	*** (ANOVA)	0.93	0.47	* (ANOVA)
2. Non-indexed publications per year of experience (up to 2006)	Avg.	0.67	0.57	n.s.	2.35	0.83	*** (ANOVA)
Prizes (cumulative number)	Avg.	5.00	1.09	*** (ANOVA)	3.96	1.20	*** (ANOVA)

Notes:
[a] 14% of female researchers are bridging researchers. The same interpretation should be extended to statistics on male researchers and South Africa.
[b] 67% of bridging researchers have studied abroad.
*** Difference is significant at 1%; * Difference is significant at 10%.

because they publish more in international journals and/or because their have received awards for their work.

Due to their characterization in terms of scientific excellence, bridging researchers may indeed play a key role in creating a gateway to international knowledge for the domestic industry and therefore they deserve more investigation in the literature.

6   CONCLUSIONS

This chapter introduces a novel idea in the flourishing literature on the opening up of innovation systems: it investigates the existence and nature of bridging researchers, who act as a natural gateway of international science into the domestic industry. The study is exploratory and the empirical analysis is constrained by the limited focus on two countries and one industry. Nevertheless the findings are interesting and, indeed, they encourage further research along the lines proposed here.

There are two main results. The first is related to the differences across the two countries, as we observe that although both the South African and the Chilean researchers are similarly open to foreign research collaborations, the balance between foreign and domestic collaborations – reflected in the indicator for scientific openness – shows that Chileans are more outward oriented than South African researchers. Also, in terms of university–industry linkages, Chilean researchers are slightly more connected with professionals than their South African colleagues.

The second more important result is about bridging researchers. A number of empirical findings are notable: bridging researchers are present in both systems under investigation and in both cases they do not differ from other researchers, either in terms of their demographic characteristics, or in their level of training and experience. Instead, they are very special in terms of their scientific excellence. Note that in these two countries emerging in the international wine market as major exporters, there are researchers with an excellent scientific curriculum creating a natural bridge from the international scientific community to the domestic industry (and this is likely to be a bidirectional link). This is particularly relevant in the wine sector, which is characterized by the increasing importance of global knowledge for the success of the industry in the international market.

These explorative findings deserve further investigation for their potential relevance in terms of policy implications. In spite of being a small number, bridging researchers are a natural gateway of scientific knowledge to the industry, and, more importantly, their activity seems not to be subject to the traditional trade-off between being involved in international scientific research on the one hand, and collaborating with the domestic industry on the other (for a discussion on this, see Giuliani and Arza, 2009). Instead, these scholars are able to achieve both objectives at the same time, probably because they have a strong personal motivation and/ or they are exceptionally talented both in doing research and in disseminating and applying scientific knowledge. At the same time, their involvement with the domestic industry implies that locally there is a demand for advanced knowledge.

Policy makers may consider the opportunity to set up appropriate incentive schemes in order to attract and adequately remunerate these talents. The presence of bridging researchers may play an important role in building up open and successful innovation systems in LDCs. Furthermore, policy initiatives that boost individual talents (rather than their institutions or networks of researchers), funding their research agendas and financing visiting schemes to strengthen their foreign collaborations, may be more desirable than the recently common funding schemes in which researchers are 'forced' to interact with other (often less talented) researchers or with the industry. Pasteur said 'chances favour the prepared mind'. In other words, governments should try to attract and nurture as many talents as possible among scientists, as their skills will sooner or later trickle down to the industry and support the success of the innovation system.

Given its explorative aim, this study has a number of methodological and empirical limitations. First, the collection of relational data through a free recall method always generates scepticism about the quality and reliability of the data collected, as missing data due to respondents' bad memory may be frequent in this approach. However, we have followed the recommendations of the established literature on network data collection (Marsden, 2005), and, although we have not used name generators (Campbell and Barret, 1991) to simulate thinking, we have carried out lengthy and detailed face-to-face interviews with the researchers. Also, the nature of the questions digs into the professional networks of researchers, which are more selective and much easier to identify than personal or private networks. This aspect should increase the reliability of our responses.

The second limitation is about the definition of bridging researchers as those who have above-average scientific openness and U–I linkages. We have tried alternative measures and we are aware that yet other measures could be developed to capture bridging behaviors. Moreover, the different nature of U–I linkages (research, consultancy, conferences and so on) could be analyzed separately, rather than treating them as a unique bundle, and explored in more depth. This can be done in future research. Furthermore, in this chapter we have considered both academic and U–I linkages only on a dichotomous scale, while in future work we would also like to include a distinction between weak and strong linkages.

NOTES

1. The authors would like to thank Aldo Geuna for very useful comments on a previous version of the chapter.
2. Many other scholars have addressed this concept. Among the many, see Freeman (1987); Lundvall (1992); Nelson (1993); Metcalfe (1995); and Edquist (1997). In addition, due to the recognition that, depending on the purpose of the inquiry, the most useful definition of innovation systems might not necessarily coincide with national borders, different concepts have been introduced in the literature: in order of appearance we can recall 'technological systems' (Carlsson and Stankiewicz, 1991), 'regional innovation systems' (Cooke, 1992) and 'sectoral innovation systems' (Breschi and Malerba, 1997).
3. Although not meant to be so in the original writings (Lundvall, 1992), much of the IS literature has been substantially 'inward looking', often losing sight of the importance of interactions with foreign sources of innovative activities and knowledge through different channels, as for example inter-firm, intra-firm and individual networks (Bunnell and Coe, 2001; Carlsson, 2006; Fromhold-Eisebith, 2007; Bell et al., 2008).
4. An autonomous research agenda is important as each country has its own specificities in climate, soil, pests and diseases, all of which need dedicated investigations to analyze and solve local problems.
5. We use the term 'researcher' to identify an individual who is professionally engaged in scientific research. Thus the term includes individuals occupying different academic positions, from research associate to assistant, to associate and to full professor.
6. Three research assistants have carried out a detailed analysis of all CVs, checking for their completeness through the researchers' web pages, cross-checking the publications in Google Scholar and ISI Web of Knowledge and then directly asking the researchers to confirm the completeness of their CV through subsequent email contacts.
7. We also asked for links with professionals abroad but the number of these collaborations is very small and therefore they have not been included in the empirical analysis.
8. Two separate questions were asked for collecting names of academic collaborators within the country and abroad.
9. By 'professionals' we mean individuals who work in the wine industry – most of whom are either employed by wineries as oenologists, agronomists or in other roles, or employed by wineries' suppliers (chemical or engineering companies) or private consultants for the domestic industry.
10. We have constructed three matrices: one including only national linkages, one including only foreign linkages and one including both foreign and national linkages.
11. This has been adapted from Gould and Fernandez (1989), whose original formulation included three different affiliations and identified more brokerage roles: five in the case of directed networks (the additional roles are 'representative' and 'liaison') and four otherwise (the additional role is 'liaison').
12. In our survey, each researcher was asked to list a maximum of 10 contacts with national researchers and another 10 links with foreign researchers.

REFERENCES

Arocena, R. and J. Sutz (2000), 'Looking at national innovation systems from the South', *Industry and Innovation*, **7** (1), 55–75.

Barba Navaretti, G. and A.J. Venables (2004), *Multinational Firms in the World Economy*, Princeton, NJ: Princeton University Press.

Bell, M. and E. Giuliani (2007), 'Catching up in the global wine industry: innovation systems, cluster knowledge networks and firm-level capabilities in Italy and Chile', *International Journal of Technology and Globalisation*, **3** (2–3), 197–223.

Bell, M., V. Arza, E. Giuliani and A. Marin (2008) 'The evolving role of MNEs in Latin American and Caribbean Innovation Systems', SPRU-IDRC scoping paper, University of Sussex, Brighton.

Bonaccorsi, A. and A. Piccaluga (1994), 'A theoretical framework for the evaluation of university–industry relationships', *R&D Management*, **24** (3), 229–47.

Breschi, S. and F. Malerba (1997), 'Sectoral innovation systems: technological regimes, Schumpeterian dynamics and spatial boundaries', in C. Edquist (ed.), *Systems of Innovation: Technologies, Institutions and Organizations*, London: Pinter, pp. 130–56.

Brundenius, C., B.-A. Lundvall and J. Sutz (2009), 'The role of universities in innovation systems in developing countries: developmental university systems – empirical, analytical and normative perspectives', in B-A Lundvall, K.J. Joseph, C. Chaminade and J. Vang (eds), *Handbook of Innovation Systems and Developing Countries*, Cheltenham, UK and Northampton, MA, USA: Edward Elgar Publishing, pp. 311–33.

Bunnell, T.G. and N.M. Coe (2001), 'Spaces and scales of innovation', *Progress in Human Geography*, **25** (4), 569–89.

Campbell, K.E. and A.L. Barret (1991), 'Name generators in surveys of personal networks', *Social Networks*, **13** (4), 203–21.

Carlsson, B. (2006), 'Internationalization of innovation systems: a survey of the literature', *Research Policy*, **35** (1), 56–67.

Carlsson, B. and R. Stankiewicz (1991), 'On the nature, function and composition of technological systems', *Journal of Evolutionary Economics*, **1** (2), 93–118.

Cassiolato, J.E., H. Lastres and M. Maciel (eds) (2003), *Systems of Innovation and Development: Evidence from Brazil*, Cheltenham, UK and Northampton, MA, USA: Edward Elgar.

Chaminade, C. and J. Vang (2008), 'Globalisation of knowledge production and regional innovation policy: supporting specialized hubs in the Bangalore software industry', *Research Policy*, **37** (10), 1684–96.

Cooke, P. (1992), 'Regional innovation systems: competitive regulation in the new Europe', *Geoforum*, **23** (3), 365–82.

Edquist, C. (ed.) (1997), *Systems of Innovation: Technologies, Institutions and Organisations*, London: Pinter.

Edquist, C. (2001), 'Systems of innovation for development', background paper for UNIDO World Industrial Development Report 2002/3, UNIDO, Vienna.

Erschberg, E., K. Nabeshima and Y. Shahid (2007), 'Opening the ivory tower to business: university–industry linkages and the development of knowledge-intensive clusters in Asian cities', *World Development*, introduction to the special issue, **35** (6), 931–40.

Etzkowitz, H. (1998), 'The norms of entrepreneurial science: cognitive effects of the new university–industry linkages', *Research Policy*, **27** (8), 823–33.

FAOSTAT (2009), Trade statistics, accessed 31 January 2010 at http://faostat.fao.org.

Freeman, C. (1987), *Technology Policy and Economic Performance: Lessons from Japan*, London: Pinter.

Freeman, C. (1995), 'The "national system of innovation" in historical perspective', *Cambridge Journal of Economics*, **19** (1), 5–24.

Frenken, K., S. Hardeman and J. Hoekman (2009), 'Spatial scientometrics: towards a cumulative research program', *Journal of Informetrics*, **3** (3), 222–32.

Fromhold-Eisebith, M. (2007), 'Bridging scales in innovation policies: how to link regional, rational and international innovation systems', *European Planning Studies*, **15** (2), 217–33.

Gereffi, G., J. Humphrey and T. Sturgeon (2005), 'The governance of global value chains', *Review of International Political Economy*, **12** (1), 78–104.

Geuna, A. (2001), 'The changing rationale for European university research funding: are there negative unintended consequences?', *Journal of Economic Issues*, **35** (3), 607–32.

Gibbons, M., C. Limoges, H. Nowotny, S. Schwartzman, S. Scott and M. Trow (1994), *The New Production of Knowledge: The Dynamics of Science and Research in Contemporary Societies*, London: Sage.

Giuliani, E. (2007), 'The wine industry: persistence of tacit knowledge or increased codification? Some implications for catching-up countries', *International Journal of Technology and Globalisation*, **3** (2–3), 138–54.

Giuliani, E. and V. Arza (2009), 'What drives the formation of "valuable" university–industry linkages? Insights from the wine industry', *Research Policy*, **38** (6), 906–21.

Giuliani, E., C. Pietrobelli and R. Rabellotti (2005), 'Upgrading in global value chains: lessons from Latin America clusters', *World Development*, **33** (4), 549–73.

Gould, R.V. and R.M. Fernandez (1989), 'Structures of mediation: a formal approach to brokerage in transaction networks', *Sociological Methodology*, **19**, 89–126.

Gu, S. (1999), 'Implications of national innovation systems for developing countries: managing change and complexity in economic development', UNU-INTECH discussion paper series 9903, Maastricht, the Netherlands.

Hou, C.M. and S. Gee (1993), 'National system supporting technical advance in industry: the case of Taiwan', in R.R. Nelson (ed.), *National Innovation Systems: A Comparative Analysis*, New York: Oxford University Press, pp. 384–413.

Intarakumnerd, P., P. Chairatana and T. Tangchitpiboon (2002), 'National innovation system in less successful developing countries: the case of Thailand', *Research Policy*, **31** (8–9), 1445–57.

Kim, L. (1999), 'Building technological capability for industrialization: analytical frameworks and Korea's experience', *Industrial and Corporate Change*, **8** (1), 111–36.

Leydesdorff, L. and S. Wagner (2008), 'International collaboration in science and the formation of a core group', *Journal of Informetrics*, **2** (4), 317–25.

Lundvall, B.-A. (1992), *National Systems of Innovation: Towards a Theory of Innovation and Interactive Learning*, London: Pinter.

Marsden, P.V. (2005), 'Recent developments in network measurement', in P.J. Carrington, J. Scott and S. Wasserman (eds), *Models and Methods in Social*

Network Analysis, Cambridge and New York: Cambridge University Press, pp. 8–30.

Mayr, K. and G. Peri (2008), 'Return migration as channel of brain gain', National Bureau of Economic Research working paper 14039, Cambridge, MA.

Mazzoleni, R. (2008), 'Catching up and academic institutions: a comparative study of past national experiences', *Journal of Development Studies*, **44** (5), 678–700.

Mazzoleni, R. and R.R. Nelson (2007), 'Public research institutions and economic catch-up', *Research Policy*, **36** (10), 1512–28.

Metcalfe, J.S. (1995), 'Technological system and technological policy in an evolutionary framework', *Cambridge Journal of Economics*, **19** (1), 25–46.

Morrison, A. and R. Rabellotti (2007), 'The role of research in wine: the emergence of a regional research area in an Italian wine production system', *International Journal of Technology and Globalisation*, **3** (2–3), 155–78.

Mowery, D.C., R.R. Nelson, B.N. Sampat and A.A. Ziedonis (2001), 'The growth of patenting and licensing by U.S. universities: an assessment of the effects of the Bayh–Dole Act of 1980', *Research Policy*, **30** (1), 99–119.

Mowery, D.C. and B.N. Sampat (2004), 'Universities in national innovation systems', in J. Fagerberg, D.C. Mowery and R.R. Nelson (eds), *The Oxford Handbook of Innovation*, Oxford: Oxford University Press, pp. 209–39.

Nelson, R.R. (ed.) (1993), *National Innovation Systems: A Comparative Analysis*, Oxford and New York: Oxford University Press.

Paul, H.W. (1996), *Science, Vine and Wine in Modern France*, Cambridge: Cambridge University Press.

Polanyi, M. (1967), *The Tacit Dimension*, London: Routledge & Kegan Paul.

Saxenian, A.L. (2006), *The New Argonauts: Regional Advantage in a Global Economy*, Cambridge, MA: Harvard University Press.

Smith, K. (2007), 'Technological and economic dynamics of the world wine industry: an introduction', *International Journal of Technology and Globalisation*, **3** (2–3), 127–37.

Srinivas, S. and J. Sutz (2008), 'Developing countries and innovation: searching for a new analytical approach', *Technology in Society*, **30** (2), 129–40.

UNCTAD (United Nations Conference on Trade and Development) (various years), *World Investment Report*, Geneva: United Nations.

Van Looy, B., K. Debackere and P. Andries (2003), 'Policies to stimulate regional innovation capabilities via university–industry collaboration: an analysis and an assessment', *R&D Management*, **33** (2), 209–29.

Wagner, J. (2007), 'Exports and productivity: a survey of the evidence from firm-level data', *The World Economy*, **30** (1), 60–82.

Wasserman, S. and K. Faust (1994), *Social Network Analysis. Methods and Applications*, Cambridge, MA: Cambridge University Press.

Yusuf, S. and K. Nabeshima (eds) (2007), *How Universities Promote Economic Growth*, Washington, DC: World Bank.

Zucker, L.G and M.R. Darby (2007), 'Star scientists, innovation and regional and national immigration', National Bureau of Economic Research working paper 13547, Cambridge, MA.

APPENDIX 7A

Table 7A.1	*Statistics on researchers and their academic linkages to foreign researchers*

Characteristics of researchers	Indicator	Chile			South Africa		
		Number of links higher than average	Number of links lower than average	Sig.	Number of links higher than average	Number of links lower than average	Sig.
Sex							
Female	Count	2	5	n.s.	5	5	n.s.
Male	Count	13	20		8	24	
Age	Avg.	45.93	49.68	n.s.	40.15	44.31	n.s.
Years of experience	Avg.	19.4	22.54	n.s.	11.46	*17.55*	* (ANOVA)
Any study abroad	Count	11	14	n.s.	2	6	n.s.
Holding a post-grad abroad	Count	10	14	n.s.	1	5	n.s.
Scientific output:							
1. ISI publications per year of experience (up to 2006)	Avg.	0.66	0.32	n.s.	0.84	0.56	n.s.
2. Non-indexed publications per year of experience (up to 2006)	Avg.	0.65	0.54	n.s.	*2.09*	.072	*** (ANOVA)
Prizes (cumulative number)	Avg.	2.33	1.28	n.s.	2.63	1.41	n.s.

Notes:	*** Difference is significant at 1%; * Difference is significant at 10%.

Table 7A.2   *Statistics on researchers and their scientific openness*

Characteristics of researchers	Indicator	Chile			South Africa		
		Scientific openness higher than average	Scientific openness lower than average	Sig.	Scientific openness higher than average	Scientific openness lower than average	Sig.
Sex							
Female	Count	3	4	n.s.	9	23	*
Male	Count	14	19		6	4	(Phi)
Age	Avg.	44.70	50.91	* (ANOVA)	42.2	43.48	n.s.
Years of experience	Avg.	18.52	23.45	n.s.	13.80	16.70	n.s.
Any study abroad	Count	11	14	n.s.	4	4	n.s.
Holding a postgrad abroad	Count	10	14	n.s.	2	4	n.s.
Scientific output:							
1. SI publications per year of experience (up to 2006)	Avg.	0.70	0.26	** (ANOVA)	0.74	0.59	n.s.
2. Non-indexed publications per year of experience (up to 2006)	Avg.	0.66	0.53	n.s.	1.58	0.90	n.s.
Prizes (cumulative number)	Avg.	2.05	1.39	n.s.	2.58	1.39	n.s.

Notes: ** Difference is significant at 5%; * Difference is significant at 10%.

Table 7A.3   Statistics on researchers and their U–I Linkages

Characteristics of researchers	Indi-cator	Chile			South Africa		
		U–I higher than average	U–I lower than average	Sig.	U–I higher than average	U–I lower than average	Sig.
Sex							
Female	Count	6	1	**	7	3	n.s.
Male	Count	14	19	(phi)	13	19	
Age	Avg.	46.20	50.35	n.s.	40.10	45.68	* (ANOVA)
Years of experience	Avg.	19.15	23.57	n.s.	14.60	16.36	n.s.
Any study abroad	Count	12	13	n.s.	3	5	n.s.
Holding a postgrad abroad	Count	12	12	n.s.	2	4	n.s.
Scientific output:							
1. SI publications per year of experience (up to 2006)	Avg.	0.54	0.36	n.s.	0.57	0.72	n.s.
2. Non-indexed publications per year of experience (up to 2006)	Avg.	0.77	0.38	** (ANOVA)	1.45	0.78	n.s.
Prizes (cumulative number)	Avg.	2.25	1.10	n.s.	3.12	1.28	n.s.

Notes: ** Difference is significant at 5%; * Difference is significant at 10%.

8. Knowledge, science and interactions in South Africa's wine industry

Jo Lorentzen[1]

1 INTRODUCTION

New World wine provides an interesting catch-up story, especially as far as developing-country producers are concerned. Although 'New World' includes, for example, both California's Napa Valley and Chile's Colchagua region, there are obvious differences between the two. Winemakers in the USA, Australia and New Zealand caught up with the European industry leaders, utilizing infrastructure and knowledge assets of advanced industrial economies. By contrast, Argentina, Chile, and South Africa are developing middle-income countries where capabilities of the private and public sectors are much more circumscribed.

Under such circumstances it is not surprising that the dynamics of the wine sector have attracted much attention. Wine is a global and knowledge-intensive industry. Hence there is scope for linkages, and learning might transcend, at least in principle, geographically limited production areas. This chapter addresses the role of linkages between growers and producers and other actors in the wine industry in fostering innovation, an important part of catch-up stories. Such linkages refer primarily to knowledge flows. The question is not only the existence but also the quality of the underlying relationship in such networks. For example, whereas Anderson (ch. 4 in this book) hails the impact and pay-off from investments in research and development (R&D) in Australia's wine industry as impressive, Aylward (2007) cautions that knowledge flows may reflect a supply bias and disregard the needs of smaller producers.

Space may play a role in the way networks come about and operate (for an overview, see Simmie, 2005; for an application to South Africa, see Lorentzen, 2009). Much relevant knowledge is tacit and therefore cannot easily be exchanged over long distances. In addition, since innovation is rarely a stand-alone activity by one actor but a complex learning process involving knowledge flows between multiple actors and also involving social and other intangible assets that are not totally appropriable by any one firm but only available to local firms, it takes place more easily in environments in which people can have face-to-face contacts (for a comprehensive summary of this type of argument, see Asheim and Gertler, 2005). However, there is controversy over the role of proximity for innovation (Markusen, 1999; Iammarino and McCann, 2006). For example, studies of global cities show that key knowledge flows are international and not local. Hence proximity may be helpful, but it is not necessarily a prerequisite for innovation (Simmie et al., 2002). The evidence for South Africa is totally unclear in this regard (Lorentzen et al., 2009).

The role played by public policy in bringing about such linkages is debated as well. For some, it enjoys pride of place. In Argentina's Mendoza region, it was reportedly not so much firm dynamics alone but deliberate public policy choices that transformed a cluster into a learning region (Farinelli, 2007). More specifically, public–private initiatives managed to overcome weak institutional resources and socio-economic fragmentation, and to build bridges between the respective participants that amplified the scale and scope of relevant knowledge resources on which firms based their upgrading (McDermott and Corredoira, ch. 6 in this book). A different finding emerges from work on Chile and Italy, which concluded that the most important feature was the resources at the firms' disposal and the innovative activities in which they engaged. Fostering networking *per se*, through public intervention, was likely to be ineffective in the context of limited knowledge resources and weak innovation activities (Bell and Giuliani, 2007). The little available work on the South African wine industry has mostly eschewed these more analytical questions and merely postulated that the effectiveness of knowledge exchange somehow matters for innovative activity, without addressing cluster dynamics *per se* (for example, Wood and Kaplan, 2005).

This chapter studies innovation in the wine industry of the Western Cape Province in South Africa, a geographically well-defined region of a latecomer economy. It includes the entire value chain from growing grapes to bottling and marketing wine. Its first objective is to understand the relationship between the relevant knowledge infrastructure and innovative activities. Knowledge infrastructure here comprises universities and research institutes whose research and training activities must reflect the requirements of evolving and newly emerging technologies. Firms must internalize such new knowledge and at the same time inform or direct the search for it (Bernardes and da Motta e Albuquerque, 2003). The second objective is to analyze whether and how linkages in and of the wine sector contribute to innovative outcomes. Although acknowledged to be significant in developed countries, linkages – for example, between producers and universities – and the knowledge flows they may (but need not) give rise to, are much less well understood in developing-country contexts (Arocena and Sutz, 2000), and notably in Africa (Kruss, 2005, 2006). Section 2 situates the knowledge infrastructure of the Western Cape Province in the national and international context. Section 3 gives a primer on the South African wine industry and introduces the regional wine innovation system. Section 4 reports the results of a survey of innovative activities in the wine sector. Section 5 concludes.

2   ECONOMY AND KNOWLEDGE INFRASTRUCTURE IN SOUTH AFRICA'S WESTERN CAPE PROVINCE

The Western Cape economy is rather diversified, with activities in the primary sector, manufacturing, and the dominant services sector. The primary sector contributes only 3 percent to the regional economy, but is still the major exporter. It also matters through its influence on land use and the links to agro-processing and tourism. The export composition of the province is in general concentrated on low-growth products with a declining share in world markets (Edwards and Alves, 2006). Innovation is therefore important to differentiate product portfolios in the traditional sectors and move them upmarket and to open up and defend niches in newer, more dynamic activities (Western Cape Provincial Treasury, 2007).

The Cape Town city-region, which includes smaller surrounding municipalities that are part of South Africa's wine-producing regions (Stellenbosch, Drakenstein, Swartland, Theewaterskloof, Overstrand), exhibits the typical agglomeration economies of large metropolitan areas and their hinterland. The city-region accounts for 90 percent of the regional GDP. Per capita GDP can be compared to that of Mexico City and Naples. In 2002 this was more than 50 percent higher than the national average. The province has among the highest education levels in the country. Dynamic sectors in the regional economy are increasingly knowledge and skill intensive (OECD, 2008).

Agro-food is among the most dynamic value chains in the area. Food processing is the second-largest employer, the biggest exporter, and produces about a fifth of manufacturing value added. In 2005, wine alone accounted for 2.3 percent of Cape Town's GDP. Structural weaknesses affecting the agro-food value chain include insufficient inter- and intra-industry linkages in distribution, marketing, tourism, logistics, and transportation. Climate change, especially its adverse effects on an already highly water-stressed area, is expected to imperil any agricultural activity

Table 8.1   *Wine sector-relevant R&D and science in the Western Cape:*
              specialization and weight of research fields (2004)

	R&D investments		Scientific publications	
	Specialization index	Share in nat. total	Specialization index	Share in nat. total
Natural sciences				
Biological sciences	1.08	18.85	1.13	37.23
Earth sciences	–	–	1.06	34.83
Agricultural sciences	1.26	22.01	–	–
Environmental sciences	1.42	24.79	–	–
Engineering sciences				
Industrial biotechnology and food sciences	–	–	1.22	40.00
Chemical engineering	–	–	1.40	46.10
Information, computer, communication technologies	1.05	18.43	–	–

Note: The specialization index denotes the relative specialization of the province
compared to the rest of the country. A value of 2.16 means that, for example, R&D
investments in mathematics are 116 percent higher than the national average. Missing
values mean that the province is not specialized in that particular field.

Source: Lorentzen (2007).

(ibid.). It is in overcoming and adapting to these challenges that innovation can play an important role in the provincial economy.

At the national level, the knowledge infrastructure in the province is second only to Gauteng Province, which dominates economic activity in the country. The Western Cape is strong on R&D spending and scientific publications, but produces few patents relative to its economic weight (Lorentzen, 2007, 2009). Nationally, the province has the highest relative share of internet connections and telephones, along with the most highly educated population in the country – and therefore diffuses innovations more effectively than most regions in the country (DST, 2005).

A number of research fields relevant to the wine industry are present in the province (Table 8.1). In addition, the agriculture and food industries also feature as important producers and users of technology. They produce and use between a quarter and a fifth of all relevant patents, respectively, in the country (Lorentzen, 2007).

The focus of this chapter makes it necessary to understand the research competences of individual universities. The province hosts four

Table 8.2   *Research profiles of the universities in the Western Cape: specialization and weight, 2004*

Research field	UCT		US		UWC	
	S.I.	Weight	S.I.	Weight	S.I.	Weight
Natural, agriculture and forestry sciences						
Chemical sciences	–	–	–	–	2.77	4.55
Biological sciences	–	–	1.04	16.90	2.23	4.40
Earth sciences	1.62	28.80	–	–	1.13	2.09
Agricultural, veterinary, environmental sciences	–	–	1.89	14.66	–	–
Engineering and technology						
Industrial biotechnology and food sciences	–	–	2.29	40.00	–	–
Chemical and process engineering	1.19	27.90	–	–	–	–
Biomedical engineering (incl. biomedical technology)	1.04	17.01	–	–	8.82	14.97
Information, computing and communication sciences	1.42	6.52	–	–	2.78	1.34

Note: UCT = University of Cape Town, US = University of Stellenbosch, UWC = University of the Western Cape. S.I. refers to specialization index; see also Table 8.1. Weight refers to share in national total. Data are based on publications in refereed journals. Missing values mean that the province is not specialized in that particular field.

Source: Lorentzen (2007).

universities, three of which keep records that allow for an analysis at the institutional level. Table 8.2 shows where research profiles cater for the demand for knowledge in the wine sector. But the Western Cape not only does well relative to a (low) national average. It has a world-class reputation in life sciences, biology, environment and ecology. South Africa is one of only three countries in the world to host a laboratory of the International Centre for Genetic Engineering and Biotechnology (ICGEB), located at the University of Cape Town. Biotechnology is an important emerging activity of particular relevance to the wine industry (OECD, 2008).

In sum, knowledge intensity is an important feature of the Western Cape economy. The province relatively and absolutely attracts more R&D investments, undertakes more scientific activity, and is better at technology dissemination than any other province in the country except Gauteng. So there clearly is knowledge, including knowledge relevant for the wine industry. The question is whether and how it flows through what sort of linkages, and if such flows contribute to innovation in the industry, because only then are linkages productively useful. At least in general, this is not the case; interactions between knowledge producers and users are weak (Kruss, 2005; OECD, 2008).

3   THE SOUTH AFRICAN WINE INDUSTRY

Until the 1990s the South African wine industry did not face much competition at home (due to the absence of imports) or abroad (because it hardly exported). Supported by a protectionist regulatory regime, it produced low-quality (mostly white) bulk wines at inflated prices for domestic consumption. Hence, as in Chile and Argentina or in Eastern Europe at about the same time, innovation played little role because there was nothing and no one with which or whom to catch up. The liberalization of the economy in the 1990s changed that profoundly. Although there continued to be very little import penetration, the withdrawal of support for artificially high prices implied that grape growers and winemakers had to change their ways to survive. All of a sudden catch-up, which hitherto had been pursued only by a handful of estates that for different reasons had remained outside the central producer cooperative, KWV, in which membership was compulsory, became a necessity and the only feasible alternative to a demise of much of the industry.[2]

Industry players got together in the late 1990s to agree on a strategy to improve international competitiveness. Among the key actors was Winetech, the Wine Industry Network for Expertise and Technology, which sought to develop an inclusive strategy for an 'innovation driven, market directed, globally competitive and highly profitable industry' (Winetech, 1999). The document had the merit of suggesting priorities that needed to be discussed by the industry in order to survive a much more competitive environment (Ponte and Ewert, 2007). Innovation was key among them. It is here that the demand for science originates. Both vineyard and cellar management required improvement in the interest of exploiting cleaner and more scientific winemaking for better styles. This included a whole array of new technologies. Since compared to their Old World competitors, South African winemakers had been relatively less regulated as far as *terroir* is concerned – that is, *terroir* is an aspiration more than a tightly prescribed limitation on who may grow what where – there was at least in this respect also more scope for experimentation and innovation (ibid.).

The industry has undoubtedly changed in the last decade. South Africa has some 4,000 primary wine producers and 560 cellars which crush grapes. In 2007 they produced 730 million liters of wine, excluding wine for brandy, distilling wine, and grape juice concentrate and grape juice, on just over 100,000 hectares. In 2005 South Africa accounted for some 3 percent of world wine production, similar to Chile (2.8 percent), and below Australia (5.1 percent) and Argentina (5.4 percent). About 50 percent was sold locally, 42 percent was exported, and the remainder added to stock. Some 95 percent of the area under cultivation is in the Western Cape Province around Cape Town; the rest is along the Orange River in the Northern Cape close to the border with Namibia. The largest and internationally best-known wine regions include Worcester, Paarl, Stellenbosch, and Robertson. The most prominent varieties are Chenin Blanc, Colombard, Chardonnay, and Sauvignon Blanc (85 percent of white), and Cabernet Sauvignon, Shiraz, Merlot, and Pinotage (79 percent of red) (SAWIS, nd).

In 1997–2007, yields therefore improved substantially. Quality also improved – between 2001 and 2007 the production of wine of origin increased by more than 80 percent and now accounts for more than half of total production, much like noble varieties. Accordingly, exports as a share of production more than doubled in 1997–2007. By comparison, imports are negligible and account for merely 4 percent of exports. From 2000 the industry faced increasing cost pressures (ibid.). Like its peers, it suffered from the global red wine glut, exacerbated by a strengthening rand in the mid-2000s. Exports decreased, and some bankruptcies ensued. Overreliance on only a few export markets and a higher exposure to less-resilient vine varieties continue to present risks to the industry. Marketing has so far not widely succeeded in pushing local wines into higher and more profitable price categories (for a detailed treatment of these issues, see Ponte and Ewert, 2009).

There are three main groups interacting in the Western Cape wine industry's knowledge economy: the producers of knowledge (universities and research institutes), knowledge intermediaries (industry bodies) and the users of knowledge (growers, winemakers, and support industries). Knowledge producers provide material for publications, which in turn disseminate this knowledge to industry. Knowledge producers are also

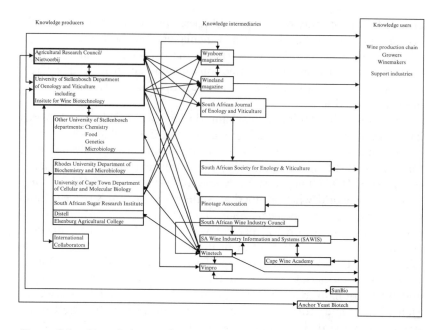

Figure 8.1   Knowledge producers, intermediaries and users

engaged in projects and commissioned research for industry bodies, which in turn disseminate this knowledge to industry. This is a two-way process, as industry bodies also feed back industry requirements to the universities and research institutions. Researchers and industry associations also form partnerships, which benefit publications because they keep in touch with industry needs, and benefit industry associations as a media channel.

In addition to these conventional flows of knowledge, knowledge producers in some cases have direct contact with industry, for example through commercialization ventures, collaborative research, joint staff, or other connections (Figure 8.1). The main producers of knowledge are the Agricultural Research Council's (ARC's) Nietvoorbij Institute and the University of Stellenbosch's Department of Oenology and Viticulture. These form the core of a network of collaborative research that includes other departments within the University of Stellenbosch, other South African universities, colleges, and research institutions, private sector firms, and international universities and research institutes.

This research is disseminated through a number of channels. The two major channels are through publications and industry associations. For example, both Nietvoorbij and the University of Stellenbosch are major contributors to *Wynboer, Wineland,* and the *South African Journal of*

Enology and Viticulture, the three major industry-linked publications. Many contributions are collaborative research between Stellenbosch and Nietvoorbij. Dissemination through industry associations includes partnerships with the Pinotage Association and commissioned research through Winetech. Winetech is at the fulcrum of many of these activities. In collaboration with all relevant stakeholders it establishes priorities for the industry, such as virus infections or *terroir* optimization. Industry players submit applications for funding for research proposals related to these priorities, which are evaluated in a competitive process.

Within the set of knowledge intermediaries there is a parallel network of partnerships and interactions. The South African Wine Industry Council, South African Wine Information and Systems (SAWIS), Winetech, VinPro, and the Cape Wine Academy form a cluster of networked organizations through commissioned research, shared projects, and shared organizational structures and affiliations. This cluster is loosely linked to the publications; *Wynboer* and *Wineland* are partner publications linked to VinPro, and the *South African Journal of Enology and Viticulture* is linked to the South African Society for Enology and Viticulture. Knowledge producers and knowledge users also have direct links. For example, the University of Stellenbosch jointly with industry partners runs a start-up venture (SunBio), while Nietvoorbij conducts collaborative research with a private firm (Anchor Yeast).

This description of the wine industry and the linkages between its various actors has been rather high level. But there may of course be a difference between how a system is supposed to work – its nominal design – and how it actually works. The following section provides a micro perspective on linkages and innovative behavior.

4   INNOVATIVE ACTIVITIES IN THE WINE SECTOR

The empirical research upon which this chapter is based analyzed innovative activities by growers, estates, and intermediary organizations in the wine industry, thus spanning primary, secondary and tertiary, and also low, medium and high, technology- and skill-intensive activities. The question is how knowledge flows in interactions between individual firms as well as between firms and other organizations in a specific sector contribute to innovative outcomes for the sector as a whole. The analysis shares a few similarities with the investigation of the Colchagua Valley wine cluster in Chile, by Giuliani and Bell (2005) but comes to a different conclusion.

Technical change in the wine sector has different sources and it does not fit neatly into Pavitt's framework (1984), according to which suppliers drive technical change in agriculture. Grape cultivation and winemaking are of course traditional activities, yet their pursuit presently also involves high technology and very advanced skills, and the driver of technological upgrading is not necessarily, as per Pavitt's suggestion, a supplier who offers an advanced piece of machinery; by contrast, the change may well be directed from within the firm (see also Hatzichronoglou, 1997; Lall, 2000; Von Tunzelmann and Acha, 2005; Alcaide-Marzal and Tortajada-Esparza, 2007). This qualification is important. If technological learning in the wine industry were only supplier driven and if the industry were not knowledge intensive, its catch-up would hardly be a spectacular tale. It would also have little to offer as a potential model from which other sectors can learn. By contrast, the dynamics of the wine industry are such that innovations also take place independently of suppliers and in direct consultation with relevant knowledge producers as well as in-house experimentation. Herein lies the foundation of the remarkable trajectory of New World wine producers (close) to the technological frontier in global wine production.

Data

Winetech helped identify innovative firms among its membership, based both on their track record and their presumed willingness to participate in the study. The survey captured 23 members of Winetech (30 percent of total membership in 2005), including some of the most innovative growers and winemakers in the industry. They consisted of small independent growers for whom grape growing is but one agricultural activity, growers who were part of former cooperatives that are organized around a joint cellar, those that are owned by vertically integrated groups, estates that cultivate their own grapes, and producers that source all their grapes externally. It thus reflected the diverse industrial composition of the industry and included both relatively small and very large players.

The firms received a 13-page questionnaire consisting of 94 questions and including an explanation of its purpose for the benefit of the interviewee, along with a glossary of technical terms, explaining the meaning of the various types of innovative activities and R&D surveyed. Following a brief profile of the firm and its main activities, the questionnaire probed information about skills and competences; sources of finance; the motivations for, effects of, and obstacles to innovation; the role of intellectual property rights; and the nature and importance of linkages to other actors in the innovation system. In addition, each interviewee described at least one innovative activity in detail. This could be a successful, failed or ongoing activity, and be new to firm, new to market, or new to world.

The questionnaire followed the *Oslo Manual* of the OECD (OECD, 2005; Bloch, 2007). One or two researchers visited each farm or estate at least once and compiled the questionnaire together with the owner (in the case of farms) or the managing director (who often doubled up as the winemaker) or another senior member of the management (in the case of cellars) between late 2005 and early 2006. Each visit on average lasted between two and three hours. The conversations were taped and summarized into protocols that each interviewee vetted for accuracy.

This process produced two types of data. The first is contained in a database similar to those generated by the Community Innovation Survey (CIS). It comprises responses that are binary (yes/no), on an integer Likert scale from 0 to 2 (for 'no', 'some', 'high' relevance), percentages, or verbally descriptive. The second is the qualitative interview protocols themselves that provide context to the quantitative data. Spatial information is elicited by questions that query the geographic location (in the Western Cape, in South Africa, in the world) of all possible determinants of innovation.

Analysis of the Empirical Findings

Description
On average, the interviewed enterprises were well established and had been in existence for almost three decades. Seven enterprises grew grapes; all others produced wine or did both. Four out of five were domestically owned. Most were small and medium-sized enterprises (SMEs) – 61 percent had fewer than 100 employees, 87 percent had fewer than 250. In line with the industry average, exports accounted for 39 percent of sales. Two-thirds of employees had finished compulsory schooling, 21 percent had completed secondary school, and 14 percent had gone on to university. Almost a third of the staff were involved in innovative activities, meaning that their pursuit was not limited to the most highly educated employees (see Table 8.3).

The most important means by which the enterprises aimed to cope with (international) competition was to increase or maintain market share, enter new markets, increase the range of goods and services as well as visibility of exposure for products. Clearly this reflects the general experience of the sector post-liberalization, which is the base of strategies for catching up. They also aimed to improve the quality of goods and services, and reduce labor costs. Finally, customer relationship management – something that was found lacking in earlier analyses (see Wood and Kaplan, 2005) – and internal communication also featured strongly in their motivations for engaging in innovative activities.

Table 8.3   Basic sample statistics

Questionnaire themes	Mean values
Profile	
Age	27 years
Ownership	Domestic: 78%
	MNC: 19%
	Subsidiaries: 9%
Employees	1–9: 4%
	10–49: 35%
	50–99: 22%
	100–249: 26%
	250–499: 0%
	500–999: 9%
	1000+: 4%
Exports/sales	39%
Human capital	
< Grade 9	66%
≥ Grade 9 to matric	21%
> Matric to undergraduate	13%
Postgraduate	1%
% employees involved in innovative activities	29%

Innovations – 75 per cent of which were new to the firm – had a positive impact on sales. In more than half the cases, innovation did not increase efficiency, and in two-thirds of the cases it had no impact on employment, suggesting that the immediate impact of innovation lies more in quality upgrading and the like. There was hardly anything that was perceived as hampering innovation; knowledge factors did not feature at all. Since all interviewed producers aim to sell in very competitive markets with a premium on knowledge assets, this implies that relevant knowledge exists and that it is accessible. Some degree of interaction is therefore likely; earlier research confirmed as much (ibid.). The following subsection provides more detail. In fact, the interviewees implicitly reported a con- ducive environment for innovation, except that there was some concern about uncertain demand. Although not directly comparable, the sample reported here gave rise to findings with a different emphasis from an inves- tigation undertaken at the beginning of the decade (Aylward, 2003). In that study, respondents reported that R&D coordination was only poorly (25 percent) or moderately (68.8 percent) effective, and a large majority (62.5 percent) charged that information flows within the industry were irregular.

In terms of the intensity of knowledge flows, the market was the most important source: competitors, customers, suppliers, and consultants attracted a medium to high score. In the public sector, only universities were of some importance, albeit nowhere near the score attributed to elements of the value chain. But what also mattered – and this is important for our analysis – was what one might call open sources of information such as conferences and journals, fairs and exhibitions, and sector associations. Intense relationships tended to be frequent, too, but the opposite is not the case. Thus, there was relatively frequent (but not intense) interaction with research institutes, innovation support services, and science councils. The internet, patent databases, regulatory agencies, and standardization agencies were also regularly consulted. Except for consultants, fairs and exhibitions, and conferences and journals, the cost of accessing relevant knowledge was low.

The direction of knowledge flows was for the most part two-way. Hence, on average, firms were neither solely the originators nor the destination of information, which, in turn, was a mixture of tacit and codified. Although codification affects the entire wine value chain, there is relatively more scope for it in the cellar than in the vineyards where idiosyncratic factors are more prevalent (Giuliani, 2007). Finally, the enterprises reported on the geographic origin of knowledge. They distinguished between regional, national and international. Both upstream and downstream and across all agents with which they interacted, regional and international mattered much more than national. For an intensely space-bound cluster with no competition and only few supply relationships from other parts of the country but with high exposure to international markets, this was to be expected. The regional context is most important for knowledge flows emanating from competitors, suppliers, universities and sector associations. For customers, conferences and journals, fairs and exhibitions as well as the internet, the international realm is equally (or more) important.

In sum, relevant knowledge exists in the wine sectors and is being exchanged and accessed, both internally and externally. This coincides with innovative outcomes and their impact on sales, which suggests that it is worth probing this point in more depth. The next subsection provides more detail.

Insights from the interviews with growers and winemakers

In its most elementary way the wine industry is composed of growers and winemakers. Both groups operate in a very competitive global market which over the last decade or so managed effectively to make quality the minimum common denominator of the industry rather than, as in the past, a selective achievement of individual estates. The arrival of new competitors – for example, from Australia, Chile and Argentina – on the world market, alongside massive technological intensification of growing, harvesting, fermentation, blending and maturation of wine, has turned up the heat on growers and estates alike. Estates need quality grapes to make high-quality wine, and growers need to escape the diminishing returns associated with producing bulk wine. This means that upstream techno-logical demands are high as well, despite the fact that grape farming is of course a primary sector activity.

The question is whether growers and winemakers are linked to each other as well as to other relevant actors through interactions that have productive outcomes, and whether science and innovation play a role in the trajectory of the industry. In general, not a single interviewee professed to operate in splendid isolation from his peers.[3] Interactions were impor-tant both as an aspiration – 'We need to exchange knowledge to learn and upgrade' – and a reality – 'When I undertake an experiment that fails I tell all the neighboring farmers so that they don't repeat it'. Not only do winemakers attend industry events such as a workshop on innovative practices in California, they also regularly visit industry leaders, especially in Australia, to familiarize themselves with their practices. There were hardly any exceptions to the scant importance accorded to proprietary knowledge. 'Open culture' and 'international fraternity of winemakers' were among the terms used to describe this phenomenon. To some extent this is obviously linked to the fact that it is ultimately impossible to repli-cate wines away from their territory which limits the possibility to exploit a competitor's insights to encroach upon their turf (as opposed to taking them on in a fair contest). The other reason is that winemakers seem to feel that cooperation, including across borders, enhances the collective returns to the industry. If the sector produces good wines, the world will drink more of them, which in turn is likely to benefit the winemakers collectively and individually.

Competitors were important in different ways. Especially winemakers from abroad, mainly in Australia and Europe, acted as senior partners or otherwise provided inspiration to experiment with new technological ideas. For example, one winemaker picked up the idea from his French peers of using a small amount of Viognier (a white varietal) to soften the harsh tannins of certain reds, in this case Pinotage. Another struck a long-term royalty agreement to absorb the tacit knowledge associated with making sparkling wines. Someone else imported from Spain the idea of designing a cellar that does away with pumping the fermenting wine, instead exploiting gravity through an elaborate overhead crane system, thus aiming to produce softer wines.

Growers also share knowledge, albeit less internationally. This includes all aspects of vineyard management. For example, one grower planted vines in between lucerne to improve soil quality. Several growers experimented with varietal specific pruning methods and passed on resulting insights to organized grower groups both in their immediate vicinity and beyond. Growers also discuss cultivars themselves. In addition, they pooled resources to strengthen complementary assets in training and in marketing.

The supply of inputs such as chemicals or fertilizers to growers, and of capital equipment such as satellite systems to estates, is often associated with training or advice. This may apply to the correct use of labeling machinery or to cold soaking during fermentation processes to improve wine taste and color, and is no different from other industries. What is special to the wine industry is that estates certainly try to improve these inputs. For example, two estates managed to contribute to the improvement of the resolution quality of infrared imagery beyond what was readily available on the market, one in-house and the other in cooperation with VinPro, a service and lobby organization of the wine industry. Another cellar undertook joint research on plastic bottles with a supplier.

Some consultants provided relatively mundane services such as label or website design. But others affected transfer of technology that estates themselves would not have been able to engineer. Their inputs covered the entire value chain from soil profiles to water management and emerging taste preferences and resulting marketing strategies in major markets. Some consultants had arm's-length relationships with the estates and were hired on an as-needed basis. Others worked with the industry through sector associations such as VinPro and therefore had longer-term relationships with their clients. Some international winemakers morphed from competitors to consultants and joined the boards of larger local estates in an advisory capacity. Hence many of these interactions were knowledge intensive.

Marketing agents and export managers played similar roles to consultants. Most importantly, they advised on market trends, including which blends to feature. Having largely mastered the quality game, the sector on the whole seemed to pay more attention to marketing. Both growers and estates had formed joint marketing companies with competitors, also to increase their bargaining power *vis-à-vis* retailers. One even set up a distribution company involving other estates from a handful of countries to retain margins, and experimented with internet distribution to cut out the middlemen. Another created a joint venture with a large global distributor to gain faster market entry without depending too much on the whims of retailers. Compared to traditional ways of marketing and selling wine, these activities are certainly innovative and reveal a profound engagement with market dynamics.

Customers – either retailers or end-consumers – also played an important role. Through their insistence on reduced customer response times, retailers and restaurants inspired estates to adopt just-in-time methods for inventory management and bottling. They also fed back comments on quality and market acceptance of exported wines. One estate used sizeable numbers of tourist visitors to trial new products before launching them in the wider market. Another remarked that customer feedback could be captured much more systematically than is currently done. For growers, the most important customer is the cellar. Cellars advise growers from whom they source – regardless of ownership – on everything from vineyard practices such as root improvement to market trends, and exercise quality control. This can be pretty high-tech, as when leading academics start working for industry and employ their expertise, for example, in support of *terroir* optimization. Estates also organize trials and experiments on associated farms from which the growers benefit in terms of yields and cost.

The previous subsection showed that interactions with the research sector were much sparser than those with the market. The interviews confirmed that only a subset of industry players engaged in R&D proper and interacted to this effect with private or public research institutes. But it would be wrong to deduce from this that university–industry linkages are somehow marginal. Thanks to the strong commitment to knowledge sharing in the industry and the existence of generally well-functioning sector bodies, the results of these interactions are for the most part widely disseminated. Users and producers of knowledge collaborate on the setting of research agendas and in part execute research projects jointly. The core technologies are generic to the industry and are disseminated to (almost) all the firms that want to benefit from them. Therefore, the role of science is collectively important, even though in our sample not every single grape farm or estate is party to a direct relationship with a university or a research institute. Similarly, Giuliani and Rabellotti (ch. 7 in this volume) show that although only relatively few South African wine researchers are linked into the international scientific community, their effect on domestic industry is widespread. Thanks to intermediary institutions such as Winetech that link producers and users of knowledge and that act as two-way conduits of information and knowledge between the sector and the universities, knowledge absorption has low barriers to entry.

For example, one estate experimented with the ARC on partial root zone drying, which resulted in 50 percent savings of water consumption. Relevant research institutes included not only those in the area, but also the University of Pretoria which engaged with one grower, supported by

VinPro, in research on irrigation management and weather stations, and with an estate on a particular virus infestation (white lice). Particularly the large operators are keen to attract graduates from the University of Stellenbosch and the agricultural vocational training institute, Elsenburg College, some of whom they might have already hosted as interns while they were still studying. Foreign students also come and share insights. Although it is rare that a farm will have an independent relationship with a viticulturist from Stellenbosch, this relationship typically exists through the cellar. Farmers do have direct relationships with scientists when the universities or research institutes undertake experiments on their farms. Some experiments yield immediately tangible results and thus benefit the farmer. Collaborative R&D does on occasion take place across borders, for example, between a local estate and French oenologists on tannin management.

The sector associations presented in this section have a mandate for the entire industry. So VinPro advises on new market trends. In addition, it supports more limited but industrywide initiatives such as the Pinotage Association as well as spatially more limited cooperations such as the Paarl Vineyard Study Group. Hence regardless of whether technology is high or low and of appeal to just a few or the whole industry, mechanisms exist to ensure that the associated knowledge reaches everybody who is interested in learning about it.

This does not mean that there are no problems. One estate was critical that the importance of R&D for the future of the wine industry is underestimated and consequently not given enough attention. What would be needed is a collective understanding how much sector entities invest in the development of new markets, how much into R&D, and so forth, in order to arrive at sectorwide strategies in favor of specific research objectives. But to achieve that, the institutional landscape is too fragmented. At the other extreme, a grower remarked that research is easy neither to access nor to digest. One grower found that in the absence of more comprehensive knowledge sharing in the industry, many players opt for go-it-alone strategies that are likely to be suboptimal. This was echoed by a winemaker who commented that while individuals talk across enterprises, there is little formal collaboration that could help address collective problems that estates battle to solve by themselves.

But none the less, on the whole the system is receptive to new ideas. Whether an estate experiments with teamwork to improve internal knowledge flows, employs gas chromatography to reveal consumer preferences in tastings, or grafts mild cultivars on wild rootstock in the interest of reducing susceptibility to disease, or experiments with cultivar-specific yeasts, it is likely that lessons learnt – whether good or bad – will eventually become sectorwide knowledge. This clearly sets the wine sector apart from many other activities.

5   CONCLUSIONS

The focus of this chapter was on the nature and role of linkages between relevant actors in the wine sector as well as on the knowledge flows such interactions facilitated, in order to understand the relationship between the knowledge infrastructure and those linkages on the one hand, and innovation on the other. It also raised the issue of spatial proximity, namely whether being close to one another was a necessary condition for such knowledge exchange or not. Finally, the question was what, if anything, policy had to do with this being a success story.

The empirical analysis showed that the Western Cape wine industry is supported by a relevant knowledge infrastructure and that the knowledge exchanged in networks to which industry actors are part is productively useful and effectively disseminated among firms that search for and are engaged in innovative activities. The economic logic of this finding lies in the collective rationale for industry upgrading. That is, the increasing vertical disintegration of cellars or producer-wholesalers and growers in the Western Cape (Ponte and Ewert, 2009) implies that effective knowledge dissemination to small players is a necessary condition to achieve and retain world quality levels. Therefore, not only do growers exert a pull effect on emerging technological opportunities, but also cellars have an incentive to push for technology transfer upstream so as to secure the viability of their value chain.

This finding suggests that there is no intrinsic logic whereby an initially low-capability grower needs to remain in the cold, provided he manages to become part of a functioning supply chain where customers look for innovations which also need upgrading upstream. In South Africa, where emerging black growers have by definition low capabilities (and were not included in the sample), this is an important insight for an industry that is still almost entirely controlled by whites. For policy it means that black growers and winemakers must enjoy access to these knowledge networks through appropriate linkages.

It is thus clear that knowledge relevant to all aspects of the value chain has been transmitted throughout the sector between the various actors. What mattered centrally to this process was that despite an undisputed differential distribution of resources and capabilities among and within growers, cellars and estates, incentives for individual learning as a precondition for collective success existed. This ensured that new knowledge, insights, and lessons were disseminated. This does not mean that access to and absorption of knowledge was cost free and unproblematic. On the contrary, the wine industry has its leaders and its laggards, and the latter evidently struggle in keeping up with technological change. But they are not alone in this because effective intermediary organizations such as Winetech, which both promote supply-driven and harness demand-driven innovation, reconciling their respective outcomes in widespread dissemination, help them not just in selecting relevant knowledge but also in understanding and assimilating it. This ensured that South African producers did not just execute so-called best practice developed elsewhere but mediated such insights through local knowledge. This is why it is so important to mirror global technological advance through appropriate science and technology policies (Giuliani, 2007).

These intermediary organizations are key for the exploitation of science for innovation. Many industry players do not have independent relationships with universities or research institutes. Such relationships would be difficult to negotiate especially for smaller players and they would also be rather costly. Hence it would be totally inappropriate to assess the relevance of science for catch-up in the wine industry only by 'measuring' the incidence and frequency of university–industry linkages. What matters is that even small growers have a voice in determining research agendas to which the wine sector commits knowledge producers by participating in the relevant bodies that discuss problems affecting all or part of the industry, and that they likewise benefit from the results of the scientific endeavor through dissemination by those same intermediary organizations. In this, the Western Cape is not alone – for example, the Italian wine-producing region of Piedmont is also home to a dense research system whose interactions involve and benefit the smaller players (Morrison and Rabellotti, 2007).

The evidence presented here also shows that the significance of spatial proximity is relative rather than absolute. How and how much it matters depends in part on the resources enterprises can avail themselves of to overcome the disadvantages distance poses for learning and upgrading. With few resources, proximity becomes more important. Thus, it is much easier for grape growers to learn from a study group set up by their peers that meets in the same neighborhood than from a grower halfway round the world. But the evidence also showed that estates with the requisite resources can and do participate in strategically important global knowledge networks. This includes peers, competitors, and even consumers in far-away parts of the globe. What matters are whether insights generated in such networks are disseminated to the local study group. In the wine sector they are, partly thanks to the mandate of sector associations.

So proximity is undeniably helpful, but it is neither a necessary nor a sufficient condition for the catch-up of the sector as a whole. In fact, if proximity came at the expense of external openness, it would clearly be detrimental.

The influence of policy on catch-up has been muted. Of course, policy played the key role in liberalizing the agricultural sector in the 1990s. It also created a framework that allowed the industry to set up organizations to support it in its drive to improve quality, gain global market share, and increase returns. It further promoted scientific capabilities that are relevant for the wine sector even though they are not directly or exclusively aimed at it. Yet although some of these organizations receive public funding, it would be an exaggeration to say that either national or provincial governments are aggressively targeting coordination or information failures in the industry. By contrast, the industry largely takes care of these issues itself. This is possible because the wine sector commands sizeable resources and avails itself of significant capabilities. It is no contradiction that until not so long ago it produced plenty of bad wine because it was none the less a highly organized industry that was largely successful in what it was trying to achieve, namely acceptable returns to all its members. The influx of new talent and sizeable investments post-liberalization only strengthened existing capabilities.

In sum, knowledge sharing was key for the success of the wine industry. That it happened had to do with the introduction of the relevant incentives through liberalization of the sector and the impressive capabilities that resided in the sector, along with new ones being built up, and the creation of new institutions aimed at identifying strategic knowledge and facilitating relevant dissemination around it. The lesson for catch-up in other activities is that very much hinges on the interaction between the exposure to global competition and the constitution and structure of the sector. If it is highly fragmented and if proprietary knowledge plays a big role in firms' success, policy will have to address much more intricate coordination and other market failures than in this case. By implication, governments will have to have the requisite capabilities to do so successfully.

NOTES

1. This research would not have been possible without the support of Winetech and the growers and winemakers who generously gave of their time. Junette Davids played a key role in coordinating the larger project on which this analysis draws. Bryan Dunn, Jeanne-Marie Tucker, and Michael Gastrow provided research assistance. Anabel Marin and the editors of this volume commented on first drafts of this chapter. The usual disclaimer applies.

2. For an account of the institutional changes in the wine sector accompanying the opening up of the South African economy, see especially Ponte and Ewert (2007) and also Wood and Kaplan (2005).
3. All people interviewed were male.

REFERENCES

Alcaide-Marzal, J. and E. Tortajada-Esparza (2007), 'Innovation assessment in traditional industries. A proposal of aesthetic innovation indicators', *Scientometrics*, **72** (1), 33–57.

Arocena, R. and J. Sutz (2000), 'Looking at national systems of innovation from the South', *Industry and Innovation*, **7** (1), 55–75.

Asheim, B.T. and M.S. Gertler (2005), 'The geography of innovation: regional innovation systems', in J. Fagerberg, D.C. Mowery and R.R. Nelson (eds), *The Oxford Handbook of Innovation*, Oxford: Oxford University Press, pp. 291–311.

Aylward, D.K. (2003), 'A documentary of innovation support among New World wine producers', *Journal of Wine Research*, **14** (1), 31–43.

Aylward, D. (2007), 'Innovation and inertia: the emerging dislocation of imperatives within the Australian wine industry', *International Journal of Technology and Globalisation*, **3** (2/3), 246–62.

Bell, M. and E. Giuliani (2007), 'Catching up in the global wine industry: innovation systems, cluster knowledge networks and firm-level capabilities in Italy and Chile', *International Journal of Technology and Globalisation*, **3** (2/3), 197–223.

Bernardes, A.T. and E. da Motta e Albuquerque (2003), 'Cross-over, thresholds, and interactions between science and technology: lessons for less-developed countries', *Research Policy*, **32** (5), 865–85.

Bloch, C. (2007), 'Assessing recent developments in innovation measurement: the third edition of the Oslo Manual', *Science and Public Policy*, **34** (1), 23–34.

DST (Department of Science and Technology) (2005), *Regional Contributions to the South African Technology Achievement Index*, Unit for Local Innovation, Government Sectoral Programmes and Coordination, accessed 28 February 2007 at www.dst.gov.za.

Edwards, L. and P. Alves (2006), 'South Africa's export performance: determinants of export supply', *South African Journal of Economics*, **74** (9), 473–500.

Farinelli, F. (2007), 'The awakening of the sleeping giant: export growth and technological catch-up of the Argentine wine industry,' *International Journal of Technology and Globalisation*, **3** (2/3), 179–96.

Giuliani, E. (2007), 'The wine industry: persistence of tacit knowledge or increased codification? Some implications for catching-up countries', *International Journal of Technology and Globalisation*, **3** (2/3), 138–54.

Giuliani, E. and M. Bell (2005), 'The micro-determinants of meso-level learning and innovation: evidence from a Chilean wine cluster', *Research Policy*, **34** (1), 47–68.

Hatzichronoglou, T. (1997), 'Revision of the high-technology sector and product classification', STI working papers 1997/2 OCDE/GD(97)216, OECD, Paris.

Iammarino, S. and P. McCann (2006), 'The structure and evolution of industrial clusters: transactions, technology, and knowledge spillovers', *Research Policy*, **35** (7), 1018–36.

Kruss, G. (2005), *Working Partnerships: Higher Education, Industry and Innovation: Financial or Intellectual Imperatives*, Cape Town, South Africa: HSRC Press.

Kruss, G. (ed.) (2006), *Creating Knowledge Networks*, Cape Town, South Africa: HSRC Publishers.

Lall, S. (2000), 'The technological structure and performance of developing country manufactured exports, 1985–98', *Oxford Development Studies*, **28** (3), 337–69.

Lorentzen, J. (2007), *Regional and Local Innovation Systems. A Study on Behalf of NACI*, Cape Town, South Africa: Human Sciences Research Council.

Lorentzen, J. (2009), 'The geography of innovation in South Africa: a first cut', *International Journal of Technological Learning, Innovation and Development*, **2** (3), 210–29.

Lorentzen, J., T. Mugadza and S. Robinson (2009), 'Innovation in South African city-regions: can we explain it?', mimeo, HSRC, Cape Town.

Markusen, A. (1999), 'Fuzzy concepts, scanty evidence, policy distance: the case for rigour and policy relevance in critical regional studies', *Regional Studies*, **37** (6/7), 869–84.

Morrison, A. and R. Rabellotti (2007), 'The role of research in wine: the emergence of a regional research area in an Italian wine production system', *International Journal of Technology and Globalisation*, **3** (2/3), 155–78.

OECD (Organization for Economic Co-operation and Development) (2005), 'Oslo Manual, draft of the third edition', mimeo OECD, Paris.

OECD (2008), *Cape Town, South Africa, OECD Territorial Reviews*, Paris: OECD.

Pavitt, K. (1984), 'Sectoral patterns of technical change: towards a taxonomy and a theory', *Research Policy*, **13** (6), 343–73.

Ponte, S. and J. Ewert (2007), 'South African wine – an industry in ferment', Tralac working paper 8/2007, accessed 17 March 2008 at www.tralac.org.

Ponte, S. and J. Ewert (2009), 'Which way is "up" in upgrading? Trajectories of change in the value chain for South African wine', *World Development*, **37** (10), 1637–50.

SAWIS (SA Wine Industry Information and Systems), (nd), South African Wine Industry Statistics, accessed 28 November 2007 at www.sawis.co.za.

Simmie, J. (2005), 'Innovation and space: a critical review of the literature', *Regional Studies*, **39** (6), 789–804.

Simmie, J., J. Sennett, P. Wood and D. Hart (2002), 'Innovation in Europe: a tale of networks, knowledge and trade in five cities', *Regional Studies*, **36** (1), 47–64.

Von Tunzelmann, N. and V. Acha (2005), 'Innovation in "low-tech" industries', in J. Fagerberg, D.C. Mowery and R.R. Nelson (eds), *The Oxford Handbook of Innovation*, Oxford: Oxford University Press, pp. 407–32.

Western Cape Provincial Treasury (2007), *Provincial Economic Review & Outlook*, accessed 28 November 2007 at www.capegateway.gov.za.

Winetech (1999), *Vision 2020*, Stellenbosch, South Africa: Winetech.

Wood, E. and D. Kaplan (2005), 'Innovation and performance improvement in the South African wine industry', *International Journal of Technology and Globalisation*, **1** (3/4), 381–99.

9. What have we learned from the wine industry? Some concluding remarks

Elisa Giuliani, Andrea Morrison and Roberta Rabellotti

1 DRIVERS OF CATCHING UP

Since the beginning of the 1990s, the wine industry has become increasingly global and knowledge intensive. Old World countries, with France and Italy ahead, have lost their supremacy in the international wine market, being challenged by New World players, such as the USA, Australia, Argentina, Chile and South Africa, which are recording stunning performances in terms of both export volume and value. This book presents a collection of original chapters aimed at demonstrating that such a spectacular example of catch-up in New World countries has not simply been achieved by copying new technologies from Old World leading countries. In fact, it has entailed a major process of creative adaptation and innovation, which has been underpinned by institutional changes and by impressive scientific achievements. Promoted by affluent New World players (essentially Australia and the USA), the research-driven transformation of the industry has rapidly diffused to emerging economies such as Argentina, Chile and South Africa, which in turn have significantly contributed to the process of technological modernization, product upgrading and marketing innovation. Traditional catching-up theories fall short in explaining the stunning success of these emerging economies as they generally treat latecomers as non-innovators and contend that their catching up is possible essentially through the import of frontier technologies and/ or organizational business models from advanced, forerunner countries (Abramovitz, 1986). As opposed to this, what has happened in the wine industry is an excellent empirical illustration of Perez and Soete's (1988) windows of opportunities opening up for lagging countries at times of relevant discontinuities.

When new types of knowledge, skills and experience are needed, the burden of structural adjustment for forerunners is heavier than for new entrants, who can take advantage of this sort of opportunity. As shown by Anderson in the case of the Australian wine industry (Chapter 4), a first significant window of opportunity in the sector opened up in the 1970s, as UK regulations changed and allowed supermarkets to retail wine, giving rise to a new market dominated by the baby-boomers. This new trend boosted Australian wine production and exports and was followed by a radical transformation in wine demand, which also included consumers with no prior experience in wine consumption, especially younger generations and female consumers and, more broadly, consumers from countries where wine had never been a traditional beverage, such as the UK, the USA and the European Nordic countries. Over the 1980s and 1990s, the consumption of wine also changed in the traditional producing and drinking countries such as France, Italy and Spain, where a shift occurred from bulk to premium wines. The quality upgrading of wine demand coincided with an increase in wine purchases made in supermarkets and the rising importance of large-scale distribution. To exploit the new rapidly growing markets, supermarkets required large volumes of good quality, easy to drink, international variety of wines such as Sauvignon, Cabernet, and Chardonnay. Australia and California were the first to step into this new widening segment of the international market, taking advantage of their favorable factor endowments in terms of land and capital. The production process was rapidly modernized with the introduction of new techniques for mechanical pruning and harvesting and large investments were directed to improve viticulture and oenological techniques, brand promotion and marketing to respond to changes in wine consumption habits across the world.

Indeed in Chapter 2, Cusmano et al. stress that in New World countries, the designs of innovation programs have been largely market driven, aimed at solving problems related to output variability, quality regularity and adaptation to international tastes. At the beginning, the reaction of Old World countries to such industry transformations has been rather inertial, relying on their accumulated competitive advantage and based on context-specific assets such as vine varieties. To exacerbate this situation, Old World countries have been held back by very severe laws and regulations, which inhibited experimentation and limited their capacity to react as flexibly as New World producers to the rapidly changing international demand. More recently, Old World producers have responded to the increasing competition from emerging New World countries, upgrading quality and adapting autochthon wines to new international tastes, also taking advantage of market niches dominated by highly educated consumers, who demand 'experience goods', that is unique wines linked to a specific heritage and *terroir*. These consumers represent a small, but culturally relevant and rapidly increasing market segment, reacting to the standardization of tastes and the dominance of supermarkets and international retail chains in the global wine market.

While the tenants of advanced knowledge remained located in Old World countries, New World countries have exhibited an impressive commitment to set up new research institutions, as well as other institutional arrangements supporting the development of their wine industry. In Chapter 2, Cusmano et al., suggest that New World countries' successful strategy of 'building up' wine products fitting with the new international tastes has been based on a mix of factors: domestic scientific and technological capability building aligned with market objectives, openness and access to foreign knowledge and technologies, linkages between local research communities and the industry, as well as the development of supportive industrywide institutions. These results are reflected in several of the chapters presented in the book.

With regard to scientific advancements, Cassi et al. (Chapter 3) give an account of the steady increase of New World countries' scientific publications in international journals, a terrain that was mostly dominated by Old World countries up until the mid-1990s. Although the first to appear in international journals were researchers working in affluent New World countries, it is striking that beginning from 2002, Argentina, Chile, and South Africa also became significant contributors to international scientific knowledge. Such an achievement has been reached through a strong commitment of these countries to strengthen domestic research institutions. In all the New World countries we have investigated, there is evidence of a well-developed system of research organizations, involving both universities and other public research organizations (PROs), employing highly qualified and active researchers. In this book we contend that the development of domestic scientific capabilities has been a critical step in the catching-up process, as scientific results obtained internationally are not likely to hold in different country contexts, where soil characteristics and climate conditions vary substantially. Hence, indigenous scientific research is needed to develop knowledge that can usefully be applied within the national context. As the wine field is one where scientific research is mostly applied, results from projects undertaken at leading universities and PROs often find applicability in viticulture and oenological practices.

A further prominent role played by universities has been to train and educate a whole new generation of experts, specialized in different fields spanning agronomics, oenology, chemistry, engineering, and biotechnology, whose skills have been critical to promote technical change in the industry, as illustrated by Kunc and Tiffin (Chapter 5). Such highly qualified professionals have played a key role both within universities and PROs as well as within firms. In Chapter 7, Giuliani and Rabellotti show that besides being critical in terms of scientific production, researchers employed in universities and PROs have proved to be important gateways of international scientific knowledge for the domestic industry. Both in Chile and South Africa the most talented researchers, that is those having the brightest scientific curricula as signaled by their international publications and awards, act as bridging researchers connecting the domestic industry with international sources of applied science, through their scientific networks. This reflects a significant proximity between science and industry. This fluid relationship has been facilitated by the fact that most wineries now employ highly qualified workers as agronomists and/or oenologists, whose language and codes of communication is very proximate to that of their peers working at universities. Therefore, the caricature of closed-minded farmers who relied only on tacit skills and past experience is no longer appropriate. Winemakers are often competent technicians and entrepreneurs, who have built their skills on both formal education and firm/territory-specific know-how.

Finally, the book confirms the importance of linkages for innovations. While most of the rhetoric about innovation systems in developing and emerging countries is that weak linkages characterize them, this study shows the opposite. In Chile, Argentina, and South Africa, firms have managed to create a web of relations that has positively affected the sector's product and process upgrading. Besides universities, intermediary bodies play a role in connecting firms to new technological knowledge. The development of supportive industrywide institutions has been one of the hallmarks of the export-oriented success of the Australian wine industry since the 1980s, and this successful model of promotion of R&D and direct involvement of the industry in the determination of the research agenda of the domestic researchers has been replicated in South Africa and other New World countries. In South Africa, Lorentzen (Chapter 8) shows that the process of knowledge dissemination is orchestrated and facilitated by intermediary bodies, which help small growers that are not directly connected to university researchers, to access, select, understand, and assimilate relevant knowledge. In a similar vein, McDermott and Corredoira (Chapter 6) show that, in the Argentinean wine region of Mendoza, public–private institutions (PPIs) acted as social and knowledge bridges among previously isolated producer communities, thus helping the weakest actors in the region to be connected and to upgrade their products.

2　LESSONS LEARNED

The successful experience of the wine industry can have implications on the understanding of development through innovation. The key lessons learned through this book are reported below.

Lesson 1: Traditional Sectors Are Not Necessarily Low-tech and Characterized by Low Knowledge Intensity; They Can Be Knowledge Intensive and Highly Innovative

The empirical evidence presented in this book clearly shows that the wine industry involves considerable knowledge-generating activities. We have shown that research undertaken at universities and PROs has enormous applications in winemaking practice and that winemakers, *vignerons* and oenologists deal with innovation activities on a permanent basis. This new way of producing wine has been possible thanks to the upsurge of a whole new generation of highly skilled professionals, holding university degrees, who have become the leading actors in the technological revolution that has occurred in this industry in the past two decades. These findings align with other recent studies on sectors such as salmon farming in Chile (Iizuka, 2009) and fruit in Brazil (Gomes, 2007), challenging the conventional wisdom of agro-food industries as traditional activities where barely any innovation occurs, mainly based on the tacit skills of rural farmers.

Lesson 2: Innovation Is Not Just the Result of Formal R&D

To account for knowledge generation in this industry, it is necessary to pay attention to different types of activities and indicators other than formal R&D and patents. R&D and patent statistics are ill suited to this industry, where experimentation, learning, trial and error and other means for generating new knowledge are mostly informally undertaken and measured.

Our case studies show that a better way to discern and account for innovation-related activities is to look into the innovation capabilities (Bell, 2010) of winemakers. They represent the key input to product and process innovation and in this sector they take the form of skill upgrading, development of new routines and organizational change. By building this set of competences, winemakers and viticulturists in catching-up countries were able to mold to their needs external best practices and significantly upgrade their wines. Our case studies also show that innovation capabilities not only correspond to scientific and technological activities; they also include competences such as entrepreneurial and marketing capabilities, which have proved to be crucial in the rise of New World countries. Indeed, as discussed in Chapters 2 and 4, the increased ability of New World producers to penetrate the world's most dynamic markets (for example, the UK and the USA) is also related to aggressive brand-promotion strategies and marketing investments. Winemakers from New World countries have been able to build and integrate a wide range of dispersed activities into complex value chains, linking domestic grape growers and wineries with export agents and international buyers. Other capabilities such as reduction of time-to-market, environmental management, compliance with food safety regulation and fair trade certification have been identified by Ponte and Ewert (2009) in the case of the South African wine industry as key for allowing developing-country players to improve their position in value chains.

Lesson 3: Access to Foreign Knowledge and Local Capability Building Are Complementary Activities

The analysis of the wine industry leaves no doubt about the importance of international connections. Experiences of other firms in both Old and New World countries suggest that contracting consultant oenologists and connections within the international scientific community are among the key channels through which knowledge is circulated globally within this industry. During the fieldwork, we frequently met with young oenologists who were often involved in harvesting experiences in wineries on the other side of the world – a clear anecdotal indicator of the global scope of this industry. In spite of the intense external connections, knowledge and technologies coming from more advanced contexts are never passively adopted. In fact, external knowledge is tested, improved and contextualized by local agronomists/oenologists both in universities and PROs as well as in the field by wineries. Through several case studies, this book shows that New World countries have been successful in building up a local scientific and technological basis, which has in turn been critical to access, adopt and adapt in a fruitful way the knowledge resources coming from other contexts. This has led to the development of significant problem-solving capabilities in the production process, as well as to the production of differentiated wines, which have gained international recognition and value in the global marketplace.

This result matches with other studies in the agro-food industry, which show that the complementary relationship between the imported knowledge and technologies and localized innovation is a key driver in the industry's dynamics and sustainability (Thompson and Scoones, 2009).

Lesson 4: Networks of Private and Public Actors Are Key to Learning and Innovation

Our study clearly points to the fact that wineries do not innovate in isolation. Various findings in this book confirm the importance of networks for learning, knowledge access and innovation. In the wine industry, networks of companies jointly with public and mixed institutional actors, networks of researchers and university–industry (U–I) networks play a key role in learning and knowledge-generation activities. These experiences of collaboration are of a new type with respect to the traditional forms of technology transfer occurring in agriculture, where farmers are often passive adopters of the know-how provided by extension agents. Our findings suggest that the wine industry is undertaking a transformation not dissimilar to the one experienced by high-tech and manufacturing sectors, in which the increasing complexity of innovation, along with the competitive pressure posed by international markets, have forced firms to rely more and more on external sources of knowledge. The case studies show that winemakers play a central role in these formal and informal knowledge and scientific networks. They actively collaborate with researchers, and in many instances they are also involved in the definition of the main lines of investigation and areas of intervention. This new system of governance between public and private actors may reduce the importance of the rent-seeking behavior of incumbents, giving more voice to the needs of the different stakeholders of the industry, in particular the more marginal ones (for example, small farmers and grape growers).

3 POLICY IMPLICATIONS

From the above discussion it emerges that skills, access to external knowledge, domestic research and innovation capability and networking between public and private actors are key drivers of the catching-up process successfully undertaken by some emerging countries in the wine sector. What policy implications can be drawn from the rich and varied empirical evidence presented in this book?

A general implication is the importance of investing in universities and PROs. Traditionally, in the economic development literature little attention has been devoted to universities and PROs, but these institutions are increasingly considered as key in the process of acquisition of technological capabilities in high-tech sectors such as electronics, software, pharmaceuticals, and telecommunications. This book shows their importance in a traditional sector such as wine. Technical colleges and universities have a clear role to play in terms of competence building that is central for the creation, absorption and use of knowledge for innovation. From the empirical evidence collected in this book it appears that human resources in wine companies have increasingly been trained as viticulturists and oenologists at universities and colleges. Universities provide advanced skills, but also and perhaps more importantly, they create opportunities for social ties, which often represent important channels to share information and knowledge. Indeed, it is very common that oenologists, winemakers, entrepreneurs, consultants and academic researchers have been former students or teachers at the institutions where they build relationships, which are key for enhancing the creation and diffusion of relevant knowledge within the wine community.

The necessity for upgrading skills of workers and farmers as well as generating networks formed by graduates and researchers, which are important means for the informal circulation of knowledge from university to the industry, call for investment in advanced educational institutions.

Moreover, in the case of the wine sector, given the specificities of wine regions in terms of climates, soil characteristics and biodiversity, the existence of peripheral research centers localized close to the production areas could be a valuable source of knowledge and skills.

The first policy implication is therefore to invest in public universities, tertiary formal education and PROs, paying a special attention to the specialization and specificity of wine regions.

Besides providing training and education, universities and PROs have a key role in the development of indigenous research capabilities and in connecting the domestic industry with global knowledge. It is a widespread belief that the building of research capabilities should not be considered as a priority in the early phases of the development of innovation systems in less developed countries. On the contrary, our empirical evidence shows that in wine-related fields, researchers from emerging countries have rapidly begun to contribute to global scientific knowledge. Argentina, Chile and South Africa have built a domestic research base, which has contributed to the catching-up process in the wine sector. Furthermore, our findings in Chapter 7 about bridging researchers, a restricted number of talented scholars who have connections with international academic scholars as well as with the domestic industry, highlight the multiple roles that a well-functioning research system can play. However, prospects of international mobility in the career of bridging researchers may raise concerns over the vulnerability of academic and U–I networks, as their exit might severely disrupt the connectivity of the national innovation system (Giuliani et al., 2010). Our implication is that policy makers should attract and nurture as many talents as possible among scientists, as their skills may be critical in the growth and consolidation phases of innovation systems. In this sense, policies could be oriented towards boosting individual talents (rather than their institutions or networks of researchers), funding their research agendas and financing visiting schemes to strengthen their foreign collaborations.

The second policy implication is to attract and support talent and to take advantage of international linkages to build domestic research and innovation competences.

The studies in this book provide some interesting policy insights on how to build a governance system that generates a positive pay-off for the industry as a whole. In particular, the Australian and South African cases offer examples of nationwide policy initiatives that enhanced the participation of the different stakeholders of the industry along with the public sector, in particular research organizations. The design and implementation of participatory systems, involving companies at different levels, even small growers, have been demonstrated to be effective in smoothing conflicts between opposed and often diverging interests, and in particular in favoring the construction of a shared vision for the future of the industry. These mechanisms, implemented in the specific context of U–I relations, also proved to be rather successful in setting research priorities that met industry needs, for closing the gap and for reinforcing the linkages with academia. Our cases also provide some successful examples of well-functioning intermediary organizations at the regional level, as discussed in Chapters 6 on Argentina and 8 on South Africa. These intermediary organizations are key for the exploitation of science for innovation because many companies, particularly small growers, often do not have direct relationships with universities or research institutes. Through their links with these intermediary organizations, companies likewise benefit from the results of scientific endeavor.

The importance of institutional innovations, in particular the role of intermediary organizations and public–private partnerships, is consistent with empirical evidence from a disparate set of developed and emerging economies (Morrison and Rabellotti, 2007; Rodrik, 2007).

The third policy implication is to experiment with new forms of governance of public–private partnerships, so as to implement participatory mechanisms in setting research agendas.

4   FUTURE CHALLENGES

This book has identified the key factors driving the catching up of New World countries in the wine industry, which started during the 1990s and has continued throughout the present decade. At the time of writing these concluding remarks, however, the wine industry is facing a severe crisis, due to a mix of internal and external factors. Within the industry, the success of New World emerging producers is attracting new competitors from both the Old and New Worlds, thus increasing competition in the global market. With regard to exogenous factors, the current global financial crisis is having a negative impact on the size of the market, particularly on the expensive segments. It is therefore highly possible that in the forthcoming years the industry will have to face a shakeout and that new transformations with new drivers for success will emerge. In such an unstable and mutable context, issues that have not been fully addressed in this book may become progressively more crucial.

One such issue is value chain management and downstream industry concentration. The chapters included in this book have not dealt significantly with the role that downstream actors, such as global buyers (for example, retailers, supermarkets), may have played in product and process upgrading – a relevant phenomenon in other industries (Schmitz, 2004), also addressed in the case of the wine industry in South Africa by Ponte and Ewert (2009). If the crisis reduces competition among wine producers, it is possible that global buyers with an established distribution network will significantly increase their bargaining power *vis-à-vis* producers, as the latter will fight strenuously to get access to the final market. The following research questions will thus become crucial: will wine companies from emerging countries be able to meet buyers' expectations and requirements, and will a consolidation in the distribution channels lead to a rising importance of multinationals and an escalation of international alliances and acquisitions? The role of global buyers for wineries' future competitiveness is an area where further research is needed.

With regard to changes in demand, there is a growing trend towards product differentiation, reflecting consumers' increasing sophistication. Old World producers, who have historically built their competitive advantage on local differences in terms of vine varieties and other local assets, have traditionally promoted differentiation. In the last decade or so some emerging countries, opening up opportunities for small independent producers aiming at niche markets, have adopted this strategy too. In this context, new questions arise: will the highly centralized, industry-wide institutional frameworks adopted by Australia and then somewhat replicated by Chile and South Africa be able to adapt to the recent need for more differentiation, and will this increasing demand for appellation wines crowd out the international varieties, which represent the bulk of the exports from New World countries? The changes in demand and the reaction of the wine industry in Old and New World countries are issues that should be addressed.

Another issue that this book has dealt with only indirectly, but that is potentially relevant to explain international competitiveness, concerns the regulatory framework. Of concern is the evolution of the agricultural policy at the level of the European Union (EU), particularly within Old World countries, such as France and Italy. European producers have traditionally been embedded in a dual layer of regulation – national level, especially in the appellation wines categories, and European level, within the framework of the Common Agricultural Policy (CAP). On the one hand, this strict regulatory framework has severely restricted the space for innovation, but on the other, the CAP has also strongly subsidized grape producers. Within the EU there is an open controversy on the recent trend for simplification of winemaking practices and labeling policies, as well as on the reduction of direct subsidies to producers. Are these changes addressing the interests of large industrial groups to the detriment of small wineries, which represent the backbone of some of the EU's more competitive wine industries, such as that in Italy? Are changes necessary to compete with emerging wine-producing countries? And how will a change in the EU regulatory framework eventually impact on the wine global market? The role of the regulatory framework and the impact on the wine industry of its undergoing changes are further questions open for future discussion and investigation.

Finally, the focus of the book is on the catching up of emerging economies, leaving mostly unanswered questions such as the impact of the growing wine industry on the livelihood of rural people and the extent to which the rents generated are redistributed in a fair way within the rural community in which wineries are located. Has the success of the wine industry in Argentina, Chile, and South Africa helped to reduce marginality and poverty in rural areas? It is well known that in many emerging economies only élite social groups, often in spite of agrarian reforms, own land. Hence, a question arises as to whether only a restricted number of powerful families and landowners have in fact benefited from these successful catching-up stories, or whether this has sparked a process of inclusive growth also involving more marginal people. In South Africa, wineries are generally owned by white people, an issue that opens up questions about the degree to which this industry has so far managed to empower the black majority of the population. Questions about redistribution of rents, diffusion of benefits, and improvement of livelihood conditions of rural people are imperative, and we encourage future scholars of innovation and development to investigate them in the context of the wine industry.

REFERENCES

Abramovitz, M. (1986), 'Catching up, forging ahead, and falling behind', *Journal of Economic History*, **46** (2), 385–406.
Bell, M. (2010), 'Innovation capabilities and directions of development', Innovation, Sustainability, Development: A New Manifesto, STEPS working paper. 33, STEPS Centre, University of Sussex, Brighton.
Giuliani, E., A. Morrison, C. Pietrobelli and R. Rabellotti (2010), 'Why do researchers collaborate with industry? An analysis of the wine sector in Chile, Italy and South Africa', *Research Policy*, **39** (6), 748–61.
Gomes, R. (2007), 'Upgrading without exclusion: lessons from SMEs in fresh fruit producing clusters in Brazil', in C. Pietrobelli and R. Rabellotti (eds), *Upgrading to Compete: SMEs, Clusters and Value Chains in Latin America*, Cambridge MA: Harvard University Press, pp. 71–108.
Iizuka, M. (2009), '"Low-tech" industry: a new path for development? The case of salmon farming in Chile', in F. Malerba and S. Mani (eds), *Sectoral System of Innovation and Production in Developing Countries*, Cheltenham, UK and Northampton, MA, USA: Edward Elgar, pp. 232–59.
Morrison, A. and R. Rabellotti (2007), 'The role of research in wine: the emergence of a regional research area in an Italian wine production system', *International Journal of Technology and Globalization*, **3** (2/3), 155–78.
Perez, C. and L. Soete (1988), 'Catching up in technology: entry barriers and windows of opportunity', in G. Dosi, C. Freeman, R.R. Nelson, G. Silverberg and L. Soete (eds), *Technical Change and Economic Theory*, London: Pinter, pp. 458–79.
Ponte, S. and J. Ewert (2009), 'Which way is "up" in upgrading? Trajectories of change in the value chain for South African wine', *World Development*, **37** (10), 1637–50.
Rodrik, D. (2007), 'Industrial policy for the twenty-first century', in D. Rodrik, *One Economics, Many Recipes: Globalization, Institutions and Economic Growth*, Princeton; NJ: Princeton University Press, pp. 99–153.
Schmitz, H. (ed.) (2004), *Local Enterprises in the Global Economy: Issues of Governance and Upgrading*, Cheltenham, UK and Northampton, MA, USA: Edward Elgar.
Thompson, J. and I. Scoones (2009), 'Addressing the dynamics of agri-food systems: an emerging agenda for social science research', *Environmental Science and Policy*, **12** (4), 386–97.

Index